Managing Learning and Communication Systems as Business Assets

How to Engineer Organizational Performance and Demonstrate Value

Diane M. Gayeski, Ph.D.
Ithaca College
and
Gayeski Analytics, LL. C.

PEARSON
Prentice
Hall

Upper Saddle River, New Jersey

Library of Congress Cataloging-in-Publication Data

Gayeski, Diane M. (Diane Mary)
   Managing learning and communication systems as business assets / Diane M. Gayeski.
     p. cm.
   Includes bibliographical references and index.
   ISBN 0-13-046261-6
    1. Organizational learning—Management. 2. Performance—Management. 3.
  Communication in organizations. 4. Intellectual capital. 5. Communication in management.
  6. Knowledge management. 7. Customer relations—Management. I. Title.

HD58.82.G39 2005
658.4'5—dc22
                                                          2004044414

Director of Production & Manufacturing: Bruce Johnson
Executive Editor: Elizabeth Sugg
Editorial Assistant: Cyrenne Bolt de Freitas
Marketing Manager: Leigh Ann Sims
Managing Editor—Production: Mary Carnis
Manufacturing Buyer: Ilene Sanford
Production Liaison: Denise Brown
Full-Service Production/Composition: Carlisle Publishers Services
Design Director: Cheryl Asherman
Senior Design Coordinator/Cover Design: Christopher Weigand
Cover Printer: Phoenix Color
Printer/Binder: Phoenix Book Technology Park

Pearson Education Ltd.
Pearson Education Australia PTY, Limited
Pearson Education Singapore, Pte. Ltd.
Pearson Education North Asia Ltd.
Pearson Education Canada, Ltd.
Pearson Educacíon de Mexico, S.A. de C.V.
Pearson Education—Japan
Pearson Education Malaysia, Pte. Ltd.

10 9 8 7 6 5 4 3 2 1
ISBN 0-13-046261-6

Contents

Preface   vii

Chapter 1   **A New Framework for Organizational Learning, Communication, and Performance Management   1**

Overview   1

Are YOU in Charge of Your Organization's Most Competitive Assets?   1

Building Credibility   3

Communication, Learning, and Organizational Performance   5

Collaboration   6

Credibility   7

Confidence   8

Culture   9

An Integrated Infrastructure for Performance   9

Challenging Our Assumptions   11

Performance Spans the Silos   14

What and Who Drives an Organization's Future?   16

Beyond HR—Managing Human Performance Systems   17

Case in Point: McDonald's Invests in Its Intangible Assets   *19*

The Big Picture: Assessing the Current Infrastructure   20

A Roadmap for this Book   22

Self-Check   22

References   23

Chapter 2   **How Human Resources, Communications and Learning Systems Can Create—or Destroy—Value   25**

Overview   25

From Personnel to Performance   25

How Human Performance Management Creates Value   26

Focusing on Systems   27

Case in Point: Watson Wyatt's Human Capital Index Research   *29*

How HR Can Create—or Block—the Ideal Organization   33

How Traditional Practices Often Decrease Performance   35
   Islands of Communications   36
   Case in Point: Various Choices in a Cruise Line:
      Organizational Internal Connectedness   38
   Outsourcing Value   40
Self-Check   42
References   42

Chapter 3   Internal and External Communication Systems   43

Overview   43
Where Does Communication Fit?   43
What Goes On in Each Department?   45
   External Communication   45
   Internal Communications   47
   Supervisory Communication   48
How Communication Is (or Is Not) Integrated   49
Theory Informs Practice   51
   *The Transportation Model of Communication, or: Don't
   Believe Your Own Words*   52
   Defining Communication "Success"   53
Case in Point: A Framework for Customer Relationship
   Communication   55
Envisioning the Ideal System   57
The Elements of a Strong Communication Infrastructure   59
   Internal Collaboration   59
   Customer/Supplier Communication   61
   News   61
   Leadership and Supervisory Communication   61
   Special Events and Sponsorship   62
Case in Point: Strategic Event Sponsorship   63
   Crisis Communication   64
   Communication Audits   65
Case in Point: Integrating Communication and HR Assessment   65
Self-Check   72
References   72

Chapter 4   Corporate Brand and Culture   73

Overview   73
What Is a Brand and What Is Your Role?   73
What Is the Value of a Strong Brand and How Is It Maximized?   74
Case in Point: How Cracker Barrel Old Country Store
   Creates "Fanatic" Customers   74
Internal Branding   78

Case in Point: Caterpillar Coordinates Its Voice 78
What Is Corporate Culture and How Does HR Engineer It? 84
Case in Point: The Implications of Managerial Leadership
  on Organizational Citizenship Behavior (OCB) 85
Engineering Culture and Brand from the Ground Up 87
Case in Point: Creating a New Brand and Culture 88
Self-Check 94
Reference 94

Chapter 5   Managing Learning, Performance, and Knowledge Systems 95
Overview 95
How Do We Conceptualize and Assess Organizational
Learning Systems? 95
What New Learning Systems Look Like in Practice 101
Linking Enterprise Training Systems to Value 102
From Training to Learning to Performance Infrastructures 104
Knowledge Management 105
Case in Point: Organizational Knowledge Management
  at Buckman Labs 106
A Learning and Collaboration Infrastructure 110
Case in Point: Intel Captures Expert Knowledge 112
Feedback Systems 114
Case in Point: Feedback and the Performer Information System 118
Self-Check 123
References 123

Chapter 6   Performance Analytics 125
Overview 125
Communication and Learning Infrastructure Audit 127
How Did You Respond? 129
How Can We "Re-Wire" Our Approaches? 130
Capacity for Change and Crisis 132
Case in Point: Communication System Key in Crisis Management 134
Conducting Communication Audits 135
Case in Point: Assessing Communication in Government 135
Assessing and Managing Communication Overload 137
Assessing and Closing Group and Individual Performance Gaps 139
The Performance Engineering Model 140
A High-Level Walkthrough of the Performance Engineering
  Approach 140
Performance Engineering in Detail: The ComADD Model 144
Getting the Results You Want 148
Self-Check 149
References 150

Chapter 7   **Translating Data to Dollars: Calculating and Communicating the Value of Learning and Communication   151**

Overview   151

Where Is 1 Million?   151

Levels of Project Evaluation   153

Going Beyond ROI—Infrastructure Analytics   156

Doing the Numbers: Methods of Calculating Value   157

After-Tax Calculations   159

Multi-Year Systems   160

More Complex Financial Considerations   160

Present Value   161

Net Present Value   161

Combining NPV and ROI   162

Working with Vendors   162

Assumptions and Calculations Applied in ROI   163

Translating This to Stockholder Value: Turning $100,000 into $1 Million!   165

Case in Point: Pitching an E-Learning System in a Company Turnaround   *166*

Are You Leveraging Your Communication and Learning Assets?   170

Summary: How to Determine the Value of an Infrastructure Project   170

Self-Check   172

References   172

Chapter 8   **Getting There: How to Start Managing and Communicating for Value   173**

Overview   173

Creating the Strategic Structure   173

Case in Point: Effective Information Sharing   *175*

How Do You Pitch a New System?   181

Making the Case for Change   182

What the CEO Wants You to Know   185

Questions to Ask the CEO   186

Case in Point: Engineering the Flow of Information Within Pitney Bowes   *186*

Valuation Concepts for Not-for-Profits   191

Reporting to Stockholders and Financial Analysts   194

A One-Year Plan   197

Self-Check   205

References   206

Index   207

Preface

"The set of tasks formerly known as human resource services is now cast as a value chain of integrated processes and functions that are strategically positioned to help the organization compete."

This quote by Vincent J. Serritella, Vice-President of Employee Development, W.W. Grainger, Inc. was featured in a white paper called *The Human Capital Challenge*, published by the American Society for Training and Development in 2003. How many professionals in corporate training, business communication, and human resources can live up to this promise—or even clearly articulate how their work adds value? Are we there yet?

I've been working in the organizational learning and communication field for all of my professional life, both as the executive of a consulting company and as a professor. Despite decades of experience and education, I still find it difficult to explain my work. In fact, it's an inside joke in the field of human performance improvement that none of our family members can figure out what we do for a living. What's *not* so funny is that frequently our clients are similarly mystified.

What used to be a set of pretty simple (but not very strategic) roles as trainers, meeting planners, recruiters, or writers has been superceded by a more comprehensive and powerful framework of methods sometimes called "human performance technology" or "performance consulting." There's abundant research to show that human behavior in the workplace can be engineered in ways that are both empowering to employees and profitable for the organizations in which they work. The struggle for many of us has been how to communicate our methods and the value we add to our employers and clients.

In my continuing effort to propel the field, I have researched the enablers and barriers to getting performance engineering accepted as a set of processes and stable professional roles. One day in 1999, my then-13-year-old son (and trusted business advisor) and I independently read news stories about intangible assets and simultaneously decided that this was "it". . . the new framework for the profession. I started talking to smart executives, reading books on financial analysis, and networking with some of my colleagues who shared my experiences and frustrations. I learned a new language of finance and spent a summer teaching at a business school in Finland.

What you'll be reading here is my attempt to help you answer the question "So, what *do* you do?" and to help us all re-wire our professional roles and assumptions. I hope it gives you some new perspectives and helps you to achieve the kind of impact and meaning that you wish for your professional work.

Many people deserve credit for their assistance in the process. My son, Evan Williams, has not only been a patient housemate while I read and talked endlessly about this book, but he's also been a great source of ideas and witty critique. He's the best business partner ever. Michael Petrillose came into my life in the midst of my research and international travel for this book and at times must have questioned his decision to partner up with such a busy woman! His love and support guided me through the challenging days of wrapping up this enormous project— and on top of this, he even contributed an essay for Chapter 4.

Gordon Rowland and Sandra Herndon, chairs of my department and of the graduate program, in Organizational Communication, Learning, and Design at Ithaca College respectively, have been supportive colleagues by giving me opportunities for research and teaching in this area. Our former Dean of the Roy H. Park School of Communications at Ithaca College, Tom Bohn, reassigned my teaching time and supplied internal grants to provide the resources I needed to get into this foreign but important field of financial analysis and intangible assets.

My valued friends Bob Stanton and Dennis Clawson served as devil's advocates and business coaches, and generously shared the wisdom of their many years as successful executives. Hundreds of clients over the years gave me the opportunity to develop and test my ideas, and a number of them were kind enough to write their first-person experiences and advice as "Case in Point" essays.

Thanks also to the reviewers of the manuscript, Stephanie Wilson of Intel Corporation and Gregory Akin of Lansing Community College.

Finally, the idea would never have become a book without the help of Roger Chevalier at the International Society for Performance Improvement, who hooked me up with Elizabeth Sugg at Prentice-Hall, my editor. Thanks to both of them.

Author Bio
Diane M. Gayeski, Ph.D.

Diane M. Gayeski, Ph. D, is an internationally recognized consultant, speaker, researcher, and professor of organizational communication and learning. She is CEO of Gayeski Analytics, and since 1980 she has led more than 300 projects for clients such as General Electric, the U.S. Department of Labor, Fiat, and Bank of Montreal, assessing and improving their information, learning and collaboration infrastructures. She maintains a full-time academic appointment as Professor of Organizational Communication, Learning and Design at the Park School of Communications at Ithaca College. She is an adjunct faculty member in Boise State University's online Masters Degree program in Instructional and Performance Technology, and is the author of 13 other books on organizational training and communications. Dr. Gayeski is a frequent speaker at professional conferences and executive briefings.

CHAPTER 1 *A New Framework for Organizational Learning, Communication, and Performance Management*

Overview

Although organizations invest considerable time and energy in communication and training projects, they are often seen as frills rather than strategic assets. This chapter defines the infrastructures that are necessary to achieve organizational performance—often called "intangible assets"—and argues that professionals in human resources, communication, and training must re-frame their competencies and contributions.

Are YOU in Charge of Your Organization's Most Competitive Assets?

The value of most organizations today lies beyond the assessed price of their physical assets and the size of their bank accounts. What some people call "intangible assets" form a substantial part of the current value and support the future vitality of every enterprise. They include:

- brand and reputation
- customer, supplier, community, investor, and government relationships
- knowledge assets (patents, formulas, secrets, tacit knowledge)
- employee ability and willingness to perform (knowledge, motivation, selection)

I call them "infrastructure assets" because they are actually quite tangible. Although it is challenging, you *can* manage and assess them. If you are in employee communications, training, recruiting, performance consulting, branding and marketing, or knowledge management, you are the developer and custodian of these strategic resources.

Almost any business magazine will include stories about how enterprises are using new online computer technologies to train their employees, how they support and solicit feedback from their customers, how their executives try to influence workers to "buy into" their new visions, and how they use information systems to manage organizational knowledge. Communication and learning systems are an organization's most sensitive and powerful tools for attracting and informing employees, customers, and investors, thereby creating value.

Because roles, technologies, and performance solutions are changing so quickly, it can be quite confusing to determine exactly who in an organization is in charge of these initiatives and systems. **Organizational learning and communication is the professional function responsible for developing and implementing "rules and tools" to enhance the dissemination, comprehension, acceptance, and application of information in ways that help to achieve an organization's goals.** In other words, people who bring the brand to life, manage the communication and collaboration systems, provide feedback and performance support to employees, and develop organizational knowledge are **in charge of the organization's intangible assets.**

It is getting easier for the competition to match or top your technology, reverse-engineer your products and sell them at a lower cost, steal your customer lists, or even create products and services that make yours obsolete. Kaarl Erik Sveiby, a noted researcher on intangible assets, describes the components of a company's market value (see Figure 1.1) These components are the tangible assets (book value) and the intangible assets (external and internal systems and employee competence). Structuring and managing these systems for communication and learning is what drives competitive profitability.

In most organizations, professionals in a variety of disciplines have responsibility for various parts of these assets (see Figure 1.2):

♦ human resources
♦ organizational development
♦ training and development

Visible equity (what's on the books)	Intangible assets (the extra factors that add to the worth of a company beyond what is on the books)		
	External communication and learning infrastructures such as brands, methods of retaining customer and supplier relationships, and technologies for expediting supplier and customer transactions	**Internal communication and learning infrastructures** such as training and feedback systems, R&D methods, intranet applications, management communication practices, and collaboration tools	**Human capital,** the collection of individual employees' knowledge, experience, and dedication

Figure 1.1
The Components of the Market Value of a Company (*adapted from Sveiby, 1997*)

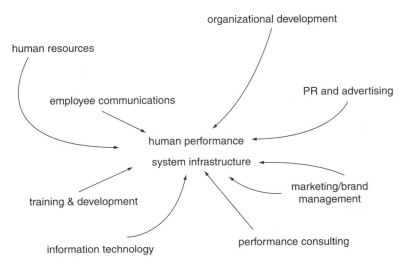

Figure 1.2
The Professions That Create and Manage Intangibles

- ◆ marketing and brand management
- ◆ information technology
- ◆ public relations and advertising
- ◆ employee communications
- ◆ the emerging practice of performance consulting

While the territory of each of these departments and roles may remain distinct, it is crucial for them to work together toward a coordinated performance vision. This book will provide some new frameworks for these roles, and will present new methods to demonstrate how they add value.

Building Credibility

The previous list of professionals includes the areas that are often thought to be "soft"—those whose impact is difficult to measure and therefore are dispensable when companies fall on hard times. These individuals struggle for credibility and parity with other professionals—even those who are supposed to be at their same organizational level. Therefore, it is more important than ever for people who engineer human performance to show how they add value. This is true not just for those professionals in large, publicly traded corporations, but also for small, closely held companies whose owners may be looking to sell out at some point, as well as for not-for-profits and government agencies who need to demonstrate value to their donors and taxpayers.

Although many people are beginning to develop some interesting models and metrics on return-on-investment for various kinds of human capital systems, there still are no reliable or accepted ways to measure these areas. In fact, when many executives, prospective corporate buyers, or financial analysts attempt to do this, they use all the wrong measures. For example, if they want to assess employee knowledge they look at how many days of training the company provides to each person. They might as well measure pounds of handouts . . . or the average size of employees' heads. If they are interested in looking at the value of the website, they look at hits, not knowing who is hitting the website or if that activity results in any economic benefit. They measure the success of their intranets using similar metrics—it makes one wonder whether this shows productivity or just demonstrates that the system is an attractive nuisance to employees.

Concepts like knowledge, reputation, and loyalty may be hard to grasp . . . that is why they are literally called "intangibles." However, we clearly need some better measures. Let's say that I won the lottery and have $1.5 million to invest. I find a little hotel in the college town where I live, and I think it is a good buy: it has a great reputation, and I think I could expand it to capitalize on the business involving reunions and graduations. I might also try to replicate the business in other university towns.

Since I am a communication and learning specialist—not a building engineer or financial analyst—I know enough to hire professionals with that expertise in order to evaluate the deal. Suppose the property appraiser has good and bad news: The good news is, the wiring has recently been redone and it should not only handle today's demands, but it also can accommodate high-speed Internet connections, as well as the addition of some new air conditioning units that I'd like to install. The bad news is that the roof will need to be replaced within two years—to the tune of over $100,000—and the foundation won't support adding the extra three floors that I planned to add. The financial analyst I retained has a similar list of pros and cons with regard to cash flow and investments for the business.

What about the intangibles? Who can I hire to inspect the infrastructure that supports employee and customer behavior? What checklist should I use to evaluate the company's training programs, its recruiting and compensation system, its brand image and corporate culture, and the way in which it communicates news and policies to employees? These are the systems—the infrastructures—that drive future earnings. For example, there may be no crisis communication plan in place, which would be analogous to having no security system or fire sprinklers. The employees may perform well, but if their training procedures and tacit knowledge is not documented, it will make it very difficult to expand or replicate their unique pattern of service in another setting. . . just like an inadequate foundation on the building will make it difficult or even impossible to add onto the physical structure.

You can see how and why we need better ways to measure intangibles. This whole idea, however, is not without its critics. Many people say that there is no way to put a number—especially a dollar number—on human performance, knowledge, or attitudes. Others say that the contributions of intangibles are already on the books in terms of excess earnings that a strong brand brings in above that of the competition or in terms of the savings that accrue from having smart and loyal employees and customers. Intangibles *do* eventually show up on traditional profit and loss statements.

Figure 1.3
Intangibles Predict Future Value

So, why develop and measure intangibles? Simply put, because they predict the future while the "books" only show what happened in the past (see Figure 1.3).

Communication, Learning, and Organizational Performance

Communication and training systems are powerful means for acquiring and disseminating information that can lead to dramatic organizational change. Organizations can create a culture that is oriented toward predictability, order, and formality, or one that is characterized by innovation, variable amounts and types of information, and spontaneity. Modern theories and technologies can encourage individuals to work in physically isolated environments aided by communication devices, or to embrace a more personal style of "management by walking around." Forces exist that impel business leaders to control the quality and quantity of messages, and equally powerful ones advocate a loosening of bureaucratic channels and chains of approval. Executives and communication professionals need to build a distinctive and powerful system that works for their own situation—one that builds the brand and culture as well as supports excellent performance.

When clients engage me to assess their communication and training functions, one of my most frequent observations of communication and training functions in organizations is that they aim too low. Generally, people in these departments are focused on individual messages or requested courses, and as a result they don't pay adequate attention to the larger factors that promote organizational vitality. For example, the training manager at one hospital mentioned that the hospital would like to turn its attention to preparing staff for the changes brought on by managed care. However, she said, they were too busy teaching time management and sexual harassment courses and would have no time for anything new for the next eighteen months. When I talked with the CEO, he was less concerned about people learning to use their expensive leather planners than he was with trying to get the organization to "move." He found that his managers were not making the changes necessary to keep them competitive, and that it was a struggle to get people to be committed, honest, and collaborative. In other words, the training department was spending its resources (and the time of hundreds of hospital staff who attended their courses) on nice-to-know material and ignoring the enormous conceptual and motivational requirements that would be necessary for the organization's survival. Unfortunately, their situation is more the rule than the exception.

So, what's the answer? Should we create courses in honesty, or newsletter articles on commitment? Of course not. However, those very fundamental attitudes and behaviors are exactly what need to be considered when designing the "rules and tools" for communication. The indicators of high-performing organizations are the **Four Cs:**

- collaboration
- credibility
- confidence
- culture

These factors need to be the driving force—the "core curriculum"—of everything a company says, models, and teaches. The core curriculum idea is *not* just about using these as topics for meetings or classes, but rather engineering the communication and learning infrastructure to make sure that these indicators are maximized. When these indicators are strong, the organization has a better internal and external infrastructure, and therefore stronger intangible assets.

Collaboration

Some of the most successful organizations today started out with a business plan more oriented toward putting together a top-notch team than marketing a product. More and more organizations are defined by their people—and the important sharing of knowledge, trust, know-how, wisdom, and social bonds between them. Collaboration and synergy are the defining forces behind high-performing and flexible enterprises.

Despite the "teamwork" management fad and sophisticated tools for collaboration, it is actually becoming more challenging for organizations to promote cooperation and idea sharing. Several reasons exist for this. One is that organizations' members are often scattered in different sites, and may frequently be on the road or work at home. Although e-mail and similar technologies do allow people to send messages, they can't promote the kind of informal chat and development of strong relationships that the old-fashioned water cooler did. Secondly, in the wake of downsizing, more organizational work is done by outside vendors, contractors, or temporary workers. In fact, one of the world's largest employers today is Manpower Inc., which employs more than 2 million people all over the world as temporary workers. Many freelancers don't even frequent the offices of the companies they work for these days. These so-called "e-lancers" may do their work from any corner of the globe simply by downloading their work over the Internet. This fragmentation of workforce locations may save money, but in the long run it can be devastating to the development of know-how and innovation. Coupled with massive downsizings and retirements in many organizations, outsourcing can be a crippling force.

Many businesses only realize the worth of their "intellectual assets" after they lose key employees. Some have had to bring people back from retirement because essential expertise, contacts, or procedures only existed in their heads, without having been shared or documented. For example, seemingly obsolete COBOL programmers found themselves having to decide among multiple million-dollar-a-year contracts to fix Year 2000 (Y2K) problems in legacy computer systems.

Tim Hicks, a Canadian communication professional, framed an elegantly powerful question to assess how well companies promote the sharing of knowledge in an e-mail conversation with me: "Ask yourself this—in your organization, is *knowledge* a gas, a liquid, or a solid? Does it diffuse everywhere? Does it have to be poured and only go downwards? Or, do people have to search for it, find it and mine it?"

Thomas Stewart (1997, p. 102), in *Intellectual Capital,* recommends that companies "foster the growth of intellectual communities in areas that are central to their competitive advantage. . . . A vibrant learning community socializes human capital, which gives the company an ownership stake in it; if Sally leaves, three other people know most of what she knows—and though Sally has left the company, she is probably still part of the community." This can be fostered by giving communities of practice semiofficial status, making resources available, creating trans-organizational communication systems, and moving employees around among business units.

Another way to express the positive and trusting relationships within companies is the term "social capital." Authors Laurence Prusak and Don Cohen (2001) found that social capital—the relationships that make organizations work effectively—result in bottom-line gains for organizations. Even within the turbulent times of working in virtual space and the volatility of the workforce, many companies invest in social capital by such activities as:

- committing to careful hiring and retention
- giving employees time and environments to facilitate conversations
- sharing expertise through professional and social networks
- letting employees know about their common purpose and that they are valued

Credibility

When people believe that their managers are credible, they are significantly more likely to:

- be proud to tell others about the organization and their association with it
- feel a sense of team spirit, ownership, and commitment
- see their own values as consistent with those of the organization

However, when they perceive their management to have low credibility, they believe that their coworkers

- perform well only if they are watched
- are motivated primarily by money
- say good things about the organization in public but don't feel or act that way in private
- would be easily attracted to a job outside the organization

Put another way, "If managers are content to pay more money to increase pro-
ductivity, to watch over people carefully, to know employees are talking behind
their backs, and to live with high rates of turnover, then credibility be damned."
(Kouzes & Posner, 1993, pp. 31–32)

To foster credibility, a company's communication and learning systems need
to be aligned with its goals and culture, and its messages need to be consistent.
Leaders need to establish ways to promote honesty. Too often, people are expected
to bluff rather than to admit that they do not know answers, or are rewarded for
outwardly acquiescing to ideas that they do not believe in or cannot follow up. Perhaps the biggest killer of knowledge in organizations is fear.

Katie Paine, CEO of the Delahaye Group, says that business culture teaches
us to bury mistakes and to blame somebody else. She has instituted a system called
"Mistake of the Month." After missing an important client meeting, she walked
into a staff meeting and offered $50 to anybody who could top that mistake. Now
at every staff meeting a half hour is set aside to write up mistakes; the person that
contributes the one that people learned the most from gets a coveted parking space
for the next month. In one year, they recorded more than two thousand mistakes
(Screw up and get smart, 1998).

Perhaps companies need to develop systems that promote open debate, support of mistakes, and raising of questions rather than the kind of communication
they tend to have today: rah-rah meetings, upbeat and superficial newsletters, and
oversimplified instruction.

In a research study funded by the International Association of Business Communicators (Shockley-Zalabak et al., 2000), five factors were found to create organizational trust:

- ◆ competence (employee and managerial effectiveness)
- ◆ openness and honesty (amount, accuracy, and sincerity of information shared)
- ◆ concern for employees (exhibition of empathy, tolerance, and safety)
- ◆ reliability (consistent and dependable actions)
- ◆ identification (sharing common goals, values, and beliefs)

In turn, organizational trust was shown to result in:

- ◆ adaptive organizational structures
- ◆ strategic alliances
- ◆ responsive virtual teams
- ◆ effective crisis management
- ◆ reduced transaction and litigation costs

Confidence

No matter how intelligent, well-trained, well-equipped, and highly compensated
a workforce may be, without conviction they are impotent. When people do not
perform up to their capabilities, it is often not because they cannot, but rather because they lack the confidence. This can not only impede progress, but also increase employee turnover.

A classic model for motivation is the ARCS model, developed by John Keller (1996). According to this model, motivation is comprised of attention, relevance, confidence, and satisfaction. In order to engineer motivation, organizations need to clearly state performance requirements, share control wherever possible so that employees can feel responsible for achieving their goals, and set challenging but achievable goals. It is not sufficient for people to succeed—they need to feel that they are personally responsible for and in control of their own success.

Having confidence and believing in one's ability to do the job are essential in promoting and sustaining high performance. "A leader's challenge is to create situations for small wins, structuring tasks in such a way that they can be broken down into manageable pieces, with each success building up the person's sense of competence. Creating a climate where learning is stressed and people feel comfortable making mistakes is also critical" (Kouzes & Posner, 1993, pp. 166–167).

Culture

Culture is, in essence, an organization's personality derived from the values, assumptions, norms, and artifacts of the organization's members. Corporate culture also includes inputs in the form of feedback, stories, and regulations. Having a strong corporate culture has been shown to create the following benefits:

◆ employee loyalty
◆ cohesiveness
◆ employee satisfaction and productivity
◆ a positive external image
◆ improved collaboration
◆ lower turnover

For example, Southwest Airlines has consistently been rated as one of *Fortune* magazine's "Best Companies to Work for in America." They have a strong and rather unique culture that was strongly influenced by their founder, Herb Kelleher. The culture is informal, hard-working, and fun-loving. Although they are very customer oriented, they have a policy that employees come first. The airline has found that by treating employees well, the spirit of Southwest Airlines shows itself in excellent customer service. They have a "Culture Committee" that generates and enlists ideas to maintain the corporate culture, and numerous articles have been written about their consistent ability to turn a profit, even when other airlines are declaring bankruptcy.

An Integrated Infrastructure for Performance

Organizations communicate to coordinate activity, improve their performance, and maintain a positive social system both within the workforce and with their various customers and publics. Some specific objectives are to:

◆ motivate employees and customers
◆ stimulate sales

- garner public support
- draw investors
- teach employees and customers new skills
- aid in decision-making
- coordinate internal activities and production
- lobby for favorable legislation
- attract qualified employees
- comply with regulations
- promote their general industry
- respond to mass media inquiries
- fulfill their roles as good community citizens
- maintain a supportive internal social system
- elicit suggestions for improvement
- capture and disseminate internal and external knowledge

Almost every organization has each of these systems in place. Some of them—typically activities like responding to the media and advertising products—are well-designed, thoughtfully managed, and carefully scrutinized. However, some of these critical functions—typically, internal processes like knowledge management and decision-making support—are just left to chance. These activities occur, but nobody is in charge, there is no systematic design or assessment, and there is no attempt to examine the costs of execution (or lack thereof).

Increasingly, communication and learning are the key infrastructures utilized to create high-performing organizations. To achieve excellence in operations, an organization needs employees that:

- understand the organizational culture and goals, and are a good "fit"
- know what is expected of them
- have the right tools to do the job (including efficient and appropriate communication tools)
- have the right environment in which to perform (including few obstacles and distractions to doing what is really important)
- have the knowledge and skills to perform
- receive regular and clear feedback on their performance
- perceive and receive rewards for good performance
- have the information and incentives to be excellent ambassadors for the company to the external environment

To achieve excellent financial performance and community/regulatory support, organizations need customers and stakeholders who:

- understand and are attracted to the company's values, styles, and products
- can find the information they need to invest in products or the company itself
- recognize the contribution the organization makes to the larger community and society
- have the information and incentives, and frequent reminders, to engineer good word of mouth referrals

---

Communication for Performance

Internal

- Understand/fit culture and goals
- Know what is expected
- Have the right tools and environment to do the job
- Have the correct knowledge and skills
- Receive regular/clear feedback
- Perceive/receive rewards
- Have the information and incentives to be excellent ambassadors

External

- Understand/attracted to values, styles, and products
- Can find information needed to invest
- Recognize contribution to community and society
- Have the information, incentives, and frequent reminders for good word of mouth referrals
- Give two-way feedback to improve use of products and services, and inform and improve products and services

---

Figure 1.4
The Internal and External Communication Drivers for Performance

◆ can give and receive feedback that improves their use of the organization's products and services and that, in turn, informs and improves the organization's products and services

Together, these factors make up a performance system (see Figure 1.4).

Functionally, this kind of environment is executed by a number of channels and strategies. Internally, it starts with recruiting and selection systems and supports employees through supervisory communications, news, and training. Externally, the communication and learning environment includes advertising and marketing programs, community relations, financial and investor communications, and other interventions (see Figure 1.5).

Challenging Our Assumptions

Traditional communication and learning practices are being challenged and replaced in many progressive organizations, and not just because of new technology. Changes in our economy and social structures are creating the need for newer and more effective communication and knowledge management systems. It is not just that new communication tools like wireless pocket computers, cell phones, interactive multimedia, and Web conferencing are available, but rather that new policies, systems, and tools are mandatory.

This book is about using communication and learning systems as management tools. However, companies can't know what kind of systems to design or how

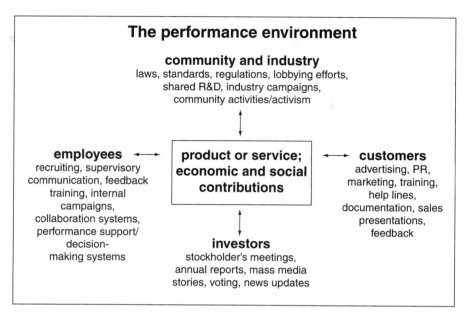

Figure 1.5
The performance environment—a systems view

to assess them unless they can articulate what success—good management—looks like. Depending on one's implicit theory of management, a particular system or situation could be viewed as a roaring success or a dismal failure.

Management theory is about one hundred years old. Before this time, very few large organizations existed other than religious groups and armies. Some early writers on this topic, like Frederick Taylor and Henri Fayol, developed what is now called the "scientific" or "bureaucratic" approach to management. Scientific management developed a set of techniques to maximize performance and manage people in ways that are not dependent upon the whims of managers, nepotism, or bonds of friendship. One example of scientific management is time and motion studies, in which workers are carefully observed and timed in their performance of each small task that make up their jobs. Management engineers then redesign the work to reduce the number of motions and amount of time needed to produce an item, while workers were held to strict standards of output and paid by piecework.

This approach to managing also created ways of scientifically selecting personnel, devised incentive plans, and created organizational structures in which there was a clear division of work, reporting structure, and orderliness. The "assembly line" approach to creating products and managing people that emerged from this school fit well into the manufacturing technology and social structure of the era. Organizations were seen as machines to be run; we still describe some companies as "well-oiled machines," and talk about people getting "gears in motion."

In the 1930s, a number of researchers began to see flaws in the assumptions of scientific management, so another set of theories, the humanistic school of management, was born. The humanistic or human relations theory asserts that structure and rules alone cannot make productive organizations. While the scientific school emphasized money as an incentive, the humanistic school emphasized the importance of non-economic rewards. This approach focuses on how workers react as a group, and stresses communication and shared decision-making.

Perhaps the most famous research that provided a foundation for the humanistic school was conducted by Elton Mayo in the 1930s. Collectively called the "Hawthorne Studies," these consisted of a series of studies conducted at Western Electric Company's Hawthorne Plant. Researchers were trying to determine what physical environment or job structure would lead to the greatest productivity. The surprising results were that no matter how the researchers manipulated the environment (light, compensation, schedules), the productivity increased. The only explanation was that the workers were being given more attention, knew that they were being studied, and therefore were more productive. Mayo also found that there were strong group norms about productivity and how work should be done; no matter what the environment or regulations, the group had unspoken standards about how much work was appropriate.

Just as scientific management tends to view organizations as machines to be built and tweaked, humanistic management leads us to develop images of organizations as families, cultures, or teams. This view has a profound impact on management communications. A number of common practices have emerged from this movement, such as team-building workshops, quality circles, employee forums with the CEO, and collaborative decision-making. These practices center on fostering good relationships among peers as well as between supervisors and subordinates, on group consensus-building, and on the plasticity of the roles and relationships among individuals. Self-directed or "high performance" work teams are another spin-off of this approach. Both scientific and humanistic management schools strove to figure out the right formula for successful management, just as the sciences like biology and physics were developing formulas to explain and predict natural phenomena. Recently, however, even the hard sciences have found that some of the traditional, simplistic notions about the behavior of objects are not really supportable.

More recently, chaos theory and complexity theory have been popularized. Chaos theory postulates that the behavior of individual elements in systems cannot be predicted; they are out of our control, despite what on the surface may seem to be orderly and well-behaved. Complexity theory is related, as its basic theme is that systems are generally not externally controllable. However, complex systems are in constant transitions—self-creating small levels of order, and then adapting and changing again. A diamond crystal, for example, with its neatly arranged atoms is "ordered"; a rose, which has both randomness and order in the arrangement of its parts, is "complex"; the movement of gas molecules is truly "chaotic." Complexity covers that vast territory that lies between order and chaos. That leaves the question, how does this relate to management and communication?

Author Margaret Wheatley (1993) coined the term "fractal organization," based on the term "fractals," or shapes derived from iterations of non-linear equations that appear everywhere in nature. Their beauty and variety emerge as a result of two contradictory processes: total freedom for the equations to evolve as they will with no moment-to-moment prediction possible, yet a predetermined final shape prescribed by the initial parameters. In any fractal object, we are viewing a simple organizing structure that creates unending complexity. Fractals illustrate that order exists within disorder, and disorder exists within order. Each individual part has within it the information to generate a larger, more elaborate version of itself—when we view a part, we view the whole.

Wheatley believes that fractals have a direct application for leadership and communication in organizations. The potent force that shapes behavior in these fractal organizations, as in all natural systems, is the combination of a strong culture that embodies mutually held values and standards for acceptable behavior, and the freedom available to individuals to assert themselves in non-deterministic ways. Leaders and communicators in these fractal organizations must have trust in natural organizing phenomena—trust in the power of guiding principles or values, knowing that they are strong enough influences on individual behavior to allow every member to reflect the desired representation of the organization. In these highly principled organizations, one can expect to see similar behaviors show up at every level in the organization because those behaviors were patterned into the organizing principles at the very start.

Therefore, the way we view management is integral to the way that we try to manage to communicate—and communicate to manage. The workforce has also changed: the diversity and level of education have increased, and employees are seeking different rewards and environments than ever before. These call for a new approach to how organizations develop and manage promotional, collaborative, persuasive, and instructional communication (see Table 1.1).

Performance Spans the Silos

While management styles, workplace environments, communication technologies, and competitive strategies have changed dramatically over the past decades, the roles and structures for managing these systems have generally not kept pace. In most organizations, functional "silos" still exist into which external communication, employee communication, and training professionals and projects are placed. This is true even when many messages and technologies actually span those functions. Consider the following example:

Suppose a large chemical company is investigating the possibility of providing tablet computers and a new CRM (customer relationship management) software package to each sales representative to help "automate" their work. These portable computers wirelessly and continuously connect to the Internet, contain a database of current and potential customers, and provide the means to track

Table 1.1

Comparison of Characteristics of Traditional and New Organizations

Traditional Organizations	New Organizations
Management by a few at the top	Self-managed teams
Stable economy and products	Highly unstable economy, products, and services
Competitiveness based on price and product features	Competitiveness based on information and services bundled with the product, organizational reputation, and timeliness
Production machinery and physical plant are most valuable assets	Information, knowledge, and commitment of employees and customers are most important assets
Homogeneous workforce and customers	Diverse workforce and customers
Workers expected to obey	Workers expect explanations and a voice and are expected to contribute to company strategy
Highly specialized workers	Broadly educated and flexible workforce
Assembly-line production of routine products	Customized production of unique products
Workforce pre-trained at school or during an initial orientation	Continuous learning mandatory
Centralized workforce and facilities	Dispersed workforce and partnerships
Work takes place from 9–5 on weekdays	Work is "24/7" (continuous)
Face to face communication was most common and sufficient	Mediated communication is more common and technology skills and infrastructure are necessary
Cost of communication failure of inefficiencies is very low	Cost of communication failures or inefficiencies is very high
Pay for status	Pay for performance
High profit margin is wealth	Access to information and innovation is wealth
Communication based on need to know	Communication is a required and continuous function
Training offered only as required to do the job or to meet government regulations	Learning is seen as a continuous process, a competitive asset, and includes more than formal training programs

leads and sales. The new initiative has been proposed by the sales and marketing department with the help of some internal consultants from information technologies. However, if these tools are provided to sales reps, how can they be best leveraged to drive performance? They are a new system for communication and learning, and the potential goes way beyond customer databases.

◆ From the employee communications standpoint: How could the tablet computers provide "instant" newsletters to sales reps around the world by downloading information from e-mails and their intranet site?

♦ From the human resources development standpoint: How can the computers be used to train reps in the field via Web-based training?

♦ From the marketing standpoint: How can the computers be used to create customized "slide shows" for sales calls?

♦ From the organizational communication standpoint: How will this new technology be accepted by the sales force, and might it reduce face-to-face meetings?

♦ From the media production department standpoint: Will these computers reduce the need for hard-copy brochures and videos for marketing and training?

♦ From the line management standpoint: How can the timely and comprehensive data collected by the computers be better used to manage and evaluate sales reps?

As organizations grapple with the complexities of automation and new technologies, the most serious problem is that few people seem to have the "big picture." Indeed, in a large company such as an international chemical distributor, many people would be involved in deliberating the previously posed questions. The problem is that those questions often do not even get raised. The "sales force automation" project is often assigned to one department or individual with little input from other areas that will be impacted by it. That individual often comes at the problem from a technical perspective, and does not have a handle on the managerial and social implications of technology. A potentially good solution often gets caught in turf wars between departments who each want to have a stake.

In other cases, technologies are put into place without any regard for future or concurrent uses. Expensive multimedia or teleconferencing systems are purchased without a thought for how they can be updated when the information changes. Sometimes, communication systems are installed without thinking about the physical and social environment. For instance, hundreds of video playback units, purchased for each branch of a bank system, were to be used to deliver new product information to the tellers and platform representatives. However, most branch banks have no training or conference area and the units generally wound up being placed in the small staff lounges used for lunch breaks. One can imagine what kind of programming is actually being played on these machines given the employees' mind-set in this space.

What and Who Drives an Organization's Future?

Spreadsheets, trend lines, and mathematical formulas are the tools that business leaders often use to predict an organization's future. They look at earnings growth, market share, demographics, and pricing models. Although these are useful, countless examples exist where a company fails despite all the right market conditions and a terrific track record—and at the other extreme, extraordinary successes have come from organizations that seemed to have everything going against them.

Although there never will be a crystal ball, most scholars and experienced executives will provide a pretty similar list of the factors that are essential for a company's future:

- resilience and maneuverability—the ability to withstand tough times and "turn on a dime"
- the ability to survive—and perhaps eventually profit from—various types of crises
- a culture of continuous improvement and innovation
- the capacity to learn, share, and apply knowledge both internally and externally
- an ability to attract and delight the right customers and employees
- a reputation as a good corporate citizen so that policymakers and the news media further the company's interests

Although professionals in human resources and performance improvement do not directly manage all of these factors, they clearly do influence them. For example, corporate communications may be in charge of media relations, but if employees and executives are not trained in how to respond to media inquiries and do not understand important facts about the business, they are likely to cause great embarrassment when a reporter grabs them for an unexpected interview. While the brand may be crafted by the folks in marketing and advertising, the employees actually live the brand and deliver it to the consumer; unless those employees are selected, trained, and properly incented, the best advertising campaign and brand identity will ultimately fail. Finally, customers need the right documentation, job aids, and training to make good use of many products today. These factors may well provide the competitive edge for many enterprises.

Beyond HR—Managing Human Performance Systems

Human resources (HR), communication, and training have gone through many transformations over the past decades. This book goes beyond the traditional models of HR as "personnel" and training as fact and skill provision. Executives need to move beyond these titles and functions and think about the value that professionals in these areas bring to the table: **the knowledge and ability to shape human performance by creating the right infrastructures of rules and tools.**

For human resources, organizational development, employee communication, training, and documentation to demonstrate value, professionals need to show how they contribute to the present and *future* performance of the organization (see Figure 1.6).

HR professionals need to move from a focus on managing and assessing interventions (like training courses, safety campaigns, or new compensation programs) to managing, assessing, and developing infrastructures. There are three reasons for this:

1. *Empowered employees.* With today's information technologies and flattened management structures, employees at all levels are able to do a lot of what HR, training, and employee communications professionals used to have to do for them. People cross-train and coach each other; individuals create their own

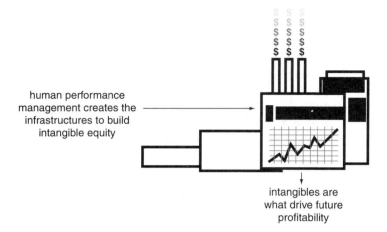

human performance management creates the infrastructures to build intangible equity

intangibles are what drive future profitability

Figure 1.6
Performance Management Drives Intangibles That Drive Profitability

personal and departmental intranet pages to share knowledge and news; employees manage their own benefits packages using online tools and develop their skills with online courses. While this may seem like a job threat, this is actually a benefit because of the second factor.

2. *Too much change to manage alone.* Most of my clients and students mention that they can't keep up with the organizational changes that imply the need for constant news updates, modifications in training and documentation, and coaching and feedback on performance. Fortunately, information technologies and more empowered employees can and are doing a lot of this themselves. HR leaders now have a new role, and that is to create the systems and guidelines—the rules and tools—to implement this change.

3. *Becoming a strategic partner.* This phrase has become somewhat of a cliché among people in communications, training, and HR. Despite a lot of talk, it still has not really happened in many organizations. As long as these professionals talk about individual projects, it is difficult for management to take seriously how they add long-term value. It is like being the decorator for a series of house parties rather than being the construction company that creates a new wing of a house. The former results in short-term pleasant experiences, and maybe even a short-term increase in positive activity, while the latter adds permanent value.

Human performance management is the engine that drives intangibles. This new professional orientation involves managing the communication, collaboration, and feedback systems that support current performance and future expansion.

CASE IN POINT

McDonald's invests in its intangible assets

Pat Crull, Vice President, Worldwide Learning Training and Development,
McDonald's Corporation, Oak Brook, IL

McDonald's invests in our staff by providing career-long development from crew through executives. For example, the standard training to become a restaurant manager requires about 2,000 hours. This program includes structured coaching, directed activities, self-study (paper-based and e-Learning), verification, and instructor-facilitated classes. Ray Kroc, the founder of McDonald's, said it best in 1976: "If we're going to go anywhere, we've got to have talent. And I'm going to put my money into talent."

McDonald's has learned that investing in our most important intangible asset, our people, leverages our tangible assets. The best example to illustrate this is the gap between our book value and our market capitalization [Figure 1.7]. Clearly the book value does not capture the important intangibles.

Figure 1.7
The Gap Between McDonald's Book Value and Market Capitalization

Results are assessed by the impact these investments have on the commitment of our people, measured regularly, and on the performance of our restaurants. The latter is measured by customer satisfaction feedback, mystery shopping, our 800 customer line and, of course, sales and growth.

HR professionals must position themselves "as business partners" to line management. The ability both to champion the people's causes and to translate the benefits into bottom-line numbers is critical. Recognizing that both are synergistic, not mutually exclusive, is a good starting point. Training, at McDonald's, illustrates this by recognizing these key success factors:

- Training is "real work" at McDonald's, not an event.
- Training is a major business initiative, not a support group.
- Training is viewed as an investment, not just a cost.
- Training requires long-term commitments.
- Training requires measurement.
- Training requires a proactive, planned approach.
- Training requires involved, committed leadership.
- Training requires shared accountability.

Used with permission from McDonald's Corporation.

The Big Picture: Assessing the Current Infrastructure

Too often, companies manage communication and training as a series of "one-off" or individual projects. They fund a sales training program, create an intranet site for benefits, or try to figure out what to do at the next round of employee meetings. While these individual interventions are important, they often fail to make a significant impact. Furthermore, when clients call me in to help them improve organizational performance, I frequently find that their problem is not a lack of projects, but rather some weaknesses in the overall infrastructure. This infrastructure includes the "rules" (policies, common practices, cultural norms) as well as the "tools" (technology, templates, spaces) for communication and learning.

What might an ideal communication and learning infrastructure look like? First off, its specifics—the company image or "voice," its media tools, its communication standards, and its learning mechanisms—should all be distinctive. There is no "one size fits all" model. The hallmarks of a good system are the three As of:

- adequacy
- accuracy
- accessibility

When enterprises take a systems view of the infrastructure, they often uncover significant barriers to performance, innovation, and commitment. Obstacles to effective corporate communication can be due to:

- inadequate rules or policies about how information should be disseminated
- ineffective networks or outdated technologies
- a management philosophy that does not support open communication and continuous learning
- too many links in the communication chain
- personnel (especially supervisors) who lack communication skills
- ineffective methods for analyzing the causes of poor performance and selecting appropriate interventions
- training systems that do not provide instruction that is tailored to the needs of individuals and is not accessible at the most "teachable" moment
- a mismatch of corporate culture or management philosophy with communication and training strategies
- a lack of knowledge about how best to address an organizations' various audiences' needs and interests

A quick picture of the infrastructure can be developed by using the following checkup.

Checkup 1: How Vital Are my Organization's Communication and Learning Structures?

Communication Element	What to consider
Communication infrastructure	What means/media are available to communicate what kinds of messages with whom?
Network flexibility	Who may easily and directly communicate with whom, and which paths and channels can be used?
Performance analysis	How are performance gaps detected (at an individual and team/department level) and what mechanisms are used to find the right solution?
Initiation of messages	Who may initiate dialogue, and who may seek information in what ways?
Communication load	What is the typical number of messages a given person, level of management, department, or customer must send and receive each day?
Learning load	How many new skills and concepts do people need to learn each week or month?
Communication and learning encumbrance	How much of an organization's time and money are expended on communication (memos, advertising, meetings, training, newsletters, etc.) versus producing its main product?
Communication efficiency	How quickly and inexpensively can a given type of message be created, stored, disseminated, and retrieved?
Communication integrity	How trustworthy, accurate, and current is the information in the system?
Communication effectiveness	How accurately can the intended audiences act on typical messages, how well can two-way persuasion and dialogue take place, and how does this impact performance?
Communication appropriateness	Do the channels of communication and typical messages fit the organization's culture and desired goals?
Organizational learning capacity	What are the systems that allow the organization to learn about new opportunities, approaches, and customer needs?
Feedback adequacy	By what means are individuals and work units appraised of their own performance, as well as the performance of the entire organization, and does the feedback allow individuals to monitor and control their own performance?

Checkup 2: How Do I Add Value?

Now suppose your organizational infrastructure not only needs to be aligned with the culture and with performance enablers, but your own skills and actions also need to demonstrate value. Here are some questions to ask yourself about your contributions to the organization.

☐ Do I know about and regularly update myself on my organization's long-term strategy and short-term goals?

☐ Do I really understand how the organization makes money and what factors make it more or less efficient?

☐ How do I plan my time? Do I have a strategy for selecting tasks that help the organization get the most value for my time?

☐ Do I look for opportunities to investigate new methods, techniques, technologies, or projects rather than wait for somebody to assign a project to me?

☐ How do I help to strengthen the organizational culture, both by my own actions and by the projects I create?

☐ Do I know who else in the organization is working on similar objectives and goals, and do I work collaboratively with them?

☐ Am I conscious of how I communicate and learn myself, and endeavor to improve my own skills in these areas?

☐ Do I know what new practices and theories of communication and learning are being developed?

A Roadmap for this Book

This book will describe what a good communication and learning infrastructure looks like, how it can get "on the books" as an infrastructure asset, and how you as a professional in HR, communications, or training can build jobs and organizational structures to manage and assess it. Moreover, you will learn how to move from managing and talking about interventions to performance—and then to dollars. You will see how to bridge the hard and soft disciplines of finance and HR, and how to sell your value to business executives. Going beyond procedures to calculate ROI, the chapters will present a methodology and best practices for managing the array of systems that form a solid, aligned, and integrated infrastructure that has a positive impact on your organization's performance and value.

Self-Check

1. Training, human resources, and corporate communications are traditionally thought of as staff functions that merely support the "line" revenue-creation components of an organization. As such, they are often considered as over-

head expenses. Discuss how these functions actually add long-term value in terms of managing intangible assets.

2. What are the "Four Cs" that characterize vital organizations?
3. Explain how management theory and styles have changed over the past decades and how that directly impacts what is seen as "ideal" communication and learning practices.
4. Why and how do professionals in HR, communications, and learning need to move from focusing on individual projects to focusing on infrastructures?
5. What factors should be considered when analyzing the overall health of an organization's learning and communication infrastructures?
6. Name at least five things that every professional in learning, communications, and HR should do on a regular basis to add value to her or his organization.

References

Keller, J. M. (1996). *Motivation by design.* Tallahassee, FL: John Keller Associates.

Kouzes, J., & Posner, B. (1993). *Credibility: How leaders gain and lose it, why people demand it.* San Francisco: Jossey-Bass.

Prusak, L., & Cohen, D. (2001). *In good company: How social capital makes organizations work.* Cambridge: Harvard Business School Press.

Screw up and get smart. (1998, November). *FAST Company,* p.58.

Shockley-Zalabak, P., Ellis, K., and Cesaria, R. (2000). *Measuring organizational trust.* San Francisco: International Association of Business Communicators.

Stewart, T. A. (1997). *Intellectual Capital.* New York: Doubleday.

Sveiby, K. E. (1997). *The new organizational wealth: Managing and measuring knowledge-based assets.* San Francisco: Berrett-Koehler.

Wheatley, M. (1993). *Leadership and the new science.* San Francisco: Berrett-Koehler.

CHAPTER 2 *How Human Resources, Communications, and Learning Systems Can Create— or Destroy—Value*

Overview

Human resources, communications, and training have a great potential to create—or destroy—performance and value. This chapter looks at why and how. You will see hard data on how smart management of human performance directly affects a company's valuation, and why an organization's "islands of communication" need to be bridged.

From Personnel to Performance

Years ago, the people in charge of hiring employees and getting them paid worked in "personnel" departments. Employees were often called "hands"—which was sadly appropriate to the kind of unskilled labor that most of them brought to the enterprise. In fact, the word "management" originally referred to the care and handling of horses!

When it became clear that workers needed more than money and threats to be productive, the human relations framework became popular. The intent was to keep the workers somewhat satisfied, motivated, and not inclined to cause union trouble. As the landscape of work became more complex through increased labor legislation, larger non-family-run companies, and more head-work than hand-work, the "personnel" function became known as "human resources." Still, in this paradigm people were seen as parallel to raw materials and cash: merely an input to the final product. Human resources developed subspecialties like organizational development, training, benefits, compensation, recruiting, and work design, but as the discipline gained depth it also became more fragmented.

Almost any experienced businessperson will tell you that HR probably has the lowest credibility and influence among the various departments in organizations, largely because the performance of humans cannot be precisely controlled, the mechanisms that are used to influence it are seen as "soft." Often, interventions like training and motivational systems are seen as perks rather than essential elements. Because managers sometimes think that anybody who is "good with people" can do HR, the field has been full of people put out to pasture, women and minorities who are hired to fulfill EEO quotas but who are not really meant to be taken seriously, as well as secretaries who, because they can type, are put in charge of the company newsletter and then become directors of employee communications. These harsh statements are not meant to disparage this important profession or demean the many competent people working in it. However, HR professionals are not well served by denying its history and challenges.

In the new economy, people are just not merely a resource; for many enterprises, they *are* the company. As a result, managing human performance so that customer value and relationships grow and the organization's capabilities expand is the key to a sustainable business. The old visions and versions of personnel, human relations, and human resources do not serve organizations well. We need a new framework. That is what this chapter will explore.

How Human Performance Management Creates Value

Human performance—based on knowledge, motivation, behavior, and work systems—are the key drivers of organizational value. In order for human resources to function as a strategic asset, there needs to be an integrated system of brand, people, and performance infrastructures (see Figure 2.1).

HR systems (selecting, compensating, motivating, developing, and communicating with and retaining the right people) are not easy to imitate. This creates a strategic asset. Brian Becker and Mark Huselid (2001) use the term "HR architecture" to encompass the HR function (HR professionals with strategic competen-

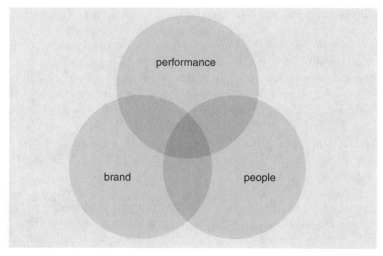

Figure 2.1
Human Resources Infrastructures

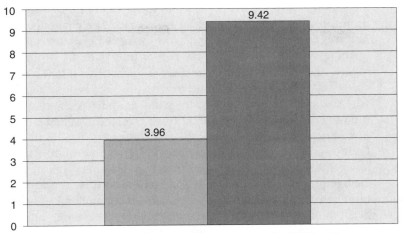

book value of companies with poor vs. excellent HR functions

Figure 2.2
Strategic HR Practices Result in Increased Stock Multiples

cies), the HR system (policies and practices), and strategically focused employee behaviors. In their study of more than 3,000 publicly held companies, they found that firms rated in the top twenty-fifth percentile with regard to strategic HR functions had a market to book value of 9.42 as compared to the bottom twenty-fifth percentile, which had a market to book value of 3.96 (see Figure 2.2).

Focusing on Systems

In today's environment of "lean" staffing, increased education and training, and empowerment, each employee carries more responsibility and therefore more value—at least, more *potential* value. Organizations cannot compete on technology alone, as competitors can generally easily replicate machinery and processes. Neither can organizations compete on price alone: consumers want innovations and relationships. Unique knowledge and relationship assets are only created by excellent human performance engineering practices.

Most corporate leaders today *do* appreciate the complex role of HR, and recognize the need to attract, retain, and train excellent employees. Given this attention, HR departments have been expanding the kinds of programs offered. These include more training and development opportunities, more sophisticated benefits and compensation systems, and quite a bit of investment in information technology products that centralize HR record keeping.

While interventions and software products like these are important, the problem is that many such products only have a short shelf-life. Because of this, a company cannot really consider them an asset or a strategy. Therefore, smart professionals in HR need to re-set their goals: **The challenge is to create value, not programs.** HR leaders can do this by focusing on developing and managing ongoing systems rather than a series of interventions. In order to get "on the books" and in parity with other areas in management, HR needs to show that it creates assets that spin-off continuing excess profits or savings.

A second reason exists for focusing on systems: many of the activities that used to be done by HR personnel (including training and communications) are now being done on a self-serve basis by employees. People and departments have their own Web pages where they provide news and training tips; HR systems allow people to check and manage their own benefits plans, enroll in courses, and change personal data. It is not just technology that is driving this movement; rather, many tactical functions in HR are being outsourced and others are being given to empowered employees and managers to handle themselves (i.e., interviewing, coaching, performance appraisal). This is similar to the evolution of cars. In the early days, few people drove because cars were so difficult to drive and because they broke down so often. There was a big need for chauffeurs. However, now that people drive themselves, the problem is coordinating all of these drivers and providing an adequate highway system. **Smart professionals in HR, training, and communications need to move from being chauffeurs who do the grunt work of driving individual projects that are assigned to them to being engineers of the human performance highway**—by deciding where and how people need to get to the right destinations.

To restate the last point: **Effective HR managers need to proactively assess the gaps between current and optimal performance and propose strategies to close those gaps.** Today, people in training, recruiting, compensation, and communications generally take a reactive role. They wait for management to tell them about their needs and instruct them what to produce. Many problems exist with this scenario. When people in organizations do not perform the way that management thinks they should, executives will generally jump to one solution without adequately diagnosing the reason for the performance gap or necessarily selecting the right solution. Suppose that a particular product is not selling as well as expected; the sales manager might order up sales training because he just read about a great new instructional technique—or he may request a new bonus system for reps who meet certain sales goals for the new product—or he may request a big product promotion campaign for the sales staff with tee-shirts, mugs, and a picnic for the sales reps. However, it is possible that none of these may be the right solution—and, as shown later, any one of them could do more harm than good.

The last change needed to achieve in order to demonstrate value is to be able to talk the language of business—and that is finance. Although it is not necessary to get an MBA or learn accounting, it is important to understand a few basic terms and at least know how to ask the right questions of the finance folks. Instead, HR usually sees finance as an obstacle—the people who somehow turn down requests for reasons that cannot be understood. Chapter 7 will discuss this financial terminology and thinking in more detail.

To sum up, in order for HR to gain credibility, three things need to happen. The HR department must:

1. focus on systems and human performance outcomes, not programs
2. proactively seek out performance improvement opportunities rather than act like an order-taker
3. talk the language of business—finance

CASE IN POINT

Watson Wyatt's human capital index research

Kathryn Yates, Global Communication Practice Director
Watson Wyatt, Chicago, IL

It pays—literally—to manage people right.

Watson Wyatt's Human Capital Index (HCI) study shows that effective implementation of certain people management practices can yield an increase in shareholder value of up to 47 percent.

Clearly, employees—and their contributions—matter.

Yet, too few companies are making the most of their human capital investments.

For the most part, the problem is the lack of widespread knowledge about which HR practices really make a difference to companies' bottom lines. Until recently, solid data showing the link between HR practices and shareholder value was scarce, so companies simply did the best they could with what little information they had.

The HCI study solves this dilemma by establishing which human capital practices have the greatest impact on shareholder value. By quantifying the expected increase in a company's market value associated with an improvement in five human capital areas, the study shows precisely which HR practices find their way to the bottom line.

Three key findings from the study underscore the importance of getting HR investments right:

Superior human capital practices are lead—not lag—indicators of financial performance. This means that effective human capital practices lead to positive financial results more than superior financial results lead to good HR practices.

Shareholder returns are three times higher at companies with superior human capital practices than at companies with weak human capital practices. The positive impact of effective human capital practices on firm performance holds whether the business cycle is in a boom period or in a recession.

Not all human capital practices drive shareholder value. Some actually diminish it. Companies must examine programs and practices such as 360-degree feedback, developmental training, and the objectives for using HR technologies to ensure they are adding to—not subtracting from—shareholder value.

HCI Study Background

The Human Capital Index is an ongoing study that quantifies the link between specific human capital practices and shareholder value. Conducted in 1999 and 2001, its objective is four-pronged:

(1) to provide HR with financial performance metrics, (2) to test the belief that it pays to manage people right, (3) to help managers assess their human capital investments, and (4) to determine whether some HR practices offer a greater return than others.

This first study, conducted in 1999, incorporated data from a survey of 405 public companies in the United States and Canada. The companies were asked a series of questions about their human resource practices, including pay, developing people, communication, and staffing.

The outcome? Thirty human capital practices were identified that, when adopted or improved, resulted in a cumulative increase in market value of 30 percent.

The contribution of effective human capital practices to market value was even greater in the 2001 study, with the inclusion of additional human capital practices and the expansion of the participant pool. Seven hundred and fifty large publicly traded companies in the United States, Canada, and Europe took part in the 2001 study, with 500 coming from North America and 250 from Europe. The participants included companies such as 3M, DaimlerChrysler, The Kellogg Company, ING Canada, Quebecor World, and Shell Oil.

The 2001 survey showed that adopting and implementing key HR practices in five broad categories can result in up to a 47 percent increase in market value. The following table breaks the contributions down by category:

Key dimensions	Increase in shareholder value
Total rewards and accountability	16.5%
Collegial, flexible workplaces	9.0%
Recruiting and retention excellence	7.9%
Communication integrity	7.1%
Focused HR service technology	6.5%
TOTAL	47.0%

Expected change in market value associated with a significant one standard deviation (1SD) improvement in HCI dimension.

Source: Watson Wyatt 2001 HCI study.

Chicken or egg?

In addition to providing data on the contributions of specific HR practices to the bottom line, the 2001 results also answered a nagging question raised by the 1999 study—do effective HR practices drive positive financial results or do positive financial results lead to better HR practices because successful businesses can afford higher quality HR programs?

Comparative analysis of the 1999 and 2001 study results found that superior HR practices drive shareholder value, not the other way around. For every available correlation calculated over time, the relation between past HR practice and future financial performance was stronger than the relation between past financial outcomes and future HR practices.

Practices that work

The results of the HCI study provide insight into precisely which HR practices—amid the ever-increasing portfolio of options—should be adopted or improved to increase HR's contribution to the bottom line. Companies that have superior recruiting and retention practices, for example, are worth 7.9 percent more in the market, according to the study. There are ten specific recruiting and retention practices that companies must implement well in order to achieve this value, as shown in the following chart.

	Impact on shareholder value
Recruiting and Retention Excellence	7.9%
Company has low voluntary turnover of managers/professionals	1.7%
Company has low voluntary turnover of employees in general	1.5%
Company emphasizes job security	1.4%
Formal recruiting strategy exists for critical skill employees	0.6%
Recruiting efforts are aligned with the business plan	0.5%
Employees have input on hiring decisions	0.5%
Company has a reputation as a desirable place to work	0.5%
Systematic new hire orientation exists	0.4%
Hourly/clerical new hires are well-equipped to perform duties	0.4%
Professional new hires are well-equipped to perform duties	0.4%

Expected change in market value associated with a significant one standard deviation (1SD) improvement in HCI dimension.

Source: Watson Wyatt 2001 HCI study.

Total rewards and accountability

The area of total rewards and accountability also is associated with a significant percentage increase to the bottom line when superior practices are implemented.

	Impact on shareholder value
Total Rewards and Accountability	16.5%
Health benefits are important for recruiting and retention	2.8%
High percentage of company stock is owned by employees	1.3%
DC and DB plans, combined, are important for recruiting and retention	1.3%
High percentage of company stock is owned by managers	1.2%
Pay is linked to company's business strategy	1.1%
High percentage of employees are eligible for stock options	1.0%
Company promotes most competent employees	0.9%
High percentage of employees participate in incentive/profit-sharing plans	0.9%
Defined benefit plan is important for recruiting and retention	0.9%
Employees have a choice regarding benefits	0.8%
Defined contribution plan is important for recruiting and retention	0.8%
Top performers receive better pay than average performers	0.8%
Company positions benefits above the market	0.7%
Company helps poor performers improve	0.7%
Company positions pay above the market	0.7%
Company terminates employees who continue to perform poorly	0.6%

Expected change in market value associated with a significant one standard deviation (1SD) improvement in HCI dimension.

Source: Watson Wyatt 2001 HCI study.

Establishing a collegial, flexible workplace

Establishing a collegial, flexible workplace is another category of practices that, when combined, are associated with a large increase in shareholder value (just over 9 percent). Among the critical practices in this category are: company shows flexibility in work arrangements (3.5 percent);

company has high employee satisfaction (1.3 percent); trust in senior leadership is actively engendered (1.2 percent); managers demonstrate company values (1.1 percent); company culture encourages teamwork and cooperation (0.5 percent); company avoids using titles to designate status and authority (0.5 percent); company avoids varying perquisites by position (0.5 percent); and company avoids varying office space by position (0.5 percent).

Communication integrity

Companies that invest wisely in practices associated with communication integrity can realize a 7.1 percent increase in shareholder value. This includes practices such as giving employees easy access to technologies for communication (4.2 percent); enabling employees at all levels to give ideas and suggestions to senior management (0.7 percent); sharing business plans and goals with employees (0.6 percent); winning high employee participation in opinion surveys (0.6 percent); sharing financial information with employees (0.5 percent); and taking action on employee survey feedback (0.5 percent).

HR service technologies

Finally, adopting focused HR service technologies can also yield a 6.5 percent increase in shareholder value. Superior practices that fall into this category are related to the objectives behind companies' implementation of HR service technologies. Companies that adopt such technologies with a goal of improving service to employees and managers can realize a 2.3 percent gain in shareholder value, as can companies that adopt the technologies hoping to achieve cost reduction. Adopting HR service technologies in order to increase transaction accuracy and integrity is associated with a 1.9 percent increase in shareholder value.

Indisputable data helps make business case for HR investments

With the release of the HCI study, human resource executives now have the hard data they need to make the case for greater human capital investment to their organizations. It is tough to argue that people management strategies are secondary when such strong linkages to shareholder returns can be made.

Awareness of which human capital strategies are most effective means HR can add greater value even without additional outlays. By retooling current strategies to better reflect the practices that bring the greatest return-on-investment, HR executives can get more value from the same levels of spending.

Take the area of communication. Many companies invest less in communication strategies than they do in other human capital areas. A look at the HCI figures shows the folly of this approach—effective implementation of specific communication practices is associated with a 7.1 percent increase in shareholder value. By failing to invest in communication, companies are missing out on a significant source of improvement in shareholder returns.

The study also makes it very clear that all communication practices are not created equal. According to the survey, companies that view online HR service delivery models merely as vehicles for conveying information, without linking them to broader HR service delivery strategies and process improvements, can see up to a 7.7 percent *reduction* in shareholder value.

That is a pretty powerful number. It means adopting communication as your primary goal for implementing HR service technologies can effectively wipe out all the gains you make from every other communication practice you successfully implement.

Counterintuitive findings

In addition to using technology solely for communication purposes, the HCI study also throws a cautionary flag in front of several other HR practices that are applauded by conventional wisdom. Two practices in particular—360-degree review and developmental training—also were associated with a decrease in financial performance.

The study notes that while nothing is inherently wrong with these practices, many organizations implement them in misguided ways. For example, implementing multi-source feedback is not likely to add value unless the program measures the behaviors that truly add value and then provides coaching and reinforcement to change those behaviors.

When it comes to developmental training, the negative effect on shareholder value is likely due to several factors, including ineffective training, poaching by competitors, and offering the right training to the wrong people. Despite its potential negative impact, companies do not need to scuttle developmental training altogether. Instead, they must retool their training programs to place greater emphasis on improving productivity in employees' current positions and eliminating factors that put a drain on shareholder value.

The 2001 Watson Wyatt HCI study clearly shows that organizations can no longer afford to operate under the traditional assumption that superior HR practices are nice to have, but not essential. Given the link between human capital practices and company performance, organizations must make developing and executing superior human capital strategies a priority.

The fact that superior human capital practices are lead—not lag—indicators of shareholder value creation means that assessing which human capital practices need to be improved and which need to be jettisoned is critical. With 47 percent of potential shareholder value on the line, and evidence that superior human resources practices are leading indicators of improved business performance, HR executives are well-armed to make the business case for moving human capital investments up in the hierarchy of organizational priorities.

How HR Can Create—or Block—the Ideal Organization

Imagine an ideal organization. . . let's call it GreatPlace, Ltd. What makes it so wonderful?

- GreatPlace succeeds—even exceeds—in enacting its well-articulated and unique mission, vision, and values. These do not simply consist of posters on the wall or sappy statements on business cards. The company's mission and its culture are focused and do not seek to imitate others in their business.
- GreatPlace has happy employees whose performance is aligned with company goals. People enjoy work when they know they are successful and get clear feedback on the results of their effort.
- Employees are loyal; they defend the company even in the face of threats or crises like market downturns or even occasional mistakes that are made by their

management or peers. Because they are treated with respect and kept informed, they feel like they have a long-term stake in the success of the company.

♦ Most recruiting and marketing is done by word of mouth; because it is known as a good place to work and for its quality products and excellent service, advertising and recruiting costs are very low. Employees and customers recruit more of their own.

♦ Customers are willing to pay more for GreatPlace's products because they consider them to have good value and they like supporting a company that is known for good employment and community practices.

♦ Similarly, many employees accept less in salary than they could make elsewhere in return for their affiliation with GreatPlace. They also really believe in its mission and enjoy coming to work.

♦ A constant stream of innovation exists. Customers and employees create new products of value by their good relationships, dialogue, and systems that track and maintain collaboration.

♦ Well-trained and motivated employees perform to their capacity and do not waste resources. Their work environment enables them to efficiently complete their tasks and find the information they need without wasting any time. While they are well-informed and trained, they are not sent to unnecessary meetings or courses.

♦ Knowledge management systems and practices reduce employee frustration because they can quickly find information and help. This also enables GreatPlace customers to get the best of the company's pooled knowledge and performance.

♦ When the company needs to expand by hiring people or even by opening new locations, it is easy because knowledge and policy systems are in place, work processes are documented, and this makes replication and expansion very smooth.

♦ Good government and community relations practices over the years provide a favorable economic and political climate.

♦ Good relationships with suppliers and industry make for smooth collaboration and consistency.

Does this sound like an ideal world? Well, perhaps no one organization has all of these characteristics, but many organizations can be described by at least several of these statements.

Extreme Logic, an IT consulting firm, improved its ability to retain star performers and align the performance of its employees with its intranet and extranet. When employees are hired away by competitors or fired for poor performance, the company spends as much as three times an employee's annual salary to find and train a replacement. Getting quick online feedback directly from customers lets Extreme Logic reward its stars and provide specific improvement goals for everyone else. The company's turnover rate is 5 to 10 percent lower than the IT industry standard. And since the company added the performance-evaluation feature to its intranet about 80 percent of its employees and managers feel that they are working toward the same goals, compared with 52 percent before.

Southwest Airlines has consistently been rated among the top five "Best Places to Work in America" and "Most Admired Companies in America" by a *Fortune* magazine survey. Southwest is selective in its hiring (only 4 percent of the 9,000 who apply at Southwest are hired; application procedures include personality tests and interviews with a recruiter, potential supervisor, and a peer employee). Once employees are hired, they are integrated into a strong culture of customer service; however, Southwest's executive management insists that employees come first. The results: they are the most consistently profitable airline; among the highest rated airline for customer service, safety, and innovation; and they have never had a strike.

Buckman Labs has created a global electronic knowledge management system for both employees and customers. One of their key customers said, "Buckman's technical support, with their K'Netix® global information system, holds as great a value to us as the chemicals they supply. When Buckman's chemicals are applied to a process, they commit their resources and skills to develop a successful partnership." Another wrote, "Buckman Labs has provided us with their chemicals, services and expertise in the water treatment area. We are very pleased with their value added services. They are not just a supplier of chemicals. We have found this ability to link, communicate, problem solve and co-ordinate all aspects of our chemical treatment programs to be the key to continuous improvement of day to day operations" (Buckman Laboratories Knowledge Nurture website).

Although these are terrific examples, it is not advisable to merely imitate what other companies have done. A healthy and interrelated set of performance systems creates strategic value because it is very hard to copy. It allows for extraordinary cost savings, excess earnings, and creates a huge barrier of entry for any organization that wants to compete. Most importantly, it is an ideal situation for all parties; a win/win for customers, management, investors, employees, and society.

How Traditional Practices Often Decrease Performance

I have spent most of my professional life designing and teaching others to design various kinds of workplace programs to improve performance—things like training programs, promotional campaigns, and employee communications. Around the late 1980s I noticed a trend: many of the projects we created for clients did not have the anticipated impact. Many of them got caught in some major corporate change that made the content or timing ineffective; in other cases, it just seemed difficult to gain the attention of those for whom the programs were designed. My professional colleagues—some of the best people in the business—reported similar situations.

As my consulting practice expanded, I found myself frequently being called in by executives, communication directors, and HR professionals to figure out why some of their critical programs were not able to effect the intended performance changes. They expected a critique of the instructional design model they used for their training programs, the formats they used for their employee meetings, or perhaps the kinds of technologies they were using for communication. The problems were rarely caused by any of those factors.

It was not until I zoomed out—took a "helicopter view" of the information and collaboration systems—that I got the picture. Most corporations have set up separate departments to do their advertising, information systems management, employee newsletters, recruiting, annual reports, documentation, media production, speechwriting, press relations, and training. The result of this fragmentation has been:

◆ a lack of coherence in (or even blatantly conflicting) organizational messages and communication styles
◆ duplication of efforts and technologies
◆ information overload

The various programs were actually competing against each other for what I call **"mindshare"—the attention, commitment, and competence of employees** (Gayeski, 2000). What I have observed is that people are spending more and more time attending meetings, participating in training courses, and reading memos and manuals. The very information that is designed to improve their performance winds up, by its sheer volume and lack of consistency, creating confusion and anxiety. Getting a better grip on workplace communication, which probably consumes most of employees' time, may be the most significant challenge of our century.

Islands of Communication

In most organizations, the various "voices" of the organization exist as "islands of communication"—even when all of them are supposed to represent the organization's official viewpoint, policy, or style. Typically, these various "islands," such as training and development, information systems, policies and procedures, employee communication, marketing, advertising, and public relations, are not only separate departments but they rarely coordinate their activities. This *dis-integration* of communication causes major performance and morale problems (see Figure 2.3).

So, what happens to communication, learning, and the corporate image and culture because of this phenomenon? As the various "islands of communication" become more specialized and compete for resources and survival, they become less connected. In many organizations, professionals in training have never spoken to their colleagues in employee communication, public relations, or advertising and are only now forced to work with the information systems department because they are attempting to use multimedia and online training systems. These separate departments generate programs and messages without any knowledge of how they relate to other messages that employees and customers regard as the "voice" of the organization.

For example, the focus of messages from the employee communication department might be organizational change, downsizing, and measures of profitability while the major themes being stressed by the training department are

Dis-integrated communication
a picture of information dissemination in typical organizations

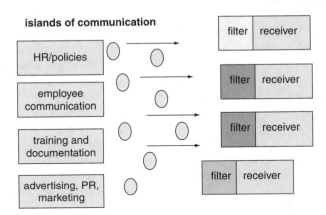

Figure 2.3
The "Islands of Communication"

teamwork and diversity. At the same time, the external communication systems like public affairs and advertising may be touting close partnerships with customers and excellent service.

In dis-integrated communication, the various islands of communication each send out their messages in the form of newsletters, Internet and intranet sites, meetings, ad campaigns, videos, or courses. Employees experience this as a barrage of data and somehow must filter it in terms of sheer volume as well as in terms of its meaning to them. Of course, each person sets up his or her own filtering system, leading to a decrease in performance and morale, as well as a less-cohesive workforce. Some short "snapshots" of case studies from my own consulting projects illustrate this concept.

- ◆ The communications department of a not-for-profit organization sent out a letter over the CEO's name appealing to its employees for donations to its research fund. This letter arrived in employees' mailboxes on the same day that human resources sent out an announcement that their benefits package would be cut. The cynicism and ill will that was caused by this mis-timing not only compromised the success of the research fund drive, but also inadvertently painted a very poor picture of the CEO. This incident was frequently cited as an example of how "out of touch" the organization was with its employees—the very *opposite* of the values and desired message of the management leaders.
- ◆ The training department at a major North American bank was in the midst of revising its training program for tellers and platform representatives. They wanted to conduct a study of what employee behaviors were most important to

customers, but they were unable to garner the resources. While meeting with the public affairs department, we discovered that they had hired an outside research company to call a sample of customers each night to ask questions about customer satisfaction and needs—but the training department was unaware of this activity or any of the resulting insights. The advertising department engaged a firm to develop a new corporate identity and image, based on an analysis of the various regional cultures served by the bank. They created an expensive series of television campaigns depicting a "new look" at the bank—without bothering to communicate the reasons behind this image to branch managers or the training department, who both continued to encourage "old" behaviors.

◆ In a large restaurant chain, I found that managers were being sent such a large volume of print, e-mail, voicemail, and other media that they could easily spend four hours a day doing nothing but processing this material. Because their jobs did not allow for such a time expenditure, they were ignoring at least half of it. The problem was that in this fast-growing company, inexperienced managers did not know what half to ignore and frequently made costly mistakes. Because headquarters staff knew how hard it was to get managers' attention, they often sent voicemail to announce that an e-mail had been sent, only to follow that up with the same message in print and another voicemail reminder. Naturally, this repetitive situation amounted to unacceptable information overload. Their chief information officer estimated that this overload of their data systems was costing them at least a million dollars a year.

This dis-integration of communication not only causes poor performance by information overload, but also by causing cynicism and an erosion of the culture and voice of the company. The poor intended receivers of all this information put up two kinds of barriers: One is a physical one—people literally throw out mail and delete voicemail and e-mail before they ever really attend to it. Obviously, this leads to the production of lots of wasted messages. The second filter is a psychological one—people will tune out inconsistent messages. They will adopt a certain stance on a topic, and just dismiss or completely ignore anything that is not congruent with it.

CASE IN POINT

Various choices in a cruise line: organizational internal connectedness

Helena Stigzelius, Associate Professor, CERS
Swedish School of Business and Economics, Helsinki, Finland

From the beginning of the 1990s, more and more companies have been shifting their strategic thinking toward customer relationship management (CRM). Some companies are driven by the possibilities that various CRM information technology solutions offer, which are implemented directly at the operational level. Others make the move out of philosophical reasoning. Either way, the road toward relationship thinking is bumpy, and not all organizations reach the goals they have set. Big money is spent on IT solutions, which unfortunately in many cases are left unused. Failure rates of implementing CRM are high; some sources claim failure rates of up to 90 percent. Yet CRM, as a guiding strategic logic, has been proven to bring competitive advantage to the firm when successfully executed.

Research findings indicate that an organization's internal relationships are reflected to the surface of external relationships with customers. When an organization is moving its strategic thinking toward a relationship orientation, the coherency in the organization's internal communication becomes of extreme importance. The real challenge is to manage the change of both the thinking and the behavior of the organizational members.

A study on the organizational change process toward customer relationship models was conducted by the Swedish School of Economics on one of the major shipping/cruising companies in Scandinavia, the Silja Line. The barriers for the organizational move toward relationship thinking were examined in a longitudinal study onboard one of the vessels employing 300 people. The marketing organization ashore was also included in the study. This case shows evidence of the importance of coherency in organizational internal communication.

The findings from the research conducted at the Silja Line indicate different dimensions of gaps in the organization's culture. The findings are summarized on the following dimensions: organizational mission, identity, values and beliefs, and skills and behavior. Three different cultures were found within this organization: the marketing culture ashore, the shipping culture onboard, and the catering culture onboard. The logic of these different cultures varies to a great extent. As a result, the internal connectedness between the organizational members was lacking. The cultural gaps, on the previously defined dimensions, are shown in Figure 2.4.

As shown in Figure 2.4, the mission of the marketing culture is mainly to make money, whereas the mission of catering personnel is to focus on providing high-quality service experiences for the customers. The third culture inside the organization has a strong tradition in the shipping logic, with the mission emphasizing the safety aspect. All these different cultures inside

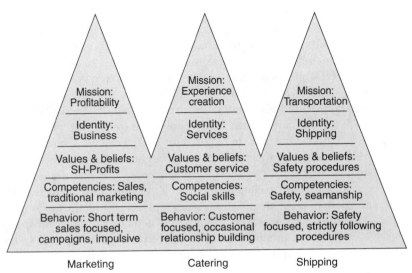

Figure 2.4
Different Functions Have Different Subcultures and Languages

the organization are a natural consequence of the firm's history and its business logic. These varying missions are a part of the organization's grand mission, and important as such.

However, the critical issue found in the study was the lack of a common language and connectedness between these subcultures. The other dimensions shown in Figure 2.4 follow the same reasoning. The different identities found within the subcultures stem from the related missions. A business identity set the frames for the values in a completely different direction than the issues valued among the catering personnel.

Without an internal common language and connectedness, these differences could lead to conflicting goal setting. This will become evident on the customer surface: the impression the customer gets during various encounters with the company can be confusing.

The lack of internal connectedness becomes extremely critical if an organization intends to move its business logic in a direction that requires a holistic customer approach from the organization. In relationship thinking, or CRM, the logic is built on this notion. Clearly, this requires a basic communication flow between different functions inside the organization. Shared meaning built on internal connectedness is required! However, it does not imply a completely unified reasoning and it does not exclude having varying opinions and subgoals. It does, however, require an internal dialogue process that enhances the development of the business logic through the emergence of internal connectedness. When the organization reaches a mode of internal connectedness, the development of customer relationship strategy has a good chance of succeeding!

Outsourcing Value

In an attempt to save costs, many HR, training, and communication departments have outsourced all or parts of some key functions. A lot of recruiting is being done online or by head-hunters, performance management and employee data systems are purchased as enterprise-wide software systems, and a lot of training is either purchased as off-the-shelf packages or is delivered by consultants. While these may be good strategies in many situations, a grave danger of losing strategic value exists.

Remember, if human performance systems are easily imitated, they are not very valuable. If pieces are merely bought from different vendors, they could easily be replicated by a competitor. Key cultural values and specific business knowledge are generally diluted when programs are not custom-designed. For example, I have done work for two major manufacturers of office equipment who were in head-to-head competition. One of them required me to sign extensive non-disclosure agreements before I could see their sales training program, which they viewed as a key competitive strategy and somewhat of a trade secret. What they did not realize was that the consultant who developed it sold an almost identical package to their competitor, and both of these organizations' sales reps were out in the marketplace using exactly the same trigger questions and probing methods with their prospects.

Moreover, this practice often exacerbates dis-integrated systems that are destructive to performance. For example, programs that are purchased from different sources generally are written from different perspectives, using different styles and personalities. This subtly makes the organization seem schizophrenic and decreases the level of trust that both employees and customers have in it.

When organizations purchase services or products from outside sources, they should perform a careful audit of not just explicit information but also of implicit cultural and value messages. Outside trainers, writers, and consultants need to be thoroughly briefed in the organization's mission, vision, value, lore, and recent events.

Checkup 3: Are You Administrative or Strategic?

Although there is no shortage of tasks for professionals in HR areas such as employee communications and training, some activities are more strategic and connected to the business. Rowan Wilson (2001) lists seven critical steps to help HR practitioners reevaluate their work and provide value-based HR functions:

1. attract and retain talent
2. master technology
3. foster a learning environment
4. define the employer brand
5. drive innovation
6. develop leadership
7. communicate strategy

Based on this framework, use the chart below to estimate the percentage of time spent in the following areas:

% of time	Administrative	% of time	Strategic
	Designing training or communication messages created by others		Benchmarking best practices in communication and learning in related industries
	Keeping records (e.g., training enrollments, responses to recruiting ads, requests for public relations materials)		Developing leadership competencies and strategies
	Attending to compliance issues (e.g., mandated training or public disclosure)		Expanding the core competencies of the organization
	Administering and communicating salary and benefits information		Defining key performance gaps and diagnosing the causes
	Monitoring the budget		Developing business cases and return-on-investment analyses for proposed interventions
	Minimizing risk		Creating opportunity
	Endeavoring to create a stable and predictable environment		Managing and leading change
	Attempting to outperform other departments		Making bridges to other functional areas to align messages and strategy

Self-Check

1. What are the three challenges that professionals in learning, HR, and communications need to take on in order to achieve credibility in the new business environment?
2. Why is it necessary to take a "helicopter view" of organizational learning and communication when a certain program or project does not seem to be working?
3. Cite research that shows how good human capital practices actually correlate to organizational performance and stockholder value, and why these are "leading" rather than "lagging" indicators.
4. What are the hallmarks of a good HR infrastructure?
5. Explain how the "islands of communication" concept helps companies understand why certain projects undertaken by corporate communications, training, HR, or marketing may actually be destructive of overall performance and value.
6. Why is it dangerous to outsource too many functions within HR?
7. What are the marks of a professional being "strategic" rather than "administrative"?

References

Becker, B., Huselid, M. (2001). The strategic impact of HR. *Balanced Scorecard Report*. Boston: Harvard Business School Publishing.

Gayeski, D. (2000). *Managing the communication function: Capturing mindshare for organizational performance*. San Francisco: International Society of Business Communicators.

Wilson, R. (2001). Seven steps to value-based HR management. *Strategic HR Review*, 1(1), 16–20.

CHAPTER 3 Internal and External Communication Systems

Overview

The way that organizations communicate with their internal and external constituencies can define the difference between success and failure. Systems that support clear, rapid, and multi-way communication between individuals and departments are essential infrastructures in today's competitive environment. In this chapter you'll explore new ways to think and talk about communication, both within an organization and with its constituencies. You'll learn how organizations can engineer communication systems that promote customer loyalty, consistent branding, and efficient employee performance.

Where Does Communication Fit?

Communication professionals can be found in many places on the organizational chart. Some people specialize in one type of communication (news, marketing and promotions, executive speeches) while, in other organizations, communication specialists are placed within individual company departments or locations and organize different kinds of products and messages based on similar content (e.g., communication for the sales department, communication for a branch office, etc.). Although there is no one best way to organize communication functions, it is important to notice where these professionals sit on the organizational chart in order to understand the ways that they are aligned with strategy and with counterparts in other departments such as training and information technologies.

Most organizations have a corporate communication department that handles external communication, such as public relations and (in public corporations) investor relations. Similarly, large organizations have at least one training function, typically situated under human resources. Sometimes, employee communication is placed within the HR department (see Figure 3.1).

In large corporations, marketing communication (such as sales brochures and trade show events) are functions that often report to a vice president of marketing (see Figure 3.2).

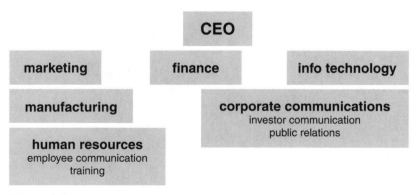

Figure 3.1
Employee Communications is Sometimes Placed in the HR Department

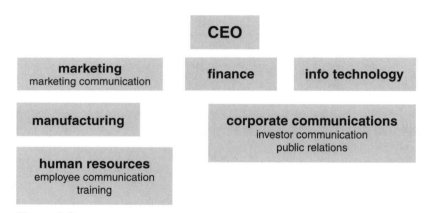

Figure 3.2
Marketing Communication May Be Separate From Other Forms of Internal and External
Communication

There is an increasing trend to integrate internal and external communications, so approximately half of the employee communication departments report to a vice president of communications and are placed in the same area as external relations. Many corporate communications departments also include marketing communications (see Figure 3.3).

In some organizations, there is a highly placed communication professional who reports directly to the CEO and provides counsel in management communications. This person is also generally the chief company spokesperson—this role is similar to the U.S. President's official spokesperson. Generally, this person provides strategic advice and may only supervise a small staff—or none at all. The more tactical and day-to-day functions of public relations, sales communications, employee relations, and training are handled elsewhere (see Figure 3.4).

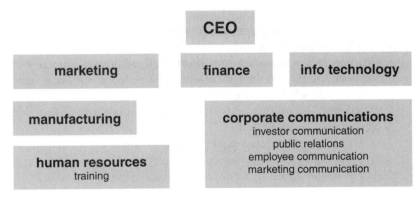

Figure 3.3
Integrated Internal, External, and Marketing Communication

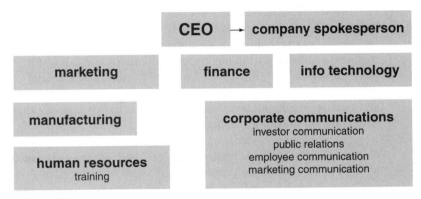

Figure 3.4
Company With a Chief Spokesperson/Advisor to the CEO

What Goes On in Each Department?

External Communication

A primary role for organizational communicators is relating to the public. This includes public relations, sometimes also called public affairs. Public relations basically involves getting "good press" for the organization by writing press releases, sponsoring events such as open houses or conference presentations, and by supporting various community and charity campaigns. For example, philanthropy is a part of the communications function in some organizations; they contribute money, products, or the time of their employees to support various charities. In some organizations, public relations is combined with the advertising and marketing function; this involves creating and placing ads and producing various promotional brochures, videos, and websites.

Not-for-profit organizations have a slightly different, but still critical, focus for their external communications efforts. Instead of sales, they rely on contributions for their support, so their PR efforts are directed toward large campaigns, as well as attracting and retaining individual donors.

Depending on the industry, separate communications functions may exist for government relations and for investor relations. Highly regulated industries, such as airlines, utilities, and pharmaceuticals, need to maintain good relationships with various agencies such as the U.S. Federal Drug Administration and the Federal Transportation Agency. U.S.-based industries often have offices in Washington, D.C., where they conduct lobbying efforts that support political parties and candidates who will vote for funding beneficial to their research agendas, or against regulations that will constrain their operations.

Investor relations, or IR, functions are responsible for communicating with stockholders and industry analysts who can influence the stock price. As many organizations are increasingly focused on maximizing their stock price, this area has become much more important. The IR department or professional is responsible for producing the required annual and quarterly reports for stockholders, arranging for the annual stockholders' meeting, and for communicating favorable company information to the financial press. The nature of financial communications for publicly traded corporations in the United States is regulated by the Securities and Exchange Commission, and professionals in this area often have financial, as well as communications, backgrounds.

The whole area of media relations has gotten quite complex. It used to be sufficient to send out the occasional press release and have a yearly lunch with reporters who cover the organization. Now, it is important to have ongoing relationships with the press, to pitch compelling stories to individual reporters, and to manage the Internet "buzz" that is generated. For example, many consumers and activist groups have set up websites where the public can discuss various organizations—as well as gripe about their experiences as customers or stockholders. There is little or nothing that a PR person can do to control this, except to threaten a lawsuit if the information is libelous, or to try to provide more accurate or balanced information. For example, if you go to Yahoo's Internet stock site, discussion boards are in place where stockholders and investment analysts can post messages about individual stocks; this can be very influential not only to the public, but also to employees who may anonymously post "insider" information here.

The measurement of public relations programs has also become much more sophisticated. Professionals in this area used to measure the effectiveness of their press relations by counting "column inches"—or the space that magazines or newspapers devoted to covering a pitched story. A similar approach these days is to count "hits" on the company Internet site. However, it is increasingly important to evaluate the *type* of story that was covered, and the *outcome* of press coverage or Internet activity, in terms of hard business results.

An important area for external communications is crisis management. Organizations need to have in place very specific procedures for dealing with crises, such as accidents, product recalls, takeover attempts, or sudden changes in management. Although a crisis is always a challenge for an organization, some actually come through them even stronger—if proper and ethical communication policies are in place. For example, when Tylenol bottles were found to be contaminated in the 1980s, the company responded quickly with as much information as they could provide to the public, and immediately instituted a recall and offered customers complete refunds. Because of the smart handling of this situation, the product's sales are stronger than ever. In contrast, when companies try to cover up problems or seem defensive, their products and company image may be tarnished forever. Obviously, a crisis is no time to start planning; external communication managers need to have in place a complete list of press contacts, a printed list of internal people and their phone numbers, a policy of who gets informed first, and a designated company spokesperson.

Internal Communications

The internal communications function is, of course, focused on employees. This usually includes producing an employee newsletter, producing (or at least organizing) the company intranet site, holding meetings where management can talk to and with employees, and producing other news and information products such as informational videos, safety campaigns, and bulletin board displays.

Although some of this function requires the design and production of "products" that are formally distributed to employees, an increasing area of focus is supervisory communication. For most employees, their relationship with their supervisors—the kind of information and feedback they get, and the opportunity to ask questions and make suggestions—is of primary importance. Certainly, it is much more critical than employee perceptions of the newsletter or intranet site. Although the internal communications manager certainly cannot control how supervisors communicate with their employees, they can provide various interventions. For example, most internal communications professionals help to coach executives on their presentation techniques, and help them plan for employee meetings. They may write speeches, help prepare them to handle tough questions or irate comments, and create presentation support materials such as electronic slides or video clips. The internal communications function may also provide training for all supervisors in skills such as coaching, giving feedback, and conflict management.

Often, important information is provided in a "cascade" model: top executives first inform a small group of high-level directors or department managers; these people inform their direct reports, and finally first-level supervisors hold meetings with their individual subordinates. Depending on the hierarchy of an organization and how spread out it is physically, there can be as many as 12 different "levels" in this chain of communication, and it can take days or weeks to get the information down to the front-line workers. In order for information to stay consistent, internal communications departments often produce meeting packages of agendas, overheads or slides, handouts, videos, or a sample of typical questions and answers; this is provided to all supervisors to help them run consistent and effective meetings.

Just as public opinion and the press have become more challenging, so have employees: they are more diverse, inquisitive, and demanding than ever. For most organizations, employees or "human assets" are extremely important, and attracting and retaining high-quality employees is critical. Good communication and training systems are major factors in keeping employees satisfied; therefore, these practices are being given more attention than ever.

Employee satisfaction with the communication system is often assessed by communication audits. Generally, these audits are conducted by outside consultants, and involve written surveys and/or focus groups with employees. They look at whether employees feel that they are given adequate, honest, and timely information by their supervisors, by top management, and by the other formal communications media such as newsletters. Sometimes an expert critique of communication products like the intranet, newsletters, and meeting packages is also conducted.

Some of the typical objectives of employee communication activities are to:

◆ improve performance and safety
◆ announce major company goals or re-organizations
◆ increase loyalty (word of mouth, retention)
◆ increase satisfaction
◆ improve the workforce's knowledge
◆ stimulate new ideas
◆ explain new programs, such as safety or quality initiatives
◆ inform about benefits (such as health insurance, retirement plans, etc.)
◆ foster social goals and participation

Supervisory Communication

While professionals in employee communication cannot control supervisors' communication practices, research has demonstrated that this relationship most affects employee satisfaction and performance. Typically, when communication audits are performed, supervisors feel that they are good communicators and that they are adequately informing their subordinates about issues that affect and interest them. However, subordinates frequently do not rate their supervisors this well, and often feel uninformed about issues that are important.

According to Roger D'Aprix, (1996) author and experienced communication professional, what employees want to know is:

◆ What is my job?
◆ How am I doing?
◆ Does anyone care?
◆ How is my unit doing?
◆ Where are we headed?
◆ How can I help?

Several ways exist for employee communication specialists to help supervisors achieve better communication. They include:

- developing training programs on supervisory communication
- assisting HR in developing metrics to measure and then reward supervisors for exhibiting good communication practices
- creating meeting templates, talking points, and presentation support materials for key messages and initiatives
- coaching supervisors in framing messages and in working through problems of conflict, teambuilding, and disciplinary communication

How Communication Is (or Is Not) Integrated

As shown in the previous chapters, various forms of communication are found in organizations, and all of them need to be aligned for performance. The corporate brand is usually shaped by marketing, but often brought to life by customer encounters with sales representatives or employees who deliver products and services. Employee attitudes and behaviors are influenced not only by what executives say in speeches but also by what they read in the newspaper, what they chat about in the lunchroom, and what they're told in training. The concept of "islands of communication" presented in Chapter 2 reinforces that a lack of alignment between the major "owners" of branding, public relations, news, and instructional communication can cause poor performance because of mixed messages and information overload.

Because of the size and complexity of many organizations today, and because of the new communication media such as intranets and online conferencing, it is often difficult to decide who should be responsible for what content or communication and learning technology. Consider a few examples:

Levi Strauss and Company's Global Communication function has four teams:

- Employee effectiveness, including internal and financial communication and business literacy
- Communication technology, including their intranet, multimedia, and video production
- Leadership effectiveness, including executive communication
- Corporate reputation, including external communication and Internet publishing

In addition to their corporate staff, field communicators reporting directly to the presidents of various divisions are placed throughout the world. We can see here an interesting integration of certain aspects of training—particularly communication training and business literacy—with the communication function. Labatt Breweries' communications department also developed and conducted business literacy workshops, based on a simulation game custom-designed for them (see Figure 3.5).

Qualcomm, a new technologies company, positioned employee communications within the learning and development department, and communicates the company's training philosophy as well as its culture and values. The vice president of learning and development supervises about thirty people who work together to manage information and skill-building components of change, such as when they sold one of their business units to a competitor. They work closely with external

Answer:

Speaking of which, do you know what you can do to influence Bob's labor efficiencies?

Anything you could do with inventory turns?

$$\text{INVENTORY TURNS} = \frac{\text{total units sold}}{\text{average inventory (in units)}}$$
(using units)

So, you want to show Bob you get it — why it is labor efficiencies are so important to him.

(Wouldn't FBI's Marty like to know more about this — but then would he know what to do with it?)

You gently pry Bob's clipboard away from him, including the Store Contribution Report, and begin to show off.

Based on his last month's results for labor efficiencies (see Scene 1), what unit sales would give an optimum labor efficiency between 104 per cent and 99 per cent?

Answer: _____

$$\frac{x}{310} = y$$
(actual labor hours)

$$\frac{y}{57.39} = 99 \text{ per cent } \text{planned unit sales per man hour}$$

$$\frac{y}{57.39} = 104 \text{ per cent } \text{planned unit sales per man hour}$$

y = unit sales per hour
x = total unit sales

What you do know is that you want to convince Bob to give you more shelf facings. (For discussion: do you think there's any difference between shelf facings and shelf feet. Which calculation would give you more information.) Meanwhile, he'd like to improve his labor efficiencies.

Drawing on your Store Grid Survey, you know he keeps 10 cases of Kokanee on the floor and sells 25 per week. But, he also stocks 20 cases of FBI beer that sells 35 cases per week.

Assuming it takes two labor hours to stock a shelf in which the inventory has turned over once, how can you demonstrate for Bob the optimal spacing to maximize his labor usage?

Answer:

	Weekly sales	units	wk. turn	labor hrs.
Labatt	25	10	2.50	5
FBI	35	20	1.75	3.5
TOTAL Hours				8.5

Optimization of Space to Sales

Labatt	25	14	1.79	3.57
FBI	35	16	2.19	4.38
TOTAL Hours				7.95
Labor Savings				0.55

Figure 3.5
Labatt Business Literacy Training Manual

communication where her counterpart, the vice president of investor relations, supervises public relations and media relations. Air Canada has an employee development and communications group, reporting to human resources. The senior director of this department supervises customer service training, organizational learning, employee communications, and incentive programs (Gayeski, 2000).

Wherever these communication functions are placed, it is important to examine exactly what functions and skill sets are necessary, to develop metrics for evaluating the effectiveness of communications, and to plan methods of collaboration with other related areas such as training and information technologies.

In order to approach the whole topic of communications assessment, we need to step back for a moment and look at theory. Often, the way that communications is organized, managed, and viewed is based on implicit assumptions that are never really discussed or even understood.

Theory Informs Practice

Communication theory attempts to describe and predict the processes and outcomes of information transmission among individuals. Although theories of persuasion date back to the early Greek civilization, communication as a system was not really conceptualized until the 1950s. The old, mechanistic models that were developed then still have a powerful hold on our thinking. Theory is important because it helps us make decisions—for example, it informs the way we evaluate the outcomes of communication processes.

There are three different levels from which we can view and evaluate communication:

◆ How accurately is information transmitted? (**technical**)
◆ How effective are our symbols in conveying the desired meaning? (**semantic**)
◆ How effectively does the received meaning affect an individual's conduct in the desired way? (**performance**)

For example, a communication manager might set up a series of meetings to inform employees about a new flex-time program. From the technical perspective, she would need to ensure that the policy gets communicated accurately—that is, that the facts are correct each time the message is told, and that the data are correctly typed and transposed among any media used, like handouts or slides. At the semantic level, she would need to be concerned about the words, tone, and images used: do they convey what the vice president for human resources has in her mind? Finally, at the performance level, the communication manager would need to consider the impact of the message: what actions should occur as a result of this information?

The root of the word "communication" is the Latin *communicare,* which means "to share." In common speech, the word is used in many ways. We may say that, after several counseling sessions, a couple is really "communicating." A manager might tell us to communicate his new expectations about sales quotas to his field representatives. When the phone lines go down, we say we have had an interruption in the communication system. We even talk about "communicating" a disease!

A common dictionary definition of communication is "information transmission," but just exchanging information is generally inadequate because there has to be a useful context in which to put it. People can't transmit information directly by "transplanting" a concept from their brain into someone else's. Rather, people have to use words, symbols, images, models, or sounds to try to encode their meanings from both the available information and their individual expertise.

As human beings, we constantly communicate. It is part of our species' inborn traits, and in fact, our use of language is part of what makes us uniquely human. We can't avoid communicating. For example, if an organization refuses to divulge any information about a possible plant closing, it is, in fact, communicating something—perhaps management's distrust of unions, or even more likely, that there will be a plant closing. As individuals, we communicate through gestures, our style of dress, and our choice of words. As organizations, we communicate through the design of our facilities, our logo, the accessibility of our executives, and the amount and kind of information we make available through various kinds of media.

Within communication systems, there are two components, message and meaning, which sometimes get confused—and this is what makes the process difficult. Messages are symbols we construct in order to create or share meanings. They are the outward acts to which a receiver can see and respond. Meanings, however, are mental images or feelings that we develop as we perceive and try to make sense of the world.

When people perceive a message, they decode or interpret it and try to create meanings for themselves. Although a message may remain constant, meanings will always vary because of our own individual responses, values, and backgrounds, and because of the inadequacy of any kind of medium whether it be the spoken word, a picture, or even a video clip, to capture someone else's meanings.

Although communication is natural, we are not naturally good at it. It is difficult enough to talk to another person and to try to share what you are feeling or what you want them to do. It is even more difficult to speak as the voice of an organization, and to try to help many different people to develop similar meanings from words, images, and sounds.

The Transportation Model of Communication, or: Don't Believe Your Own Words

Sometimes we believe our own words, and we wind up confusing and frustrating ourselves. Consider, the metaphors we commonly use for communication: We talk about *packaging* a message, *covering* a topic, or choosing a *vehicle* and *sending it* (maybe even *driving* the point home) in order to *convey* the information, hoping that the *receivers get it*. You would think we were in the freight business.

To think of it, we use a lot of automotive analogies in business. We say a poorly performing company is *off track* or *stuck in low gear*. Executives and consultants try to *drive change* and *get people on board* by *putting the brakes on* old behaviors and by *shifting into high gear* in order to lead enterprises on the *road to success.* Sometimes, the *wheels of change* turn too slowly for us, and at other times we may even *spin out of control.*

Communication is not just about transmitting messages as if they were packages to be shipped. Rather, it's about attempting to coordinate behaviors and to share meanings. It's not one-way. We can't just transplant our ideas and intentions into the brains of other people. We know these things, but we're often tricked by our own words into thinking that if we just choose the right words or package design, the most powerful medium, or a charismatic speaker, we can get others to see things the way we do.

You act on your communication theories all the time, even though you don't realize it. You make choices about how to inspire, teach, reprimand, and convince people all the time. But often the model or theory of communication we hold *backfires* (oh no, a transportation word again!).

The bottom line is, do not conceive of communication as an attempt to use a "vehicle" to "send" a message so that people *"get it."* Try to think of the process another way: your goal should be to develop shared vocabulary and experience, to effect coordinated action, and to slowly increase the overlap between your set of experiences and ideas and those of your communication partners (see Figure 3.6).

Defining Communication "Success"

We need, most of all, to define "success." Our old transportation models of communication defined success as getting the message—quickly and accurately. The process was something like filling up an empty bucket, or hitting a target. But step

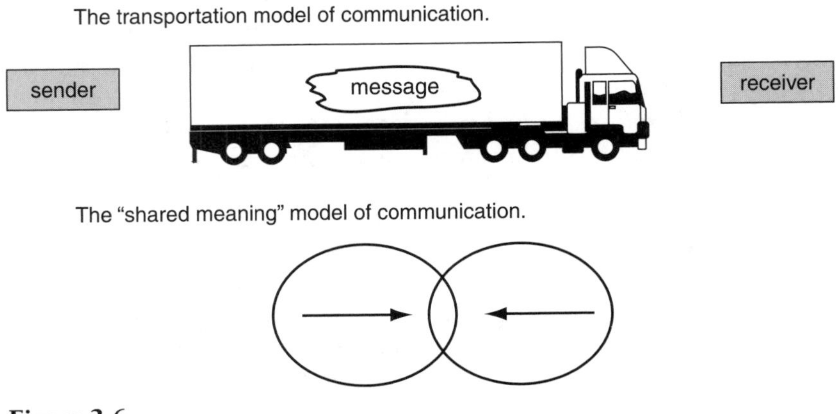

The transportation model of communication.

The "shared meaning" model of communication.

Figure 3.6
Two Contrasting Models of Communication

back. Are employees vacant receptacles, and are customers bags full of hay? We hope not. What **do** you wish of your business partners? I would expect that you would say something like intelligent participation, energetic input, and informed debate.

One of my favorite metaphors of the communication process came out of a college class I taught on organizational communication and technology. I explained that we traditionally thought of an organizational message as a beautiful, fragile vase that needed to be sent to somebody. The courier service was the communication department; it was their job to get that beautiful ceramic piece to the right receiver quickly, cheaply, and most importantly, looking just like it did when it left the sender, no matter how many hands it passed through. I speculated that, in organizations, we might actually wish to have some value added to that message as it passes through various receivers. One of my students came up with an elegant extension of my analogy. She remarked that instead of a fully formed and hardened vase, organizational messages were more like clay. The original person might have an idea for a great shape for that clay, so he would start out by molding it into a tentative form. But then he would pass it onto somebody else who would see other possibilities and who would re-shape it a bit. By the time it got to the last person, it would not look much like it started out. **It would be much better**, having had input from many different people and perspectives. It's interesting to step back and note that this interaction in class is a perfect example of my point. I started out with an idea to share, but it was greatly enhanced by the interaction.

What difference does it make whether we use the "clay" versus "vase" metaphor for organizational communication? Is this just an academic exercise, or a semantic game? It makes a big difference. If we see communication as shipping messages, we are ignoring the value and input of our intended receivers. We think of the process as all-knowing "senders" who need to package, charm, and cajole "receivers" into taking the message unto themselves without question or added value. We expect people to "get it," and when they don't we often shoot the messenger. However, if we think of our colleagues and customers as "communication partners" from whom we want to extract valuable ideas, our picture of success is something quite different. In fact, **we don't want people just to get messages; rather, we want them to actively shape meanings, develop relationships, and coordinate more mutually shared orientations to the world.**

This concept of shared meaning is critically important as we shape the performance of those individuals who deal directly with customers. Organizations are investing increasing amounts of time and money in branding and customer relationship management software systems. Those assets of brand and technology infrastructure are essential—but only if it is supported by the kind of interpersonal communication that builds loyalty and innovation. One of the leading research groups dealing with these areas is CERS at the Hanken School of Business and Economics in Helsinki. Their findings and models help to illuminate the importance and future direction of customer communications.

A framework for customer relationship communication

Kirsti Lingberg Repo, Senior Researcher,
Hanken Swedish School of Business and Economics, Helsinki, Finland

Over the last few years, organizations have faced the ineffectiveness and inefficiencies of traditional marketing communication practices and concepts. As more firms adopt a customer relationship management (CRM) approach to their business, the need for new communication concepts and methodologies to develop, manage, and implement marketing communication activities has increased exponentially.

The role of customers has changed in the twenty-first century marketplace. There are two important factors affecting this:

- First, the growing empowerment of customers through information technology has created the interactive marketplace.
- Second, the new pressures have caused the relationship marketing paradigm, customer relationship management, or CRM. This is characterized by a search for mutual value between the firm and its customers as the basis for a long-term relationship.

From this perspective, all relationship communication processes should form an integrated effort to build value and create benefit for all parties.

For the purpose of being able to generate more value in the new market scenario, a new process model was developed in the Swedish School of Economics in Helsinki. This model is an outcome of a three-year North American study.

Besides functioning as a new managerial tool for the various companies in expanding communication tools, it helps the company to understand the consequences of different processes that form the relationship base between the company and the consumer.

The Essence of the Model

This framework outlines a holistic model in which the company and the consumer perspectives are considered as co-equivalent parts of what we term a relationship communication system. The model is based on the assumption that a relationship evolves through building, enhancing, and maintaining stages between a buyer and seller (see Figure 3.7).

In the same vein, to achieve better outcomes for both parties in the relationship process, a closer connection between the relational parties must be developed through the three separate modes of communication: planned communication, contact creation, and connectedness.

The last mode, defined as connectedness, reflects a mutually strong and committed relationship. In a sense, this is the outcome of the shared understanding generated by the systems-based interaction model. This interaction level is reached by connecting consumer participation and contact back to the marketer through a feedback loop. These connections are manifested in the various levels of dialogue that enable mutual understanding and reciprocal value generation.

Connections are developed through the empowered engagement of both participants in a two-way interaction process. Dialogue is thus a central construct in bringing dynamism to the relationship's value generation process.

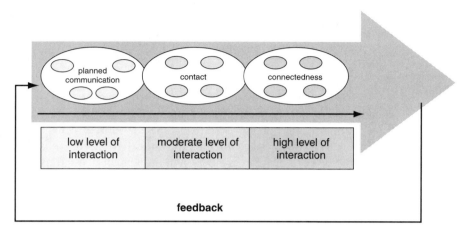

Figure 3.7
The Tri-Model Conceptualization of Customer Relationship Communication

Our recently conducted study in Finland, *Communication Excellence,* reported that a dialogue with customers formed the cornerstone in creating connectedness between parties at the Hugo Boss store in Helsinki. Customers were willing to participate in the value-generation processes in the store and, because of the high level of participation in the mutually beneficial dialogue between the buyer and the seller, the store was positively positioned in the customers' transaction memory. This contact with the Hugo Boss store was seen as the most important relational benefit of the overall brand offering.

Managerial Implications

This new framework that lays out the three stages of communication, contact, and connectedness provides a means for managing customer-perceived relationship value in a way that identifies the change of consumers' communicative behavior as

◆ their participation increases
◆ the level of two-way interactivity increases
◆ interrelatedness between the parties reaches the state of connectedness
◆ all these features provide possibilities for a new, measurable approach to communication programs

This model serves as a starting point in marketers' and academics' search for more understanding of the communication processes needed in today's new market realities. This new conceptualization is critical in managing the different stages of the relationship and determining how to best generate mutual value in each process stage.

Envisioning the Ideal System

What is an "ideal" system for organizational communication? What do the best departments and functions look like? Who is doing this really well?

I'm asked these questions by clients and students almost every day. There really aren't any general answers that apply across the vast array of companies, or any "proven" recommendations for individual organizations. Even though there is no recipe for success, there are guidelines and characteristics for high-performing communication and learning systems that appear consistently across research studies and among experienced practitioners and consultants. According to many studies on "best practices" in external employee communication, the primary factors related to effective corporate communication include:

- The senior executive is a communication exemplar.
- There is alignment between rhetoric and action.
- The organization's policies and culture support a lot of two-way, face-to-face communication.
- Executives and formal communication media deal effectively and honestly with bad news.
- Communicators support supervisors in being credible and effective communicators.

Similar conclusions were found by James Grunig (1992) in his research study sponsored by the International Association of Business Communicators (IABC).

- The communication department is headed by a manager, rather than a technician.
- That manager is a member of the organization's top decision-making group (the dominant coalition).
- Together, the communication manager and executive team use a communication model that sends messages as well as listens and acts upon messages from the audience.
- The goal of communication is to attain satisfactory outcomes for both groups, pre-supposing ethical, open behavior as part of the process.

A 1999 study sponsored by Watson Wyatt Worldwide and IABC identified traits possessed by organizations that have successful communication programs.

- Senior management recognizes the importance of communication in achieving business results.
- Management bases communication efforts on a clear, well-defined communication strategy.
- Managers tie communication initiatives to business objectives.
- The organization provides information to employees about how the firm is doing in meeting its goals, helps them understand the business, and provides information and feedback to motivate and improve job performance.

- ◆ Communication programs are developed proactively rather than reactively.
- ◆ The organization has a well-defined two-way communication philosophy.
- ◆ A comprehensive communication program is an essential part of the business strategy.
- ◆ Managers at all levels are rewarded for communicating effectively (Watson Wyatt Worldwide, 1999).

Finally, some other factors that frequently are cited as characteristics of excellent communication and learning systems include:

- ◆ The system fosters an approach in which messages can easily travel up, down, and laterally through an organization.
- ◆ Feedback and collaboration are supported.
- ◆ Communication within and between all levels and departments is frequent, honest, and symmetrical.
- ◆ Communication load is optimized (neither overload nor underload).
- ◆ Accuracy and speed of information are optimized.
- ◆ The system is sensitive to human and environmental needs (flexibility in time and mode, respectful of individuals' rights and feelings, ecologically sound).
- ◆ Policies and interventions revolve around a consensually determined and unified corporate culture and image.
- ◆ Rules and tools are articulated clearly, and made available to all members.
- ◆ Communication practices and interventions add value to the organization's products and members' lives.
- ◆ New technologies and techniques are continually examined and employed strategically to support individual and organizational goals.

An example of some of these principles in action comes from Emerson Electric, which has enjoyed more than thirty years of consistently increasing earnings. One of the core principles of the firm is open communication. Division presidents and plant managers meet regularly with employees to discuss the specifics of the business, methods of cost-control, and an analysis of the competition. As a measure of the success of communication, Emerson claims that every employee can answer four questions:

1. What cost reduction are you currently working on?
2. Who is the "enemy" (who is your competition)?
3. Have you met with your management in the past six months?
4. Do you understand the economics of your job?

You will note that there is a tight link between formal communication, good management practices, and opportunities for learning—all with a direct link to business strategy and performance objectives. The lines between communication, collaboration, and training blur.

At Springfield Remanufacturing Corporation, every employee is taught the basic rules of the business and the bottom line—how the company makes money.

By practicing "open book management," employees are given access to financial statements every month, and are taught how to read income statements and understand other financial analysis concepts. Supervisors get together in weekly meetings to present their financial reports and, within thirty-six hours, virtually everyone in the company knows what each department will need to do to improve their performance. Having this kind of open system and immediate feedback increases motivation and productivity.

> *Likewise, Sears realized that employees could perform better if they understood more about how the business works and how critical business factors interrelated to affect performance.*
>
> *To convey the larger strategic picture to every employee, the company uses learning maps—large murals with elaborate legends on the borders—to communicate essential business conditions to small groups of employees working with a facilitator. One map takes people through the shifts in the competitive environment from 1950 to 1990. Another map, laid out like a game, asks employees to place bets on the sources and uses of funds as they flow from customers' wallets to the bottom line. Sears then asks its employees to use what they have absorbed from the learning maps to come up with a list of three or four highly practical actions that can be taken immediately at the store level to correct deficiencies and improve customer service. Sears anchors the proficiency side of the discipline with training to improve the interface with customers, then adds performance measures that focus attention on individual and team performance with respect to customer satisfaction. Together, these initiatives enable employees to perform to high standards and to understand how they each contribute to Sears' success.*
> (Pascale, Milliemann, & Gioia, 1997).

The Elements of a Strong Communication Infrastructure

What elements should make up an organization's communication system? As shown at the beginning of this chapter, there may be a number of separate communication functions within an organization: PR, employee communication, investor relations, and so on. But these don't really make up the infrastructure. Rather, a communications infrastructure consists of rules and tools that engineer high performance. These elements of the infrastructure are somewhat independent, but they are also interdependent and, like individual bricks in a foundation, need to be aligned and individually robust to support performance (see Figure 3.8 and Table 3.1).

Internal Collaboration

Effective organizations create and maintain structures and practices that promote internal collaboration. Especially as firms become larger, it's more difficult

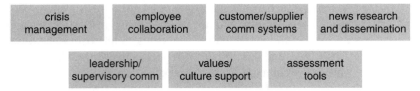

Figure 3.8
The Elements of a Strong Communication Infrastructure

Table 3.1
Elements of a Communication Infrastructure with Examples

Communication Infrastructure Element	Examples
Internal collaboration tools	Groupware, regular interdepartmental meetings, policies and templates that reduce overload
Methods for two-way communication with customers and suppliers	Websites that offer opportunities for feedback, user group meetings, visits to suppliers, extranets
Processes to uncover and disseminate relevant news	Portals that deliver customized news, company libraries, closed-circuit TV updates
Leadership/supervisory communication practices and culture	Regular executive presentations, all-company meetings, coaching on best practices for supervisory communication
Events and communication styles that support the organization's values and culture	Open houses, events that celebrate company history or achievements, company participation in community events
Crisis communication plans	Procedures for handling internal and external communication for various types of crises, technology systems to disseminate news quickly and comprehensively
Assessment practices and tools	Regular communication audits, systems that track use of intranet and Internet Web pages

for employees to share ideas and expertise because of physical constraints as well as the inevitable competition that arises between divisions or departments. It's the responsibility of professionals in human resources and communications to promote collaboration because

◆ They are not themselves embroiled in the turf wars of line departments.
◆ They can develop organization-wide infrastructures, policies, and practices.

◆ They should be the professionals who stay current on technologies and management practices that can promote collaboration.

Some of the ways that internal collaboration is supported include

◆ groupware (software systems that facilitate the sharing of ideas and the coordination of projects)
◆ training on skills that promote group interaction, such as team building, facilitation, and problem-solving techniques
◆ meetings and recognition practices that enable groups to update each other on their projects and on lessons learned

Customer/Supplier Communication

In order to maintain customer loyalty, to stimulate innovation, and to promote efficiency in the supply chain, it is important to establish systems that promote two-way communication with customers and suppliers. Some of the techniques that are used include:

◆ interactive websites that provide multiple mechanisms for customers and visitors to ask questions and leave comments
◆ user groups that invite customers to participate in meetings, online discussion groups, and advisory councils
◆ extranets, which are specialized websites that allow suppliers to access company data so that ordering and project management can be done on a real-time basis

News

A traditional role for corporate communication departments has been creating internal news vehicles, including newsletters, electronic banners, management updates, and intranet sites. Some newer developments include:

◆ portals, which are customized personal home pages that display news and other information tailored to the role and interests of individuals
◆ closed-circuit TV and intranet broadcasts that consist of slides and headlines that continuously loop. These are displayed on computer monitors (often as a screensaver) or on TV monitors in strategic locations such as lobbies, elevator areas, or cafeterias
◆ video news updates, usually produced monthly or quarterly and distributed via videotape, satellite, or on privately rented cable TV channels.

Leadership and Supervisory Communication

Although formal communications media such as intranet sites, newsletters, and meetings are important, what matters most to employees is the culture and effectiveness of communication with their supervisors. Employees who have strong communication relationships with their supervisors are usually better informed, more involved, and more satisfied with their jobs. According to many research studies, the elements of effective supervisory communication include:

- *Co-orientation.* This refers to the alignment of perceptions between two people (such as the supervisor and subordinate). Research shows that even if two people disagree, if they are *accurate* in their perceptions of each other's position and if they exhibit respect for each other, this leads to a positive relationship. In fact, open expression of disagreement is much better than relationships in which parties suppress their opinions.
- *Lack of upward distortion.* The culture and management practices of an organization should try to reduce the natural tendencies of subordinates to withhold or soften bad news when they are communicating with their supervisors.
- *Supportive communication behaviors.* These are skills and practices that support respectful and open communication, including keeping the conversation oriented to the problem rather than the person, keeping an openness to change, listening actively and rephrasing what the other has said, and trying to maintain equality in the relationship.
- *Effectiveness of upward communication.* Employees value the ability of their supervisors to effectively communicate their positions and maintain positive relationships with top management. This is often called the Peltz effect.
- *Negative feedback is related to lower job performance.* Supervisors can gain more compliance from giving compliments about what is done well than by focusing on criticizing what is not done well.

Professionals in human resources and communication can promote these behaviors by providing supervisory training and by organizing regular meeting formats that promote two-way information sharing. For example, Intel chip manufacturing plants schedule regular business updates and management meetings where plant managers share business results and goals with all employees.

Special Events and Sponsorship

Most companies sponsor special events for their employees and the public, such as open houses or celebrations of company milestones. In addition, they offer money or other in-kind donations to local not-for-profit groups, community events (like holiday parades), and schools. Finally, companies underwrite other large-scale public events such as golf tournaments.

For example, Southwest Airlines sponsors annual culture days in which employees celebrate and learn about the company's unique culture. The airline also encourages its employees to donate their time and skills to community organizations on paid company time; for example, Southwest Airlines' employees work on building and maintaining Ronald McDonald homes where families can stay near hospitals where their children are being treated. Wegman's Food Stores, which has been named one of the top 100 companies to work for by *Fortune* magazine, is very generous in donating food and money to many local community charities and schools. The ACE Group of Companies, a large international insurance group, sponsors a variety of special events that directly tie into the image and relationships they cultivate for their unique business situation.

CASE IN POINT

Strategic event sponsorship
Michael Slepian, Assistant Vice President of Communications,
ACE Group of Companies, Philadelphia, PA

At the ACE Group of Companies, our goal is to carefully consider and develop sponsorship activities to reflect our global position as an international leader in insurance and reinsurance. Committing corporate resources to a sponsorship is a serious responsibility, and we are refining an exhausting selection process. Among the criteria we will consider are:

◆ *Demonstrating Value*   The sponsorship must show measurable results and benefit to ACE.
◆ *International Value*   Does the activity reflect ACE as a truly international organization?
◆ *Longevity*   Can the sponsorship provide ACE with a long window of opportunity? For example, can we expect to gain at least several months of productive activity?
◆ *Corporate-Wide Benefit*   Can the sponsorship provide value to all ACE business units?
◆ *Earning Business Unit Support*   Each ACE business unit should be made aware of the potential for the sponsorship to improve their relationships with their agents, brokers, customers, and potential customers.
◆ *Developing Support Among ACE Employees*   ACE employees need to be fully aware of the sponsorship and its value to ACE. In addition, the entire ACE team should have the opportunity to enjoy some of the benefits of the sponsorship.
◆ *Demonstrating How the Sponsorship Supports the ACE Brand*   An overall strategy should be developed for selection of all ACE sponsorship activities. The ACE values should be reflected in all sponsorships.
◆ *Commitment to Well-Planned Risk Taking*   Commitment to highly trained, dedicated, hardworking professionals with excellent leadership qualities. Everyone concerned, including employees, senior management, customers, vendors, and stockholders, should be able to look to our sponsorship activities with a sense of pride and admiration. Our sponsorship activities should reflect our highest ethical standards.
◆ *Does the Sponsorship Provide ACE with:*
  ◆ Long-term media value for ACE
  ◆ Considerable promotional value to the entire ACE organization
  ◆ Worldwide interest
  ◆ Value as employee incentive
◆ *Media Interest*   What is the likelihood that the media will be interested in covering the sponsorship? This is especially true for media that reaches the ACE target audiences.
◆ *Public Service*   The sponsorship should include a charitable element, to demonstrate the ACE commitment to supporting our communities.
◆ *Perceived Expense*   Will the sponsorship look extravagant to our constituents? Can ACE easily justify the actual cost?

◆ *Multiple Locations*   Can the sponsorship provide ACE business units with support throughout a very wide geographical area? Does it generate as much excitement in Chicago as it
might in Los Angeles or London?

◆ *Exclusivity*   Can ACE claim exclusive ownership of the sponsorship, or at a minimum, be
positioned as a major, intrinsic part of the sponsorship?

◆ *Branding*   Will ACE have unlimited use of the sponsorship logo and other identification?

The picture in Figure 3.9 was taken just as
the Chairman and CEO of the ACE Group
of Companies announced their sponsorship of Team Dennis Conner and their
plan to send thirty-three firefighters from
New York City to New Zealand, to cheer
Conner and his crew to victory in the
Louis Vuitton cup, as part of their quest to
compete for the Americas Cup, the most
coveted trophy in international yacht rac-
ing. While in New Zealand, ACE would
also make it possible for the firefighters to
participate in the World Firefighter
Games, in Christchurch, New Zealand.
The 2002 games were dedicated in part to
the New York City Firefighters, and their
heroic efforts during and after the 2001 at-
tack on the World Trade Center.

Figure 3.9
A jubilant Dennis Conner, Skipper of Stars & Stripes
(center, wearing cap) and Brian Duperreault, Chairman
and CEO of the ACE Group of Companies) accept jackets

Crisis Communication

Having a solid crisis communication plan is just as important as having smoke de-
tectors and fire extinguishers in a building. Crisis communication plans should
cover various types of negative events, including accidents, large business losses,
the death or departure of important executives, tainted or dangerous products, or
lawsuits.

Organizations that deal well with crises can actually profit from the situation
previously shown as from the Tylenol example. By contrast, many journalists believe that when the accounting firm Arthur Andersen was involved in improper
accounting practices with some of its clients (like WorldCom), its defensiveness
actually led to its demise. An important principle for dealing with crises is to always take full responsibility, state the facts, and emphasize that you are doing
everything possible to fully cooperate with any investigations that are going on.
The public is willing to pardon mistakes and even isolated examples of wrongdo-
ing, but they are unforgiving of organizations that seem to avoid responsibility and
appear less than honest.

Good crisis communication preparedness includes:

♦ training executives and all employees in how to respond to press inquiries
♦ identifying phone numbers and contacts for key executives, including a plan (such as a phone tree) for how key executives and the public should be notified
♦ naming key spokespersons who would be responsible for communicating with the press and others directly affected by a crisis (such as families of employees)

Communication Audits

In order to keep an accurate pulse on the communication climate and to be able to make strategic decisions on communication policies and media, successful communication departments conduct regular evaluations or audits. These audits measure such elements as:

♦ employee satisfaction with supervisory and leadership communication
♦ use and usefulness of various communications media and practices, such as newsletters, intranet sites, and meetings
♦ credibility of various sources, including leaders and newsletters
♦ knowledge and awareness of critical business information, such as company goals and important events
♦ efficiency of communications media, including how easy it is to find necessary information, and how accurate and up-to-date the information is
♦ how communications affect actual performance, such as how news items shape employees' decisions and prioritization of action items

Generally, audits are done on a company-wide basis, but it is also useful to do more regular, targeted (and inexpensive) studies at a site or departmental level.

Many organizations resist conducting audits because they feel that employees are over-surveyed. Indeed, when communications assessments are done poorly they can raise problems or expectations and actually decrease performance and satisfaction. However, measurement activities can and should be integrated and their aim should be to assess how performance is impacted.

CASE IN POINT

Integrating communication and HR assessment

Andy Brown, Global Practice Leader, Research and Diagnostics; & Nathalie Harris, Senior Analyst, Research and Diagnostics,
The Empower Group, London, England

Many companies conduct their measurement like they conduct their business: in silos. We are often called in by clients where the HR function is looking to conduct a climate survey while the communications function is embarking on an audit of their own practices. Meanwhile, customer data is being gathered by marketing while profitability data is held within the finance function.

As in business, research can benefit when these barriers are broken down. Indeed, combining HR and communications measurement in the same research has several mutual benefits. Apart from cost efficiencies, there are also advantages in terms of:

- *Research Design*   While two separate pieces of research may generate interesting data, they often cover similar areas or ask questions that are broadly the same but, due to question wording differences, cannot be compared. Integrated HR and communications research helps to coordinate question design, improve the efficiency of sampling methodologies, and ensure that strategic issues can be addressed in a holistic way.
- *Metric Comparisons*   Often, two pieces of research have incomparable data. For example, if one uses four-point scales to assess employee climate and another uses five-point scales to investigate communications issues, comparing levels of, say, employee motivation and satisfaction with the availability of upward suggestion channels can be problematic. Asking the same questions under the same piece of research and using the same response scales addresses this problem head-on.
- *The Ability to Make Linkages Between the Measures Taken*   In essence, the best research aims to identify linkages. In the previous example, what we would ideally like to know is "Does satisfaction with upward suggestion channels lead to increased staff motivation?" Again if the two metrics are gathered from within separate pieces of research, these linkages are difficult to identify. However, if measured within a single research project, techniques such as correlation and regression analysis can help to answer such questions.

Case Study

A recent case study with a European-based retailer used a census survey of over 24,000 employees to investigate both communications and HR issues within the same piece of research. The findings prove interesting, as do the linkages. In particular, three insights stand out:

1. Positive communications create a highly motivated staff

The survey looked at three aspects of communication within the organization:

- *Downward Communication*   How well did the company inform its employees about how the business was performing and how much basic information did the organization provide to employees in order that they could perform well in their jobs?
- *Upward Communication*   How well did the company listen to the opinions and ideas of its employees and to what extent were staff involved in critical decision-making?
- *Lateral Communication*   How well did the company help employees across different parts of the organization (between stores, distribution, and head office) to communicate with each other and understand the implications of each others' activities?

The results found that positivity among employees on all three aspects of the communications led to significantly higher levels of employee motivation. By contrasting those staff who strongly agreed and strongly disagreed with particular communications statements within the survey, motivation levels could vary by up to 65 percentage points.

Communications question statement	Communications aspect	% motivated among those who strongly agree with the communications statement	% motivated among those who strongly disagree with the communications statement
I receive enough information to perform well in my job	Downward	88%	28%
My opinions count at ABC	Upward	93%	28%
Communication is good across different parts of the business	Lateral	89%	33%

2. *Good communications have a positive impact on the business*

The study went on to investigate how communications impact on issues that directly affect the strategic understanding of the business and behaviors that can impact on customer service and retention.

The data were analyzed using linkage modeling (a more sophisticated form of correlation and regression analysis). The retailer discovered significant positive relationships between how employees felt about various aspects of the communications mix and culture and the outcome behaviors of interest. For example:

a. the transparency of communications within the organization had a high impact on employee positivity about the overall aims and objectives of the organization (with a linkage coefficient, similar to a correlation, of 0.60)

b. equally, staff who felt that communications were open and honest were much more likely to feel that the senior management team had a clear, strategic vision of the future (with a coefficient of 0.57)

c. employees who believed that their line manager genuinely communicated well with them were much more positive about the corporate values being lived within the organization (a linkage of 0.71)

It seems, then, that delivering well on internal communications can have dramatically positive impacts on key HR measures such as strategic understanding among staff and a more coherent approach to behaving according to the corporate value set. Given the costs of **not** enhancing these behavioral aspects through the employer-employee relationship, the benefit of making linkages between the two sets of metrics can be clearly seen.

In addition, communication measures were found to be consistent drivers of one of the most common factors in terms of employee motivation, retention, and advocacy: perceptions that employees are valued by the company.

In the vast majority of employee research studies, "feeling valued" emerges as a top influencer on these behaviors that lead to direct bottom-line benefits. Where employees feel more positively valued by their organization, they are much more likely to:

◆ be motivated on a day-to-day basis in their jobs
◆ feel a stronger allegiance of loyalty and commitment to the organization
◆ speak highly of the company as an employer in the recruitment marketplace

In this particular case study, positive communication is found to be a solid basis for making staff feel valued. The subsequent benefits to the business are equally strong.

Our analysis found that all three aspects of the communication hierarchy (downwards, upwards, and lateral), as well as the transparency of the communication culture were strongly associated with the key outcomes previously described (see Figure 3.10).

The linkage coefficients between the communications measures and whether staff feel valued are all positive, strong, and statistically significant. A 10 percentage-point increase in any of the communication metrics over time would result in a rise in the "feeling valued" score of between four and six points.

As an illustration, among those employees who felt their opinions count within the organization, close to eight in ten felt valued by the company (78%). However, among those who felt their opinions were not really listened to or acted upon, only just over one in ten (12%) felt valued as an employee. The "value gap" created by good listening skills within the company is huge.

In turn, feeling valued has a strong impact on levels of motivation, employer advocacy, and loyalty within the organization.

◆ Motivation levels are over twice as high among staff who feel valued (86%) than among those who do not feel valued (at only 36%).
◆ Employees who feel valued are more than three times as likely to speak highly of the company than those who do not feel valued.
◆ Levels of loyalty toward the company are almost three times as high among staff who feel valued compared with those that do not.

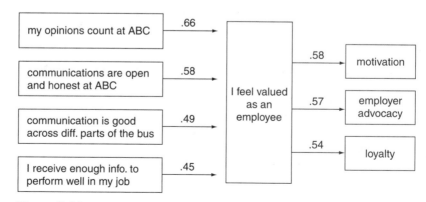

Figure 3.10
Linkage Coefficients Between Communication Measures and Their Outcomes

	"Feel valued as an employee"?	
	Agree	Disagree
% motivated	86%	36%
% would speak highly about the company	76%	22%
% loyalty felt toward company	77%	27%

The loyalty gap between those feeling and not feeling valued is particularly marked. For instance, when we look at these two groups with regard to their long-term career aspirations, the consequences for the company are enormous. As can be seen from the following table, those staff feeling valued are almost twice as likely to view their current role as a long-term job in which they would like to stay or as an opportunity for career advancement within the same company. Meanwhile, those employees who do not feel valued are over twice as likely to simply view their current role as a "job for now" or as part of a career that will take them to different companies.

	"Feel valued as an employee"?	
	Agree	Disagree
Percentage who perceive current role as long-term job to stay in or as opportunity for in-house career advancement	63%	32%
Percentage who perceive current role as "just a job for now" or part of career moving between companies	32%	66%

Good communication, then, can create a strong retention link for the company and significantly reduce staff turnover. This will have two potentially positive effects on the bottom line. First, by suppressing turnover, it will stem talent loss and recruitment volume for the business, lowering both opportunity costs and direct costs (such as recruitment, advertising, etc.).

Second, by improving retention, a greater proportion of staff are likely to act as employer advocates, strengthening the organization's employer brand in the recruitment marketplace. Again, in turn, this will minimize recruitment spending as the company improves its "employer of choice" reputation.

This is a great example of how internal effects (i.e., good communication with employees) can have a positive effect on external branding (e.g., among potential recruits) via a motivational impact on current staff (i.e., increasing the perception that the company values its people).

3. However, communication is patchy

We know good communication is a measurably positive input to the business, but how does the organization perform on it?

The results found that the picture was, at best, patchy. Although, in overall terms, it is unusual to get large percentage scores on communications issues in employee surveys (averages are at only around 50 percent), it is the undulating nature of the communications landscape that is often the greatest problem. For example, take how this particular retailer was doing in terms of its communications across various employee grades. Two key problems were found.

◆ *Communications "Privileges"*   Across several key metrics, positivity about communications was found to increase according to how high up the managerial ladder employees were. This suggested that the closer you were to the top, the more information you received and the more your views were taken into account.

	% agreeing among:		
	Non-managers	Team leaders	Management team
Communications question statement			
I receive enough information to perform well in my job	58%	62%	80%
My line manager listens to my ideas	40%	59%	75%
My opinions count at ABC	27%	31%	40%

◆ *Mid-Management Communications Gap*   Secondly, on other key communications metrics, a positivity "dip" was found at the team leader level. Ironically, this grouping had been strategically identified as being critical to the implementation of change in the business.

	% agreeing among:		
	Non-managers	Team leaders	Management team
Communications question statement			
Communications are open and honest at ABC	48%	43%	59%
Communication is good across different parts of the business	42%	36%	42%

Lessons for HR and Communications

Linking HR and communications measurement has obvious benefits. The retailer in question is now focused on communications as a critical improvement area within its HR strategy. In particular, lessons included the following items.

◆ *Communication Has a Positive Impact on Motivation Levels Among Employees*   In turn, motivation is positively associated in many businesses with productivity and resultant profitability, especially in a retailing environment with high numbers of customer-facing staff. Our research has found that, in general, unit improvements in overall satisfaction with communication can have around a 20 percent impact on motivation levels. Communication and HR professionals then need to work out the cost of improving their communications channels, content, and culture in order to conduct a true cost-benefit analysis. However, the returns are undeniable. Communicate well and your employees are likely to feel more positive about their work and more positive toward their colleagues.

◆ *Internal Communication Can Play a Key Role in Improving External-Facing Behaviors* Higher levels of pride among staff can significantly impact on customer service and brand promise delivery, while employer advocacy can be critical in attracting talent into the organization. In almost every single company where we have studied internal communication positivity among staff and external provision of customer service, there is a strong and significant link. Equally, where we find high levels of understanding of the corporate objectives among staff, customer perceptions of whether they have received the brand delivery that they were promised is higher by almost threefold. Meanwhile, where we find staff positive about how they are communicated with internally, there is over three times as great a chance that those same employees will talk highly of the company as an employer to potential recruits in the external market.

◆ *Communication Needs to Be Consistently Delivered to Leverage the Benefits Identified* Communicating poorly with the large numbers of staff at the sharp end of a company is a huge missed opportunity. Messages need to be delivered to customer service representatives as quickly and openly as they would be to senior managers and team leaders. If this consistency is achieved, HR will begin to see the benefits of positive communication. For example, in companies where a major restructuring or radical changes in product portfolios are communicated quickly and evenly across all grades, we inevitably see greater leverage of the types of benefit we have described.

Overall, then, our message is simple: Get out of your silos, combine your measurement approaches, and see how HR and communication can work together to deliver high-performance cultures.

This article was originally published in *Strategic HR Review,* volume 2, issue 1 (2002), published by Melcrum Research.

Checkup 4: Essential Communication Systems

To conclude, it's important for organizational communication systems to be more than a one-way mouthpiece for executives and the corporate spokesperson. Two-way, collaborative systems for external and internal news, brainstorming, conversation, and work partnership need to be in place. Check to see how your own organization rates.

☐ Does your organization support training, environments, and technologies that promote internal and external collaboration?

☐ Do you frequently collect and use input from customers and suppliers?

☐ Does your website actively solicit two-way communication with important publics?

☐ Does your organization have a strategic plan for sponsoring community events and other charities?

☐ Do you have a crisis communication plan, including training for executives and mechanisms for disseminating news quickly?

☐ Are your employee communications interventions designed to directly impact performance?

☐ Do you measure your communication activities to link them to satisfaction and performance?

Self-Check

1. Where do external and internal communication functions reside in organizations and what are the relative merits of various approaches to positioning this function?

2. What do employees want and expect from their supervisors in terms of information and communication style, and how can professionals in learning and communication assist in supervisory communication?

3. Why is it important to develop consistency in internal and external communication?

4. How do our underlying theories or models of communication influence how we judge the success of a message or a communications project?

5. How can, and why should, we engineer relationships with customers and how does communication style and infrastructure influence this decision?

6. What are the traits and building blocks of a strong communications infrastructure?

7. How are special events used to build brand equity and customer relationships?

8. What is a communication audit, what is its goal, and how can it be integrated with an overall HR audit?

9. How does employee satisfaction with internal communication and management affect their behavior with customers and therefore the bottom line?

10. List at least five essential communication systems that every organization should have.

References

D'Aprix, R. (1996). *Communicating for change*. San Francisco: Jossey-Bass.

Gayeski, D. (2000). *Managing the communication function: Capturing mindshare for organizational performance*. San Francisco: International Association of Business Communicators.

Grunig, J. E. (Ed.). (1992). *Excellence in public relations and communication management*. Hillsdale, NJ: L. Erlbaum Associates.

Pascale, R., Milliemann, M., & Gioia, L. (1997, November–December). Changing the way we change. *Harvard Business Review*, 127–139.

Watson Wyatt Worldwide. (1999). *Linking communication with strategy to achieve business goals*. San Francisco: IABC.

CHAPTER 4 *Corporate Brand and Culture*

Overview

Products and services come and go, as do employees and even facilities. The most important and enduring asset of an organization is its brand and culture. While brand is more consciously created and externally oriented, culture tends to evolve in an often unplanned way among members of an organization. Both of these critical factors need to be examined and nourished for a company to succeed.

Companies with a strong brand are able to spin-off successful related products, license the name, and charge more for their product. Strong internal cultures are associated with high performance and low cost, especially because of easy recruiting and higher retention rates.

What Is a Brand and What Is Your Role?

When you hear the word "brand," you probably think of a product name like Big Mac, a store name like The Gap, a logo like the Nike "swoosh," or even the distinctive packaging of a product like a Coke bottle. Beyond those attributes, a brand is really a set of associations and expectations for a company, product, or service; an implicit promise of what the buyer can expect and what meaning it has in a customer's life. For many customers McDonald's has the meaning of predictability and economy. It is a safe place to choose no matter where the restaurant is located. Being the owner of a status symbol like a Mercedes or Rolex may enhance one's self-image, and these items are often bought to make a statement about one's success and position in life. Many people are fiercely loyal to local stores where they can count on personalized service, or support certain companies because of their employment or social practices.

You may think that branding is the responsibility of advertising and marketing departments and the agencies they hire. While they may develop the strategies and positioning, a brand is built by much more than advertising and packaging. Especially in the case of services, a customer's relationship with a company and brand is the result of communication with employees: a purchasing agent, a restaurant server, a salesperson, or a repair person. While initial exposure and awareness can be built by traditional advertising and marketing programs, more significant relationships are built by two-way interactions.

What is the Value of a Strong Brand and How Is it Maximized?

Much research has been done recently on measuring the value of a strong brand. Overall, it is evident that a strong brand drives customer loyalty (which reduces advertising, marketing, and administrative expenses) and increases the price at which products can successfully be sold. Some statistics include the following.

◆ Every year you keep a consumer's loyalty, the benefits earned from that consumer will be considerably higher—a 5 percent increase in customer loyalty can lift lifetime profits per consumer as much as 100 percent.

◆ Around 72 percent of consumers say they'll pay a 20 percent premium for a brand that owns their loyalty, while 25 percent say that price doesn't matter if they are buying a brand that owns their loyalty!

◆ There is a direct relation between stock performance and brand equity—every one point increase in brand recognition results in a 1 percent increase in stock return (Davis, 2000).

CASE IN POINT

How Cracker Barrel Old Country Store® creates "fanatic" customers

Julie Davis, Director of Communications,
Cracker Barrel Old Country Store, Inc., Lebanon, TN

Cracker Barrel Old Country Store® has become a part of both the ordinary and the extraordinary moments in many people's lives; we know because of the letters we receive on a regular basis. There is room here for just a couple of examples: one letter from a couple told us that the special attention from a server in one of our South Carolina stores was the reason their grandson started talking again. He had stopped when his mother died in the September 11th, 2001, tragedy. Another letter detailed all the excitement of a wedding party held at a Cracker Barrel unit. We hear all the time from folks just wanting to share their opinions about their local store because, well, it's **their** store.

Cracker Barrel is fortunate to enjoy intense customer loyalty. Many guests use our map of all Cracker Barrel locations to plan their vacations, and we received so many e-mails from people asking for a store close to their hometowns that we finally developed a standard electronic reply letting them know we got their message (crafting that standard reply so that it fit closely with our overall image of hospitality involved many, many people—including the President of the company!). Our guest relations department increased to eleven people in order to handle all the customer contact. Six years ago, there were only two people at the home office handling this function.

We like to think that this attention to detail (some would call it obsessive) is an important reason for the loyalty felt by our guests. Every aspect of the in-store operations is examined on a regular basis at several levels of oversight, and we look to our hourly employees to speak up about the details of their jobs and how to improve things. Every item served in our restaurants and every product sold in our retail stores is reviewed to ensure that it is consistent with guests' and employees' impression of Cracker Barrel. We've identified some words, such as "nostalgia," "value," "honest," and "unique," that we think describe the Cracker Barrel brand, and we check all our store offerings against those words to ensure a good fit. We believe that "Cracker Barrel fills your hunger for the way things used to be," and so everything has to match up with that brand idea.

Our marketing department is always driven to create external communication pieces that support this strong brand identity. The "table tents" that talk to customers as they decide what to order, the "brand book" that is given out by hostesses free of charge several times a year, and the in-store signs that tell stories about the retail products all have the same look and feel, the same conversational tone-of-voice (see Figure 4.1).

One of the strengths of our communications approach is that we place the same emphasis for brand consistency on our **internal** communications pieces. The training materials that our new managers and employees use, the videos on how to prepare and serve new food items that employees watch, and the brochures outlining health benefits that employees rely upon all follow the deliberate tactic of clear, conversational language and simple "Cracker Barrel" graphics.

Half Restaurant.
Half Store.
All Country.[SM]

In 1969, we opened the first Cracker Barrel Old Country Store® on Highway 109 in Lebanon, Tennessee. Aside from the gas pumps out front, it was a lot like the Cracker Barrel you'll find today on I-75 in Gainesville, Florida, or any of our more than 450 locations. There was a restaurant in back serving hearty meals and a country store up front selling things at fair prices. Today, we also try to keep you entertained and informed, with things like this summer booklet and, soon, our new 2003 Cracker Barrel Old Country Store® Travel Almanac. (Be sure to stop by starting Thanksgiving for a copy.) So when you're on the road, we hope you remember there's a place nearby to relax, get a good meal, and do some browsing. Because that's what we had in mind when we started, back in '69.

In the spirit of Pleasing People, we invite everyone to enjoy our restaurant and our old country store. We attempt to provide both in ways that uphold our traditions of genuine quality. We hope you'll be pleased. If you have any comments, suggestions or complaints, please let us know. Home Office • P.O. Box Box 787 • Hartmann Drive • Lebanon, TH • 37087 • 800-333-9566 • www.crackerbarrel.com

"Half Restaurant. Half Store. All Country." is a service mark of CBOCS General Partnership

Figure 4.1
Cracker Barrel Old Country Store Customer Book

When employees receive a communication from "corporate," we want them to know it's from **Cracker Barrel** corporate, not from some generic two billion dollar a year company (see Figures 4.2 and 4.3).

Creating a consistent look and feel among the large amount of communications products produced each year has required a great deal of commitment, not to mention inter-departmental coordination! Senior management has made it clear that we must speak to our employees with one voice, and the individual department heads have been charged with ensuring that this happens through coordinated designs and approaches. Much emphasis has been placed on the timing of messages as well, to ensure that managers at individual stores are not regularly overwhelmed by too many different but simultaneous directives and pieces of information.

It seems likely that the desire to coordinate our internal messages to employees with our external messages to guests stems from our mission statement of "**pleasing people.**" Here is an excerpt from a statement by our founder sent to all employees about what pleasing people means:

Figure 4.2
Cracker Barrel Recruiting Brochure

Pleasing people is all about mutual respect among the individuals representing the groups of people who make up the constituencies. The four groups are employees, guests, vendors (suppliers), and shareholders. Make no mistake, our goal as a company is to make a profit; however, how we set about to do this is very important . . . and that is by effecting a balance in pleasing these four constituencies through the concept of mutual respect. It could be said that it's "showing the same face to everyone."

So, what is this brand consistency and loyalty worth? Many companies have financial models that put dollar amounts on these intangibles. Most do not usually discuss the details publicly for fear the competition will learn too much. However, all companies understand that it costs much more money to acquire new customers than it does to keep the ones you already have happy. That simple principle is the basis for the relatively recent functional specialty called "loyalty marketing," and it is something Cracker Barrel has known and acted upon for over thirty-three years.

Pleasing People With Product Knowledge: Fried Apples & Apple Crisp Mix

As a Cracker Barrel Old Country Store employee, you know a thing or two about great taste. That's why you'll likely find the taste of warm, juicy apples tucked under a crispy oat crumble topping one that's hard to beat.

Cracker Barrel is featuring this tantalizing dessert, Apple Crisp, in our Fall Seasonal Menu promotion, which runs September 17 through November 4 (see related article on page 7). What's unique is that guests who'd like to whip up this treat at home can find the "core" makings for it right in our retail stores! A jar of Fried Apples and a package of Apple Crisp Mix will do the job nicely!

The companies who produce these items know "a thing or two" about good taste too.

Apple Crisp Mix
A Product of Kari Lee's
Country Mix Company™ (Kari Lee's)
Homemade with a little help™

Founder **Kari Lee Beutell** explains that the idea for creating ready-to-use mixes came from trying to save time in her own kitchen.

It didn't take us long at Cracker Barrel to recognize the quality and convenience of her products, and we began carrying Kari Lee's Apple Crisp Mix in the fall of 1996.

"As a busy mother of two little girls, I designed our mixes for myself! I'd blend and package big batches," Kari says. "Friends began asking to purchase my tasty treats, and my business began!"

She explains that all Kari Lee's products are made with "the busy home cook" in mind. In addition to the Apple Crisp Mix, she offers a variety of muffin, cake, pie and cobbler mixes.

"Our mixes offer the 'on the go' home cook the convenience of a mix with 100% all natural, homemade flavor," Kari says.

Cracker Barrel Country Fixin's™ Fried Apples
A Private Label Product
Packaged by
Knouse Foods
Cooperative, Inc.®
(Knouse Foods)

Knouse Foods packages several of Cracker Barrel's private label items, such as Fried Apples, Spiced Apple Butter and Cobbler Fillings.

From a small beginning in April 1949, Knouse Foods has grown to become one of the largest apple processing companies in the world. The cooperative was formed when a group of prominent fruit growers from four states joined forces to purchase the processing plants once owned by **M. E. Knouse**. It is now owned by more than 150 fruit growers throughout the Appalachian region and a small number of growers in Michigan and produces under the retail labels of Lucky Leaf and Musselmans.

In 1984, **Mark Tanzer**, Vice President of Product Development, met with Knouse's salesmen at one of our Nashville, Tennessee stores. Mark asked them to create a quality fried apple with the peel left on. Though the request sounded bizarre to a company that had spent a lot of money on equipment to remove the peel, they accepted the challenge and presented the quality product we still sell today.

Apple Crisp Recipe
- One 28 oz. jar Cracker Barrel Country Fixin's™ Fried Apples
- $1/2$ cup cold butter
- 1 bag (16 oz.) Kari Lee's Apple Crisp Mix

Directions:
Preheat oven to 350° F. Place fried apples in buttered 9" pie pan. Cut $1/2$ cup cold butter into small cubes. In a mixing bowl, combine Apple Crisp Mix with butter. Mix with fork or fingers until the mixture looks like coarse crumbs. Sprinkle topping evenly over the fried apples.

Place on middle oven rack. Bake 45-50 minutes or until topping is golden and juices are bubbly.

Serve warm with whipped cream or ice cream. Serves 6-10.

Reader Survey Results To Come

Thanks to everyone who responded to our June/July 2001 Reader Survey! The results are being tabulated, and we'll report the findings to you in the next issue.

"L. P. Carnes" Winner Announced

Hostess **Lorraine Peters** of Store #416 Kingman, Arizona knows quite a bit about L. P. Carnes, hero of the new Loss Prevention Adventure comic series. She answered all the trivia questions from the first issue correctly, and her name was drawn to receive a $25.00 gift certificate.

"We had an awesome response to the contest, with over 540 entries," says **Gary Alford**, Corporate Manager of Loss Prevention. "We're planning to start putting out an issue every quarter," he says.

This comic series offers an entertaining way for our employees to learn more about preventing loss and theft in their stores.

Be sure to look for future L. P. Carnes antics and more ways to win soon.

Answers to Last Issue's Trivia:
1. Lacey Portnoy Carnes
2. Harry the Heist
3. 1-888-894-4262

Sharing's Not So Nice When it Comes to Swipe Cards

Company policy states that servers, cashiers and managers must not allow anyone else to use their Micros Swipe Cards. So be nice - don't share.

Figure 4.3
Page From Old Country Store's Employee Newsletter

Courtesy Cracker Barrel Old Country Store, Inc.

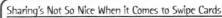

Internal Branding

"Internal branding" is a term referring to initiatives that attempt to align corporate culture and external brand. They are typically projects that help to communicate brand identity to employees and, in some cases, to involve employees in creating the brand and developing ways in which they can "live the brand." An internal brand helps you easily describe your organization to a current or prospective employee. It helps illustrate your company culture, and reinforces why your company is a great place to work. Most importantly, it helps employees to act in ways that support the brand identity when collaborating with partners and customers.

CASE IN POINT

Caterpillar coordinates its voice

Bonnie Briggs, Manager of Corporate Identity and Communications, Caterpillar, Inc.

When Caterpillar reorganized in 1990 and became a decentralized company, it became easy for the different areas of the company to produce messages that were unique to themselves and not reflective of the company as a whole. That led to fragmented, mixed messages. Instead of having a number of different communication groups throughout the organization coming up with their own ideas of what Cat is all about and issuing communication based on those varying ideas, we realized we needed some consensus.

We embarked on a project to define a global communication strategy in 1992. After a three-day brainstorming session, we identified some key issues.

- Employee confusion existed concerning the direction of the company after the reorganization.
- The potential existed for a brand trademark to be misused and misinterpreted.
- Customers, because of changes in the terms of products offered and markets served, were not clear about how and why to work with Caterpillar.
- Finally, we had to be sure we were communicating clearly to investors and the general public.

The next step was to be clear about what made Cat different. We went back to strategic planning and asked, "What are our competitive strengths? What are our values?" We looked at the company's history and learned there was a heart and soul that still exists.

We wanted to maintain some elements of our corporate personality. For example, we are a maker/builder (and we are good at it), and we're proud. In addition, there are some elements we aspire to, or "wannabe." We want to continue to be a global leader and fierce competitor. We want to be innovative, confident, assured, flexible, customer-responsive, and an up-front effective communicator.

We began to see that one role of communication is to help people understand how to help move the company from where it is to where it wants to go. In the process, we also began to get a pretty clear picture of the characteristics we wanted to communicate about the company—almost how we would describe it if it were a person. That led us to Caterpillar's "voice." Voice is an easy way to refer to a focused communication strategy based on a sound description of who and what a corporation stands for.

Caterpillar is unique. Like other companies, it has a distinctive personality shaped in part by the products we make. Our products and engines are often described as "powerful" or "rugged." These same words describe our company.

Therefore, when we speak as a company—regardless of whether it is an ad or a memo—we ought to use the messages and visuals that reflect who we are. Doing that makes communication easier and more believable because it delivers what our various audiences expect from us.

To introduce the concept of voice throughout the company, we offer a workshop to employees (and some employees from Cat dealers and suppliers) called "Communicating Caterpillar: One Voice." Think of it as Caterpillar 101. In the workshop, we focus on company values, core competencies, attributes, and positioning. The idea is to help Caterpillar people (and people who work closely with the company) to speak about the company in a way that is powerfully, distinctly "us." We don't want every communication we issue to look and sound the same. However, we do want them to be directionally the same.

Actually, the workshop is an outgrowth of a brochure entitled "Communicating Caterpillar: One Voice" (see Figures 4.4 and 4.5). It is a great brochure, but we felt it could be dismissed too easily. Plus, we were concerned people might think of this whole effort as a program—with a beginning and an end. Or they might think of it as a negative, controlling thing rather than something enabling. There was also a danger of interest and participation waning without reinforcement. We had to build in acceptance and support. Therefore, a "voice" training program seemed pivotal (see Figure 4.6).

The result is a workshop we built from scratch that relies on "hands on" rather than lecture or "show and tell." The workshop is one full day of people learning how to recognize "voice" and analyze their way to effective applications of voice principles. We use a series of demonstrations and exercises to focus on teaching voice concepts, not communication skills, because we already expected attendees to know how to communicate.

One way we measure the success of "One Voice" is in cash. For example, the marketing communicator in Cat of Australia says that she can save $50,000 to 100,000 per year in advertising expenses because the ads that dealers develop are usable. In "the old days" quite often the ads weren't quite right, and the dealers and their ad agencies didn't quite "get it" because there was no agreed upon approach for them to "get." For examples, pictures didn't show product in the preferred context, or language didn't reflect corporate's philosophies and key messages. Now, after "One Voice" training, everybody knows the messages, the attitude, the look, the style, and the feeling Cat wants to convey.

Applying "One Voice" principles also allows us to achieve efficiencies in creativity. We can create a template to produce a family of materials, say, specalogs (which give the features and specifications of Cat products). Once we have agreed on the look and messages, the designer just produces the various pieces for all the products in a family (say, track-type tractors), always using one set of design criteria. Therefore, the designer saves time and the company saves money. In addition, the user can pick up the specalogs for the various products in a family and easily do comparison shopping—knowing exactly where to find information from one specalog to the next—because the information is presented the same way each time. Therefore, we may save up to $100,000 per specalog (because of language translation we produce 100 to 200 pieces at $4,000 to $5,000 per piece), plus the reader saves time using the literature.

Caterpillar's voice is the total expression of who we are and how we work. When we use the elements that make up our voice—our values, our personality and attributes, our competencies, our positioning and the images and words that express them—the overall effect is unmistakably Caterpillar.

When we view many communications that are "in voice," there is a compelling harmony. Our messages are heard more clearly and more effectively. Within our organization, our voice gives us the power to create better and more appropriate materials, as well as providing the standards to measure their effectiveness. Among our customers and external audiences, a clear voice helps us accomplish our goal of differentiating our products and services in the market.

Figure 4.4
Caterpillar's Explanation of its Voice

Ask someone to describe Caterpillar in human characteristics and you're likely to hear the words in the boldface type on this page. And it's not surprising that they're the same words that describe the products we manufacture and the services we provide—as well as the things we believe as individuals and as a company.

This isn't language you have to use in your communications, or a list of approved words. They're words you should keep in mind when creating communications. A filter, if you will, for making sure your communications capture Caterpillar's personality.

Stop and think how we say what we say, not just what we say, and we can project Caterpillar's personality more accurately and effectively. These words should only be used to help guide the appearance and tone of our communications, so they look and sound more like who we really are. You don't have to use them literally.

Attributes

Caterpillar products are **down-to-earth,** straightforward, gritty and **rugged.** The Cat name is **enduring.** To meet our customers' expectations, our products have to be **strong,** powerful and reliable. We are **genuine** and **accessible** and act as an **honest partner** in our relations with dealers, customers and each other—and we're **responsive** and **global** enough to meet our customers' changing needs. We're **serious,** thorough and **professional** about our business, **active** and highly **industrious, dedicated** to helping our customers succeed. Our **commanding** engines and machines are of the highest quality, and that is what makes us **competitive** and our industry's **leader.**

Use these words to help "color" your communications. These are criteria for judging the effectiveness of our creative work. Does the photo of a piece of equipment look rugged? Can copy be written to be more straightforward? Does the design communicate our dedication to our work? Is an image realistic and serious? You can express these and other attributes in words and images without being literal.

Figure 4.5
The Adjectives That Describe Caterpillar

Are You Communicating Caterpillar?

By now, you should have a basic understanding of Caterpillar's personality and how it is reflected in the Caterpillar voice. So it's time to ask yourself if you are clearly communicating Caterpillar.

Collect and review examples of your communications. Then answer the following questions and decide for yourself how close you've come to using Caterpillar's voice.

Planning

1   Do you have a clear communications objective?

2   Does this communication help solve a business problem?

3   Have you taken a global view?

4   Have you looked for related material to ensure support for other communications?

5   Have you considered all of our audiences?

6   Are you supporting Caterpillar's positioning?

Writing

1   Are your sentences written in the active voice?

2   Are your sentences short and to the point?

3   Are the words you use, especially the adjectives and verbs, clear and strong?

Photos and graphics

1   Do your photos or videos portray Caterpillar people as active, professional and competent?

2   Do the photos or videos you've chosen portray a powerful, active, rugged image of Cat machines and engines in realistic settings?

3   How often do you use illustrations and drawings? Are they compatible with Caterpillar's image?

Layout and design

1   Do your publications have a strong and clear design?

2   Do you position and crop photos so that they capture the focus of action?

3   Do colors you use in your publications fit the Caterpillar personality?

4   Do your graphic elements communicate the personality of Caterpillar?

5   Does your video contain production elements that viewers will associate with Caterpillar?

Figure 4.6
A Checklist for Communicating in Caterpillar's Voice

An educated workforce allows us to more easily spot counterfeit Caterpillar merchandise. Voice involves standards for using our trademarks and logos. Counterfeiters don't know the standards and often apply our colors and marks incorrectly. Fake Cat stuff is easy to spot, if you know our rules. When we spot the bogus merchandise, we take action on the counterfeiter. This protects the market for genuine Cat goods and assures us higher sales. This translates, of course, into more long-term value for the brand itself.

Other ways we can measure "One Voice" applies to internal communication efforts. These internal measurements don't focus on money. Then again, we didn't start applying "One Voice" *primarily* to save money (although we do save). We apply it because it improves our ability to send consistent messages and carve out a differentiated message that is uniquely Caterpillar's. For example, at Cat we think of our company in terms of adjectives like "down-to-earth, gritty, rugged, strong, powerful, global, reliable, straightforward, genuine, accessible, honest, active, industrious, commanding, competitive and leader."

The key message of our positioning statement (Caterpillar makes progress possible) is "big picture" and speaks to our role in enabling our customers around the world. It's also a message employees embrace. The message helps them to feel good about their role in helping the company make progress possible. So, when we develop a communication item, we mentally lay it against the "One Voice" filter to determine if it is "us" or not. Is this language or the photo active enough? Does this look commanding? Do you feel this appears to be honest? Yes or no. It's a go/no go process that leads to a consistent outlook and forces us to apply discernment.

Having said that, here are some ways to measure the impact of voice on internal communication.

a. Our internal media, like employee newsletters, are much more consistent in appearance. Years ago, we tried to get newsletter editors to make all of the publications conform to a single look. We met resistance, because they felt that our request stifled their creativity. (They were probably right, too.) After taking a Voice class, their publications don't look the same, but they all tend to look similar. Now, they like the corporate look, because Voice allows great flexibility and creativity, and as a result the publications are better looking than ever. Applying Voice is like writing a sonnet: you have rules—but it is up to the "artist" to apply the vision and fill in the details.

b. We can work with designers more easily. They know what we want and what we don't want—so our assignments to them are easier to comprehend and their initial deliveries are closer to the target. Therefore, they can work faster and the entire developmental process is speedier. That saves us both money and turnaround time. In addition, we enjoy working with each other better, too, because there is less friction caused by creative differences!

c. Communicators find it easier to sell their ideas. They are not often the decision-makers, but when they present their ideas, because of Voice principles, they have lots of background to back up their recommendations. Many times, it is not a case of what communicators like (or what someone else likes), but rather a case of whether it's "in Voice" or not. Everyone can agree on that rather easily now. Therefore, management doesn't tend to resist communicators' ideas so much now, because the managers who have had Voice training "get" what the creative people are trying to accomplish.

d. Subliminally, our audiences understand what is happening. They know our materials are consistent and share a similar attitude, although they might not be able to put their fingers on why this is so. However, after someone points out the voice characteristics, you can see the light bulbs go on and they "get it." I have shown students copies of our annual reports before and after Voice and asked them which were better. They always pick the ones after Voice. Why? The look is more dynamic, more "muscular" and powerful, which proves that Voice "works." As another example, one of our facility communicators recently redesigned her newspaper, using Voice principles, and it won an award. Other pieces of Caterpillar's Voice-influenced literature have also won awards.

Internal communication exists to help the company make money, which happens when everyone works to his or her potential—and that means they must have the knowledge needed to do excellent work. They must be motivated to not only give the company their time, but also their creativity, their passion, their pride in their work, their sense of humor and friendliness, and their integrity. Our intent is to help employees feel so good about the company that they'll speak of Cat with pride and affection wherever they are—after church on Sunday morning, in a shop while they are on vacation, or just talking with their friends. We want to give them as much positive news about the company as possible.

The future of internal communication doesn't lie with figuring out how to produce the best-looking videos, newsletters, intranet sites, and so forth. The future lies in identifying exactly what the company stands for, its culture, what is the mission—and then what employees need to be successful on their jobs. The future also lies in recognizing that formal communication (videos, newsletters, intranet sites, etc.) are more powerful when used to support face-to-face communication. The best communication plans will involve orchestrated messages working in concert. Communicators then play the role of ensuring that all employees embrace the culture and pursue the mission. The ultimate success is to influence people to take actions that lead to the enterprise's success.

What Is Corporate Culture and How Does HR Engineer It?

Culture is, in essence, an organization's personality derived from the values, assumptions, norms, and artifacts of the organization's members. The benefits of a strong culture include

- cohesiveness
- employee loyalty
- increased employee satisfaction and productivity
- a positive external image
- collaboration
- lower turnover

A company's culture may be associated with its brand; for instance, a high-tech firm noted for its innovation may have a very informal culture that emphasizes creativity over conformity. However, many organizations have a variety of brands associated with them, and their culture may have nothing to do with the personality of the brand. Actually, in most large organizations there are really subcultures in various locations or departments.

There is no "right or wrong" culture. Culture is something that is enacted—it is more of a verb than a noun—and it's continually in transition and defined by each person who is a member.

One aspect of culture that directly impacts performance is leadership behaviors, and in turn, how these relate to fostering a climate that encourages excellent service and good organizational citizenship. The following essay presents some fascinating research on what is called "organizational citizenship behavior" or OCB.

CASE IN POINT

The implications of managerial leadership on organizational citizenship behavior (OCB)

Michael Petrillose, Ph.D., Assistant Professor, Hospitality Management,
Delhi College, State University of New York, Delhi, NY

In recent years, many demographers have commented on the increasing sophistication of today's consumer. Education, discretionary income, and leisure time have all risen. It is also widely acknowledged that today's consumers are more demanding, better informed, more assertive, and have a substantially lower tolerance for poor-quality products and services. This trend has been enhanced by increased competition in all areas of the economy. In addition to pursuing price value, customers have more selection choices.

Given these increasingly innovative and aggressive business trends, prudent business operators have realized the importance of providing quality service to ensure that all their existing and new customers become loyal and satisfied repeat customers. As a result, a variety of creative strategies based on service excellence have been developed in order to create a competitive advantage for a company. That is where organizational citizenship behavior (OCB) and leadership come in.

Organizational citizenship behavior is constructive behavior that is spontaneously exhibited by organizational members and, in aggregate, promotes the efficient and effective functioning of the organization. It is not directly related to individual productivity or specified in the enforceable or formal requirements of the individual's role. The employee personally chooses to go beyond formal job descriptions and performs extra-role behaviors on his or her own discretion and without expectation of explicit organizational reward. OCB has five categories: (1) altruism, or helping behaviors, which are voluntary actions that help another person with a work-related problem; (2) conscientiousness, or discretionary behaviors that go well beyond the minimum role requirement; (3) sportsmanship, or any behaviors that demonstrate tolerance in less-than-ideal situations without complaints; (4) courtesy, or efforts to prevent work-related problems with others from occurring; and (5) civic virtue, which are behaviors that indicate that an employee responsibly participates in and is concerned about the life of the organization.
Examples of OCB are:

- helping a new front desk clerk who has difficulties in handling a computerized reservation system (altruism)
- staying late to finish a project even though there is no overtime or direct payment (conscientiousness)
- refraining from complaining about the disruption elicited by renovation of a facility (sportsmanship)

◆ contacting shipping and delivery personnel before making a non-routine commitment to a customer (courtesy)
◆ taking the initiative to recommend how company operations or procedures can be improved (civic virtue)

All these organizational citizenship behaviors have important relationships with service quality. Service quality is enhanced to the extent that employees view each other as customers and thus willingly assist each other to better serve the external customer. For example, the new front desk clerk, as previously described, will be able to efficiently serve customers in a long line if a more experienced coworker assists him or her with handling the computerized reservation system. Altruism behavior is directed toward the external customers and can take the form of helping a customer with a problem, even though doing so is not within one's specified job duties. A bellman within a hotel may help a visitor to find his or her way. These actions, while seemingly trivial, create an overall sense of goodwill and thus enhance the customer's experience of service quality. Additionally, through suggestions from front-line employees, who interact with customers on an ongoing basis, organizations can continually improve their level of customer service. Besides, employees who exhibit high levels of courtesy and sportsmanship are respectful and considerate to each other, have a positive attitude, and avoid unnecessary complaining. Therefore, the positive climate created among employees with high levels of courtesy and sportsmanship will directly or indirectly affect customers' perception of service quality through their cooperative and courteous interaction with customers.

In practice, the employees in the companies noted for the quality of their service excellence have engaged in not only exceptional levels of in-role behaviors but also extra-role activities that are not formally required. Consequently, those companies enhance high levels of customer satisfaction and internal effectiveness and efficiencies through those employees' organizational citizenship behaviors. These organizational citizenship behaviors, however, cannot be either fully specified in advance by an organization or easily ensured through traditional techniques such as training and job descriptions or contractual economic exchange with organizational immediate compensation. Therefore, a manager's leadership has significant implications in fostering employee organizational citizenship behavior because leadership has been recognized through the ages as a primary means of influencing the behaviors of others.

Charismatic leaders have the ability to influence subordinates through their considerable self-confidence, strong convictions, and infectious enthusiasm. Admired subordinates then internalize the leader's attitudes and behaviors as guiding principles for their own behavior. Transformational leaders should direct subordinates toward mutually desired results, and subordinates then reciprocate by providing increased status, esteem, and support for the leaders. As a result of this leadership style and its emulation by their subordinates, leaders can play a mediating role to change employee behaviors and produce higher levels of employee organizational citizenship behaviors.

The importance of delivering service excellence by leadership and employee OCB is more important for service industries, such as hotels, manufacturing, and non-service-oriented organizations. This is influenced by the hotel industry's two unique characteristics: service-oriented and labor-intensive. In the absence of machinery and other forms of technology that reduce the need for human labor, employee behavior plays a vital role for service excellence in the hotel industry. The hotel industry's product is the result of the interaction between its employees and customers. Therefore, employees' behaviors and attitudes can influence customers' perceptions of the service rendered and ultimately the overall perception of the quality of the hotel's product.

The intangibility of service can be expressed in terms of the tangible behavior and attitude of employees. In addition, the successful performance of an employee's service work depends frequently upon the cooperation of other persons, including co-workers and supervisors. These interdependent relationships of the hotel industry place immense importance on employee OCB and a manager's leadership.

Reprinted Courtesy of Michael Petrillose, Ph. D.

Engineering Culture and Brand from the Ground Up

We have seen how the brand and culture affect performance and how various types of communication and training interventions can help to sharpen and strengthen an organization's identity. But exactly what decisions need to be made when you have the opportunity to create a new brand or culture?

A first step for the company is to determine whether to establish one umbrella brand for all the products and services in the company, or establish a number of independent brands. For example, Xerox bundles its various products under the one Xerox brand, adding the tagline "the document company" to refer to the fact that it produces more than copiers. Other corporations, such as the global beer company, Interbrew, encompass a number of individual brands that actually compete with one another.

One trend is for companies with many brands to eliminate the weakest ones and build up the ones with the strongest reputation, creating what are called "megabrands." Dove is one example. For many years, the Dove brand was limited to bar soap; today, Unilever has expanded the brand to include body washes, facial wipes, anti-aging products, shampoo, and deodorants. This expansion puts Dove far ahead of the competition. However, brand extension is not without its risks: if the extension products don't fit in with the customers' image and experience with the core product, the newly branded products can fail, and the overall brand can be tarnished. In fact, in the 1960s, Unilever introduced a Dove brand dishwashing liquid, but it didn't sell well because it was not perceived to carry the same promise as a creamy, gentle skin cleanser.

When organizations create a new brand, they face a number of challenges. This is especially true in situations of mergers and acquisitions. Should the company build on one of its strongest names or should they create a new name and brand? How will the various corporate cultures be reconciled? How will current customers be informed and kept, and how will new customers be acquired? What mechanisms need to be in place to align employee behaviors and values with the new concept?

All of these considerations went into effect when a new banking group, Nordea, was formed from the merger of several large Nordic banks. The following case study points out important strategies in building both the external brand and the internal culture.

Creating a new brand and culture

Philip Wegloop, Ph.D., Head of Brand Management,
Nordea, Denmark

Nordea is a recent merger of four major banks in the Nordic area—Nordbanken in Sweden, Merita in Finland, Unibank in Denmark, and K-Bank in Norway. As a result of these mergers during 1998–2001, Nordea is now the leading financial services group in the Nordic and Baltic Sea region operating through three business areas: Retail Banking, Corporate and Institutional Banking, and Asset Management and Life. The Nordea Group has nearly 11 million customers, over 1,200 bank branches in 22 countries, and it is a world leader in Internet banking, with over 3.5 million e-customers. The aim of the merger has from the start been to create a new bank that is Nordic in operations, but at the same time both local and personal in character and service delivery. The corporate brand and culture have from the outset played a central and strategic role in the merger process, illustrated by the fact that the merger negotiations included discussions of and agreement upon a corporate statement that set out the strategic and operational, as well as cultural, direction of the company.

What's (in) a Corporate Brand?

Quite simply put, a corporate brand is a name, as well as what this name signals to customers, employees, shareholders, and society at large on the basis of a company's performance and communications. More specifically, it is a promise to meet (or exceed) expected quality, benefit, and performance standards between a company (with its services and products) and its stakeholders—based on its relationships with its most important audiences.

Corporate Branding: More a Way of Thinking than "Just" Advertising

The force and challenge of corporate branding is its holistic approach. It is simply impossible to build a strong brand without having a strong customer relationship, which in turn is crucially dependent on committed employees (especially in a people's business like banking) and competitive products and services. Therefore, building a strong brand is more than securing exciting advertising. Rather, it is about linking how to say things with what actually is said and thereby ultimately contributing to the corporate agenda for what to do. As such, the brand should be expressed in everything we do with each other and with our customers. Every touch point, whether it is a written or spoken word; the way we answer and deal with customers; how our products are positioned and offered; the visuals in our advertisements; the look and feel, user-friendliness, and navigability of our online services and sites; our personnel policies and incentive schemes; the sounds we provide while a call is waiting; and the look and feel of our offices and branches, makes an impression that is linked to our brand. Only through consistency across this wealth of touch points will we be able to build a brand that supports our business and deserves a place in the hearts and minds of our stakeholder groups.

This need for consistency is increasingly recognized; the notion of integrated communications has especially contributed to this. In Nordea, we aim at integrating communications across media (e.g., press, intranet, Web, advertising), business areas (rather taking the outside-in view), and national borders. However, while integrated communications is a crucial and important step in brand building, it is not enough.

Good corporate branding ultimately is a managerial approach—a way of thinking—and is intrinsically linked to the way concepts are developed, the way the organization is set up, and the strategic direction it follows. However, it must also be a "compass" for all strategic brand building communications and provide an appropriate brand umbrella for the tactical communications that support sales.

As corporate branding must address this need to link short-term and long-term thinking in the organization, it is clear that without top management commitment it is both impossible and probably counterproductive, since overpromising probably is the most severe of all sins to be committed in branding. Slightly paraphrasing David Packard, cofounder and former CEO of HP, "Branding (marketing) is far too important to leave to the marketing department." Ultimately it is about **conducting ourselves in a way that matches the way we would like to be perceived.** This demands, of course, a holistic approach only possible with the total commitment of top management to abolish "silo thinking" and the distorting silo-based incentive schemes that are so widespread in many organizations.

A New Name as a Start of Building a New Brand

Very early in the merger process, we decided that a new name for the group had to be found, even though some of the old names were quite good and functioned well in all languages. There was an awareness that a new name would be slightly more costly and time-consuming to implement due to legal registration.

This was simply done in order to signal that we were building something new and different from the past and that we would measure our performance in relation to our goals and vision, rather than past accomplishments.

The name Nordea—short for Nordic Ideas[1]—was presented at a press conference in November 2000, about six months after the merger. On December 8 of the same year, it was announced that the name change process would be conducted in several stages. The first stage began in December 2000 and meant that the group, Asset Management, as well as Corporate and Institutional Banking assumed the name Nordea and thereby a unified brand strategy. In April 2001 Investment Banking (previously called ArosMaizels) became Nordea Securities, followed by the adoption of the Nordea name the regional banks in Poland and the Baltic countries.

During the same time the retail banks—by far the most important and visible part of the group in the Nordic home market—were working under an integrated brand strategy. This meant a name change in stages (i.e., the original brands of the local banks were complemented gradually with the new name). Parallel usage of the brands sent out signals both of being Nordic as well as genuinely local.

---

[1]The press release announcing the name read: "Nordea stands for Nordic Ideas. We share Nordic values and exchange Nordic solutions in order to create value for our customers, hence also for our shareholders. Nordea endeavours to help the customers in realising their dreams and ambitions, and we are better positioned to do this with a strong, common brand. Unified branding facilitates communication both in-house and externally, and signals that we are firmly determined to deliver synergies across borders. We intend to build the Nordea brand into a valuable asset for the Group". *Thorleif Krarup, former Group CEO Nordea.*

On June 19, 2001, group CEO Thorleif Krarup announced that:

> *The Nordea brand is going to be implemented when it is commercially appropriate. In all of the Nordic countries there is a growing desire, among both customers and employees, that the retail banks should adopt the Nordea name. After thorough analysis we have found that the time is ripe to proceed further and send out a strong signal that we have come a long way in our integration efforts.*

The last phase of implementation began on December 3, when all of the banks in the four Nordic countries began to operate fully under the Nordea name. However, already during that autumn the customers began to notice some improvements in conditions and service, (e.g., the customers of Nordea are now able to use their cards for withdrawals on the same terms in all of the Nordic countries.)

From Name to Brand

It is obviously impossible here to try and give an overview of all the consecutive efforts needed in the process of building a strong corporate brand. The often-painstaking internal networking and "missionary" efforts can hardly be put on paper, yet are a key success factor. In addition, working the brand and values into core documents like the corporate statement and internal measurement and reward systems like the balanced scorecard are crucial.

One of the key elements was to engage all the employees in a discussion around the brand and its implications: What does this mean for me in my job? In order to try and ensure that all 38,000 employees first of all would understand the brand, then begin accepting it, and finally would start "living" it, we organized a group-wide internal management cascade where the brand values and their implications were addressed on an individual level. This program, called "From Words To Action," was based on a combination of material that was centrally produced (a brand book, explaining the mission, vision, and values) and locally produced material regarding what is in it for me on a highly decentralized level. The management of the FWTA project was done in close cooperation between HR and communication professionals and with a direct link to the group's executive management.

Of course, much more can be explained about the FWTA process, and the branding and culture process are continuing. However, the limited space left available will be used on something rather unique to harmonize our understanding of branding and values—a tool called IMPSYS©.

IMPSYS©—The Method

One of the key issues we have tried to address internally is the difference between name and brand. At times we have defined a brand as being a name plus the values, performance, and mission. The very tricky question arises of how to measure this brand on these "soft" values, and especially in a way that is comparable across different countries, cultures, and media. Especially in our multicultural post-merger setting, a common language for discussing this was paramount. A very interesting tool which has helped us in creating a common language for thinking about branding is called IMPSYS©.

The IMPSYS© system is founded on the theory that people's perceptions of their own needs and of brands include *both* conscious, rational considerations *and* unconscious, emotional impressions. The brands studied are projected into a system of coordinates formed by an *I—we ori-*

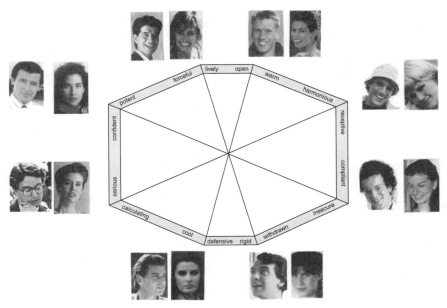

Figure 4.7
IMPSYS© Chart

entation (social) axis and an *outward—inward (biological orientation)* axis. Results of the IMP-SYS© study are presented in Figure 4.7 as positions in this system of coordinates.

The set of photos that can be seen in Figure 4.7 represents the most important human archetype personalities and are the cornerstone in facilitating this approach. The photos are validated in many countries, which for instance allow for direct comparison of the results between all the Nordic countries and the other countries in which Nordea operates. The technique is projective (i.e., interviewees are not expressing their own views but are giving their expressions on behalf of the different human archetype personalities shown in the photos).

The brands are positioned as a result of these answers. For each archetype, the interviewees are asked which financial institution he or she is using to achieve what is important in regards to his or her personal economy. If a financial institution is tied to one specific archetype, the position will be right at the particular corner of the frame. If, however, an institution more or less randomly is tied to many archetypes, the position will be close to or in the center of the map.

Attributes, (e.g., core values) are positioned indirectly, (i.e., through the brands associated with these attributes). Figure 4.8 shows the IMPSYS© platform, which is characterized by:

◆ being fixed over time
◆ being ethnographically and culturally neutral
◆ enabling comparison of all kinds of different issues, as they are positioned in the same platform

A brand's personality and its position in the map can change over time, with or without the influence of the brand owner. In general, it is much easier to move a brand on the right side of the

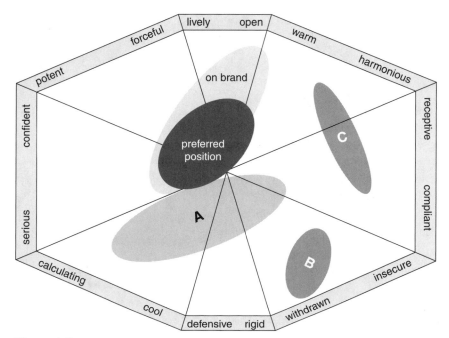

Figure 4.8
Nordea's Preferred Brand Position

map than one on the left side, where the personalities normally are more distinct. This is because the personal or corporate economy is regarded as a necessary task (evil) on the right side which people are not committed to as much as on the left side. On the left-hand side, the interest in economy is higher and plays an important role; it may, therefore, be expected that people are less willing to change.

How We Have Used IMPSYS©—A Common Language

Following an extensive IMPSYS© base study with 1,200 personal interviews in each of the four Nordic countries and a further 800 observations per country among corporate customers, the so-called preferred position of Nordea was determined. This preferred position is the location of our mission and values in the hearts and minds of our (potential) customers. It simply answers graphically the question: If we, as Nordea, make it possible, create value, are innovative, and are empowering, what then is our position on the IMPSYS© chart? The result, in the form of a chart, becomes a central focal point for discussion and directing how to align our efforts for building the brand (see Figure 4.8).

Nordea's preferred position is a true focal point. Sponsorships are tested as to their degree of matching the brand and values of Nordea—clearly showing one type of sponsorship such as tennis is on brand, whereas sponsorships A, B, and C are not.

On this basis it then becomes possible to test whether campaigns sponsoring HR concepts support the building of Nordea's desired profile and provide a lot of insight on how to move the old profiles toward the position that reflects our mission and our values. In addition to the very concrete cases like the example shown with sponsoring above, the findings regarding the preferred position and how various elements are placed in the map have facilitated a healthy dialogue between all communicators and HR professionals in Nordea. Being as simple and visual as it is, this new language easily transformed highly theoretical discussions where each "side" had its own vocabulary to concrete discussions of real substance.

Obviously this research tool is only a tool and cannot drive our business strategy. However, it truly has helped us a lot in bringing otherwise very intangible issues to the surface. It is better to agree to disagree than mistakenly believe that you agree only to find out later you meant different things at too late a stage! IMPSYS© has helped to reduce that risk and, as such, marks an important step in our journey to gradually build a strong financial services brand. Many steps and challenges remain, but with the right level of commitment, these will be tackled.

Checkup 5: Creating and Protecting the Brand and Culture

To create an effective and profitable brand, you need to consider a number of factors.

1. What is the strategic positioning of the company or product?
2. What makes the company or brand distinctive?
    a. Is there something about the company (its location, founders, history) that you can build upon to create a unique culture or identity?
    b. How does the product compare to its competition in terms of quality, image, price, reliability, or other factors in its promise to consumers?
3. How will the brand image (its reputation and its reality as seen through the eyes of customers and employees) and its identity (its graphical and physical representation) be developed and carried out consistently through both internal and external communication?
    a. What research exists about the current perceptions of the company or brand in the eyes of its constituencies?
    b. How can negative perceptions be changed, and positive perceptions be built upon?
    c. What needs to be done to reconcile differing opinions or values?
    d. Who will decide on the brand image and company values and cultures?
    e. What mechanisms will be put into place to ensure a consistent tone and voice?
4. Is the proposed brand and image meaningful to all constituencies?
5. Is it recognizable and distinctive from its competition?
6. Is the brand proprietary, and do you have the mechanisms in place to protect it as a trademark?
7. Is the brand logo, name, and any taglines consistent with the organization's current and future goals and products?

8. Have you checked to see if the brand and all of its dimensions work well in other cultures?
   a. Is it meaningful?
   b. Do the words translate well?
   c. Do the colors have any negative connotations in other cultures?
9. How will you protect and develop the brand and culture?
   a. What research mechanisms do you have to measure brand perceptions, organizational culture and climate, and customer loyalty?
   b. What communication campaigns and infrastructures do you have to keep the brand consistent and refresh its meaning and value?

Self-Check

1. What is a "brand" and how does it relate to long-term corporate profits and value?
2. How can professionals in employee communication and learning maximize the value of a brand?
3. Give three examples of how organizations strengthen their brand by explicit structures that help to coordinate their "voice" and positioning in the marketplace.
4. What is a corporate culture and how can it be engineered?
5. What are organizational citizenship behaviors—and how do these translate to improved customer service and efficient functioning?
6. What research tools are available to help organizations identify their voice and market position, and how can HR professionals use these in hiring and training?
7. What are factors to consider when building an internal and external brand when dealing with different cultures and languages?

Reference

Davis, D. (2000). *Brand asset management: Driving profitable growth through your brands*. San Francisco: Jossey-Bass.

CHAPTER 5 Managing Learning, Performance, and Knowledge Systems

Overview

The ability of organizations to specify goals and then to engineer the desired performance by training, sharing knowledge, and providing feedback is one of the most important factors in success. While these decisions and tactics are part of every executive's and front-line manager's role, the systems that support them are usually engineered by human resources, training, and knowledge management functions. Contemporary organizations have gone beyond providing training classes: a more comprehensive and participatory notion of organizational learning helps us to create systems that are modern and effective.

How Do We Conceptualize and Assess Organizational Learning Systems?

In the previous chapter, we looked at some theories and definitions of communication, and examined how they influence our decisions about "success." Just as we typically use models and metaphors about communication, we also operate on theories of learning.

The typical ways that people conceptualize training center around thinking about knowledge as something that's packaged and given by one person to another. We say (at least in the United States) that we "give" or "take" a course, implying a one-way, top-down model. We hope that our learners "absorb the material" as if they were dry sponges, ready to uncritically soak up whatever is given to them. We say that someone has "received an education" as if it were a letter.

Interestingly enough, Canadians say that they "go on a course." What's the underlying difference in the word "go?" Is a course something you "get" or is it more like a journey? Are you a passive receiver or an active participant and shaper?

A lot of corporate training has been influenced by behaviorist approaches to learning theory; the underlying principle of this theory is that our conduct is shaped by what is reinforced. Learning is defined as a relatively permanent change in behavior. To change behavior, the instructor provides a stimulus and reinforces or rewards the desired response until it gets ingrained (see Figure 5.1).

Figure 5.1
A Behaviorist Model of Training

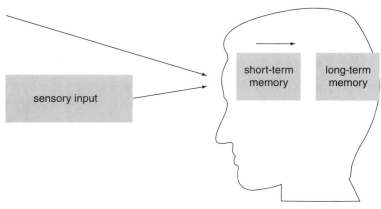

Figure 5.2
Information Processing View of Learning

This view of learning, of course, has its shortcomings. How can we account for our ability to form rules and concepts when they have not been explicitly presented to us? How can we explain why we remember some things only briefly, and forget others? An alternative set of learning theories are categorized as cognitive approaches. These models see the human brain as an information-processing machine. These theories emphasize the process of how we get information from short-term memory to long-term memory (see Figure 5.2). Here, learning is viewed with the idea of the brain as a computer, with inputs, storage areas, and outputs. One of the concepts that represents the cognitive approach is "chunking," or our ability to organize information. For example, a novice sees a chessboard as a complex arrangement of pieces on a board; a master is able to "chunk" that same image into patterns and to quickly memorize it. While it may be difficult to remember a ten-digit phone number, we tend to "chunk" the three numbers of the area code into one unit.

Both behavioral and cognitive approaches to learning theory emerge from the objectivist view that the physical world exists in one correct and complete form, and that the job of learning is to come to an understanding of these external objects and processes. Although objectivists acknowledge that different people "see" the world differently, this is considered to be a shortcoming in their experiences or learning. A newer set of theories, called constructivism, argues that people impose their own structures on the physical world; therefore, there are different

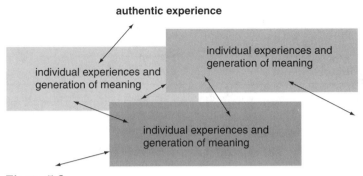

authentic experience

Figure 5.3
A Constructivist View of Learning

meanings and perspectives on any object or event. Constructivists feel that there is not any one "correct" meaning that we should strive to discover and teach (see Figure 5.3).

The constructivist approach has many implications for the way that we design instruction and view the learning process. Rather than uncovering the "facts" and teaching them, the role of instruction within the constructivist framework is to present concepts within authentic experiences. Constructivist approaches seek to help learners develop their own plans and concepts rather than force a shared reality—which will simply never exist anyway.

Organizational training has been heavily influenced by the American public school model. We tend to think about learning in terms of courses, objectives, curriculum, and even certification. There's a growing trend for corporate training departments to expand themselves into "corporate universities," complete with Deans. However, let's look at some different assumptions about what makes a good instructor, a good student, and a good learning experience. Traditional assumptions are based on a rather behaviorist approach to learning (and a rather scientific view of management). Alternative approaches emphasize a constructivist view of learning and a more participatory view of organizational management (see Table 5.1).

So, what does this say about what "good" training looks like, and how does this relate to the new concepts of management and communication that we've reviewed in the previous chapters?

The changes in the business environment and management styles of most organizations mean that less can be predicted. Many kinds of rule-based decision-making processes have been automated, requiring people only for the creative, unusual, and sophisticated kinds of services and problem-solving. For example, one of my clients processes Medicare claims. While every claim previously had to be handled by a clerk, a computer program now scans them first and the ones that are not unusual are automatically processed. The only ones that are presented to people are the ones that are somehow "problematic"—they don't follow any simple rules, and call for creative applications of many different rules, policies, and

Table 5.1

Characteristics of a Good Instructor, a Good Learner, and a Good Learning Experience

What are the characteristics of a good instructor?

Traditional assumption	Alternative paradigm
Explains the content clearly and makes it easy to learn	Offers authentic challenges to learners and what may be simple explanations or common assumptions
Is well-organized, in control, and follows a predetermined lesson plan	Is flexible; knows when to abandon the plan to address some new or urgent issue
Is impartial and gives every member of the class a turn and the same amount of attention	Gives learners authentic feedback on their performance and behaviors, providing a realistic preview of work situations
Presents information in an unbiased manner	Knows and presents alternative viewpoints, but can also articulate and model her/his own views and values
Is a skilled presenter who can follow content developed by others and offer it to learners in an entertaining way	Is a content expert and a willing coach, although learners must be active in eliciting and organizing information themselves

What are the characteristics of a good learner?

Traditional assumption	Alternative paradigm
Cannot contribute much as a novice until more learning is mastered	Is very valuable as a set of fresh eyes
Soaks up knowledge like a sponge	Is active in acquiring, contributing, and questioning information
Complies with instructor and accepts what is taught	Often acts as a polite "devil's advocate" and works with instructor to form the experience
Is oriented toward a body of knowledge or profession	Is a protégé of one or more masters of the field and is oriented to their approaches
Continually develops more in-depth knowledge of a particular area	Becomes a knowledge integrator and becomes more of a generalist

What are the characteristics of a good learning experience?

Traditional assumption	Alternative paradigm
Predictable	Flexible
Homogeneous output in terms of learner approaches	Learners enter with different approaches and learn even more perspectives
Training will sort out the "poor" from the "excellent"	Learning experience is aimed at developing mastery in all learners
People will learn content	People will learn how to learn

even experience and wisdom. Instead of looking in thousands of pages of manuals for guidance, there is now an online reference tool that acts as a job aid and somewhat of an expert system. A lot of what used to be covered in training classes has now been simplified by technology, overcoming the problems of memorization and hard-to-use computer systems. However, there's an increase in the complexity of the situations covered, as well as higher demands for pleasant and efficient customer service behavior.

Since the specific content in many jobs changes so quickly, it is more important to teach people how to problem-solve and where to find information. Both instructors and learners must be more flexible in their approaches to methods and content. Learning is seen as much more of a two-way process, mirroring the more contemporary approaches to employee communication.

Checkup 6: Reflect on Your Last Learning Experience

Let's see if you can put some of these ideas into context and practice analyzing the underlying learning theories that inform many instructional projects. Think back to your last formal learning experience: this would ideally be training conducted by your company, but it might be a course you've taken in a professional degree program, or even a short lesson you took to further one of your hobbies or volunteer activities.

Describe the role of the instructor (lecturer, facilitator, coach, etc.).	Was the instructor effective?	What do you think was his or her underlying learning theory?
Describe the role of the learners (what they expected, hoped, and actually did).	Did the learning design match their needs and expectations?	What do you think was the underlying learning theory of the learners?
How would you describe the design of the instruction in terms of flexibility, content, testing, etc.?	Did the design of the learning and any learning materials (handouts, visuals, tests) fit the instructor and the learners?	What do you think was the underlying learning theory behind the materials and the overall design?
Were there any disconnects among expectations and styles of the instructor, learners, and materials?	Did the styles promote the performance that was desired?	Did the styles promote the overall voice, brand, and culture of the organization sponsoring the learning event?

Recent research has shown that, sadly, less than half of what is typically taught in corporate training actually translates to changes of behavior on the job. There are several possible reasons for this:

◆ Training is offered either too early or too late to make a real impact.
◆ Training may be offered to the wrong people; either they already know the content, or trainees may not be in a situation to apply the new knowledge.
◆ The training methods may be ineffective; too much information is presented at once and there's no time to apply or absorb it.
◆ Supervisors may not actually allow the learners to apply new skills or approaches on the job.
◆ Learners may not be rewarded (or they actually may be inadvertently punished) for changes in their performance, so they will continue to do what is traditional or easy.
◆ The content or methods taught may not be realistic, given the actual job situations, time, and resources available to the learner.

Because of the growing realization of these limitations of traditional approaches to training, there is increasing pressure to change methods, to streamline the budgets and time frames for courses, and to put training into a larger context of employee and organizational needs, development, and accountability.

John Gatto, an award-winning scholar and critic of educational systems, wrote a powerful essay called "The Seven Lesson Schoolteacher" in his book *Dumbing Us Down* (1992). In this essay I read about what kids really learn in the typical structured classroom and thought that it related just as well to corporate training. Regardless of their purported content, here are some of the inadvertent lessons that are uncovered in typical training systems.

◆ *Dependence.* The organization will figure out what you need to learn, and will provide it for you. Learning is our job, not yours. If there's something important for your job, the HR department or your manager will send you to a course that will teach you what you need. They know best, and they'll help you manage your career.
◆ *Distrust.* Your fellow workers can't be relied upon to know the right way to do anything. Believe what the trainer says instead. The trainer (or whoever created the course) is the *real* expert. And while we're at it, forget the concept of teams. The class is taught by one expert, and you're being evaluated as an individual, right?
◆ *Compliance.* The only real way to learn is to attend a course, soak up the knowledge, comply, and get certified. The way to prove your knowledge is to show people the list of courses you've attended; the longer and more expensive the list, the better (learning is measured by days and certificates). Evaluations will go in your file and will be looked at if you're being considered for a promotion, so don't give the trainer a hard time or get creative in answering questions on the test.
◆ *Low self-esteem.* Sharing what you know is not a part of your job; you're not the subject matter expert. Besides, not everyone can teach; it takes showman-

ship and train-the-trainer courses. Don't try this at home (or on the job); leave it to the experts.

◆ *Suspicion.* If you're singled out for training, you'd better think about why. Perhaps you're not performing well and you're being punished. If the training is at some exotic location, your manager is probably just trying to give you a "perk" and doesn't really care how it affects your performance. Or maybe— like one attendee we had in one of our seminars—your manager is trying to get you out of the office because you're a bit of a troublemaker.

◆ *Uniformity.* Creative thinking and diversity are not really valued. Our courses will tell you the one right way to do something. Your job is to ingest what we've already digested for you. We don't really want to hear your opinion or get confused by too many different approaches.

◆ *Cynicism.* Don't take what they say in training too seriously. Your manager, who really has the power, probably has no idea of what you're being taught and won't support it anyway. The organization is just providing this training because it's mandated or it wants to seem progressive. It's likely that the course was just bought at some trade show, and the content will probably contradict what you'll be taught in other courses.

◆ *Dishonesty.* Mistakes are bad, so you'd better never admit to one. Your job is to figure out what the organization wants, even if it's a bad idea or impossible, and to pretend that you're performing as expected. Answer the questions according to our expectations and please evaluate the training highly. Remember, one hand washes the other.

◆ *Risk-aversiveness.* Don't take a course that may stretch you too much because a low grade will be on your record forever.

What New Learning Systems Look Like in Practice

Yesterday's training department was typically a "little red schoolhouse," staffed by good performers who were somehow not fit to be promoted to executive positions in the line organization (this was typically true for women in prior decades), or employees whose supervisors wanted to give them a developmental assignment. For example, when I did consulting work to help a large pharmaceutical company begin work in multimedia training, all of the people on their training staff, including their director, were on temporary "developmental" assignments. It was a way to bring promising young sales representatives into corporate headquarters to look them over, let them share their expertise with new hires, and wait around until a sales territory opened up for them to manage. If they were still in the training department beyond eighteen months, they (and their director) were considered failures.

Typically, training is one of many functions housed within a human resources department. However, in larger organizations, individual training departments might be found in various line functions (to provide training on technical topics related to the business unit) and even within marketing (to serve customers). Figure 5.4 illustrates such a decentralized training function.

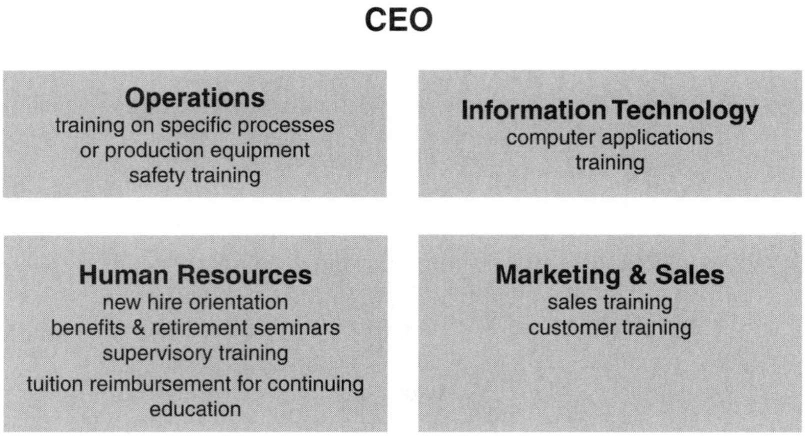

CEO

Operations training on specific processes or production equipment safety training	**Information Technology** computer applications training
Human Resources new hire orientation benefits & retirement seminars supervisory training tuition reimbursement for continuing education	**Marketing & Sales** sales training customer training

Figure 5.4
Decentralized Training Departments

A challenge for many organizations is to coordinate these various training efforts. One of my clients in a large bank endeavored to identify all the people who had training responsibilities and bring them together in a training council. Guthrie Healthcare System, a northern Pennsylvania-based organization that consists of local physician offices, two hospitals, a research center, and a large clinic, also recognized that many individuals had training either as their official function or as a partial responsibility. To identify them, they had a "Star Search," an enjoyable social function to which everybody who did any sort of training within the system was invited. Because it's important for organizations to be able to leverage training systems and to identify who's being trained, this kind of coordination is essential.

Linking Enterprise Training Systems to Value

In order to better manage training, identify existing and lacking skills in an organization, and coordinate learning with performance management, many organizations have established "enterprise systems," which are coordinated databases that are usually managed by human resources. These software systems provide a number of functions, including:

- identifying educational backgrounds, skills, and particular certifications of employees
- tracking skill sets needed for existing and open jobs
- matching employees with job vacancies
- managing performance appraisal forms
- training course management, including functions for employees to enroll themselves in appropriate courses

◆ tracking of attendance and scores in various training programs
◆ providing a platform for e-learning, including authoring tools, methods of tracking and updating content, and enrolling users

Creo, one of Canada's leading employers and the world's leader in graphic arts technology, installed a learning management system as a foundation for their corporate university where all training-related activities and processes would be efficiently managed and integrated. After a limited pilot project they realized a 374 percent return on their investment; mostly due to automating the process of enrolling in courses. There was also a 90 percent savings in time by offering courses online instead of in the classroom. Of course, there were large savings in travel and expenses, which is generally how the biggest impact on ROI is made when training is offered online.

Naturally, just reducing training costs is not a convincing enough argument to make the switch from traditional to online learning—it must be shown that the training is at least as effective (if not more effective). Some organizations do track this. For example, Century 21 realized a 33 percent increase in productivity, as measured by revenues per agent, in their switch to online learning. With the old training, revenues per agent averaged $7,500. With online learning, average revenues jumped to $9,800. Century 21's director of training stated, "The greatest value we plan to realize is not in simply reducing the costs, it's in helping to increase the amount of money that our franchisees are making; which translates into market share, making affiliation with the Century 21 brand even more valuable. It offers us a concrete, tangible way to check the ROI" (click2learn.com website). Their LMS (learning management system) enables Century 21 franchised offices to track, by name, individual performance regarding productivity year over year, and see what effect it has had on their production.

Not all changes in the training landscape are technology related. Even if technology can enhance the administration and delivery of training, there will always be a place for traditional classroom training as well as education that takes place in traditional academic settings. Research shows that training is an attractive benefit to employees and that good opportunities for learning are associated with enhanced recruiting and retention. However, too much of a good thing can also be problematic. In some situations, employees can become overloaded with training, and attending corporate or university courses may add stress and actually contribute to burnout and turnover.

Skandia, one of the largest global insurance companies, is rated one of Europe's best places to work and is a leader in putting intellectual capital on its balance sheet. While they encouraged continual education and training, they noticed an increase in turnover. Research showed this was due to "burnout." The new benefit is a competence savings account, into which employees can put some of their salary, matched by Skandia. Employees can then use it to take time off while the company uses the funds to hire a temp to cover for the employees. Skandia has a website, The Competence Marketplace, where they manage their development plans; this is now offered to other companies (Hawkins, 2002). Some organizations, such as Intel, offer sabbaticals to their employees—time off from work to learn new skills and engage in broadening experiences, such as travel or community service.

From Training to Learning to Performance Infrastructures

From these examples, it's clear that this field has migrated from creating and delivering courses to orchestrating the learning and development that supports performance. In fact, a trend in this field is to broaden the practice into a more holistic approach of interventions, sometimes called performance consulting or human performance improvement. Practitioners in this area include training as one of their many tools in a larger toolkit that consists of:

◆ job aids and manuals
◆ compensation and motivational programs
◆ job and work setting re-design
◆ communication and feedback systems
◆ collaboration and coaching/mentoring programs

The focus of performance consulting is to look at the desired end results or accomplishments, and then to "engineer" performance by providing people with the knowledge, skills, tools, and motivation to perform at a high level. (More about this approach is presented in the next chapter.)

Once we move beyond the bounds of training classes and think more broadly about organizational learning, it's quite apparent that increasing the collective knowledge in an organization also requires careful design of the culture and of the communication system. Peter Senge (1994), known for his popular books on the learning organization, has stated that to become a "learning organization," an enterprise must become proficient in what he calls five "disciplines":

1. Building a shared vision, so that the organization may foster a common commitment to long-term results and achievement.
2. Creating and challenging mental models—techniques for building new concepts and for challenging assumptions to foster creativity and openness for change.
3. Fostering team learning so that the learning is passed on from individuals to teams (i.e., the organization as a whole).
4. Nurturing personal mastery, or individual's skills and motivation to learn.
5. Systems thinking, a way of more holistically looking at the organization, its components, and its external environment so that it's possible to see relationships, impacts, and how changes in one subsystem affect other subsystems.

While these disciplines in themselves consist of concepts and tools that can be learned, it is more important in creating a "learning organization" to create a climate for openness, sharing, critical thinking, clear and accurate feedback, and collaboration. Many organizations have attempted to become "learning organizations," and while this concept is better thought of as a goal than a destination that one "gets to," the past decade of case studies have shown that it's easier to conceptualize than to create this type of climate. The barriers to achieving mastery of these five disciplines are often more related to the infrastructure of policies and tools than to a lack of motivation.

Knowledge Management

Knowledge management is one of many terms related to practices that attempt to build, codify, and share experiences, approaches, facts, and general "know-how." Its various manifestations combine approaches to training, collaboration, information science, computer technologies, and business process development. As organizations began to realize the impact of the "information age" in which human knowledge and behaviors were more important than mere products and facilities, leaders became more interested in mechanisms to build their intellectual capital.

Knowledge management means attending to processes for creating, sustaining, applying, sharing, and renewing knowledge to enhance organizational performance and create value. Companies are doing this by:

- encouraging collaboration and sharing of knowledge through meetings, teamwork, and presentations
- developing mentoring and coaching systems that especially focus on orienting new employees and sharing the experiences of people who are about to retire
- developing computerized databases that capture best practices and lessons learned
- creating formats and templates for reports, proposals, sales presentations, and other frequently created documents
- archiving important documents and processes so that they can be re-purposed by others
- developing strategies for interviewing, de-briefing, and documenting the thinking processes and actual behaviors of exemplary performers

There are several important concepts that are related to knowledge management:

- *Intellectual capital*   is the sum of everything the people in an organization know that can be formalized, captured, and leveraged. This is harder to put a value on unless you can define exactly how this either reduces expenses or increases revenues as compared to your competition.
- *Intellectual property*   is explicit knowledge that can be protected by standard legal constructs including copyright and patents. This is more amenable to valuation, because it can be well-defined and incorporated into pricing agreements or licensing. Examples of intellectual property are patented formulas or processes, as well as copyrights on books, music, or presentations.
- *Human capital*   includes both the knowledge and commitment of your employees; it is perhaps the hardest to define because it is broadest in scope. Human capital is driven both by the intellectual assets of individuals as well as the various cultural and human resource factors that make them loyal and motivated.

One important question raised in this domain is whether knowledge really can be shared and communicated, no less managed. To understand this problem, we need to make a distinction between explicit and tacit knowledge.

- *Explicit knowledge* can be expressed in words and numbers and shared in the form of data, scientific formulae, specifications, manuals, training, and so on. Examples of this include the calculations necessary to figure out a break-even analysis, the process used to turn on a new machine, or the decision process in figuring out whether a particular medical expense is covered by a given insurance policy.
- *Tacit knowledge* is not made explicit because it is highly personal, not easily visible or expressible, and usually requires joint, shared activities in order to transmit it. Examples of this would include how managers decide on the right job candidate among a pool of qualified applicants, how scientists develop an innovative new product, or the skill of an accomplished skier in adapting to new ski runs and snow conditions.

Most experienced practitioners and researchers agree that knowledge is not something that can be explicitly managed. Rather, executives and human resources professionals can create the conditions and tools that promote the exchange of ideas and documents that underlie knowledge. The concept of **knowledge markets** was developed by Laurence Prusak, based on an analogy to traditional commodities exchanged in external markets. Prusak (1997) believes that knowledge can be exchanged, bought, bartered, found, and generated and that what drives the knowledge market is **reciprocity**, the expectation that one will receive valuable knowledge in return for giving it. This means that people willingly share knowledge because they think the knowledge they gain in return will have present or future value.

One of the most widely cited success stories in knowledge management is Buckman Laboratories. They have created both a culture and the infrastructure tools to learn and apply knowledge that the organization considers a key to its success. In fact, Buckman Labs has an entire website devoted to sharing general research on knowledge management.

CASE IN POINT

Organizational knowledge management at Buckman Labs

Sheldon Ellis, Vice-President of the Bulab Learning Center,
Buckman Labs, Memphis, TN

In 1945 Dr. Stanley J. Buckman founded Buckman Laboratories. Initially, the company focused on research and development. From the very beginning it was clear that our ability to create knowledge as well as our capacity to learn, share, and apply knowledge, both internally and externally, was critical to our success. One early sign of our emphasis on knowledge was our Idea Traps, small notepads used to capture ideas as they occurred. The unspoken message was that the ideas of all our associates were needed, so we had a notepad that could fit easily into a pocket or pocketbook to capture them and put them into practice. As we grew globally and our need to create and share increased, we sent experts around the globe to learn and share best practices. However, that approach proved to be too inefficient as we continued to expand across the world.

Our corporate headquarters have always been in Memphis, Tennessee. Initially, our business was limited to the United States. However, we soon expanded to Canada and Mexico, and over the years we have added operating companies in such locations as Australia, Brazil, Mexico, Europe, Singapore, China, and Finland. We also have associates working in over ninety countries around the world. This gives us the standard, but still difficult challenge of how to support and manage a global business.

Our corporate headquarters is the home for such functions as IT, finance, and human resources. However, since our beginning our U.S. company, Buckman Laboratories Inc., has also been located in the same Memphis facility. Unfortunately, the co-location had created a situation over the years that our supposedly corporate human resources department primarily supported our U.S. company and corporate headquarters. Our HR department hired and fired, and did other HR functions within the United States, as if the department only encompassed operations within the United States. Unfortunately, despite our global status there was limited support and involvement with our other companies worldwide, which usually had at least one person locally assigned to the HR function. Given that there was little coordination, there was also no development of coherent, worldwide HR policies and systems. From operating company to operating company, the face of HR changed.

In addition, our "corporate" HR department was not integrated into the overall activities of the company. They remained bounded by the traditional view of HR departments, and were limited in their functions and applicability.

This became more apparent in 1992, when we created our knowledge sharing system, K'netix©. This system gave us a global communications infrastructure that enabled us to have global e-mail, a globally accessible database, and also discussion areas with threaded messages for all our associates. We organized our discussion areas, which we named forums, into topics. Some applied to everyone, such as IT and human resource announcements. Others focused on less-defined areas of interest, such as general corporate news and informal chat. While informal chat may seem like a waste of business resources and time, those informal areas have proven critical in fostering a shared sense of belonging to our company and thus increasing overall participation.

Some forums directly addressed our key customer industries like pulp and paper, leather, and industrial water treatment. Such forums were open to anyone in the company, although normally associates were involved in those forums applicable to their jobs. We also created private forums so that we could protect such sensitive information as not-yet-patented formulas, proprietary research, financial information, and senior leadership team discussions. However, regardless of the privacy or subject areas in all forums, our associates shared information, asked questions, and posed solutions.

By sharing our knowledge we provided faster and smarter service to our customers, and it paid off. We do not have a conventional measurement system for our knowledge management efforts, as we believe that the value is self-evident. We are much smaller than our competitors, who have vastly more resources of all kinds than we do. When we formed our K'netix system in 1992, our competitors were eating our lunch. Through our knowledge sharing system we not only have survived, but during 2002 we were the only company in our industry to have double-digit growth.

However, there are some measures that we do consider to be indicative of the value of knowledge sharing. One key measure is our percentage of sales from new products, which we view as a measure of innovation. Over the years of our K'netix system our percentage of sales from new products has risen by about 51 percent. Sales alone per associate jumped 51 percent, while our operating profit per associate has soared by 93 percent. These figures also are undoubtedly influenced by other factors such as the power of our information technology infrastructure; it also would be impossible for us to factor out the influence of knowledge sharing even with the help of multivariate statistics. Nevertheless, we feel these results offer compelling evidence for the value of our knowledge-sharing activities.

Yet despite our continuing success we recognize that we have learned some lessons along the way. Being a pioneer means that there are no maps and no road signs to follow. A critical lesson learned for us was the need to not only involve human resources, but also to have them as a strategic partner.

When we started K'netix in 1992 we had a traditional hierarchical organization. Information flowed up and flowed down, going through the chain of management. Additionally, despite our global nature we thought of ourselves as belonging to our individual functions, not Buckman as a whole and certainly not as part of a global company. Sharing knowledge in the way we wanted to required a significant change of our organizational culture, which was always a showstopper in organizational change.

One way we communicated our desired new state was to tell associates that they no longer needed to go through management to ask questions. In fact, we wanted them to directly ask anyone in the company any question, regardless of their position and location. We believed that by going directly to the source we would receive the best possible information. While many responded positively to this direction, our middle managers were confused about what their new role should be. They resisted change, with some going so far as to forbid their subordinates to participate in our knowledge-sharing system.

Up until that point we had not involved our HR department. We soon realized we had made a mistake, since their particular skills were what we needed, and we enlisted their help. They taught us how to coach and counsel our associates. With their help we learned to clearly communicate the expectations for their new roles. We also made it clear that change was mandatory, not optional. Those who refused to change after counseling were assisted in finding new roles or in leaving the company. Historically, our turnover has been outstandingly low for our industry, but at that time our turnover rate was the highest it has ever been, since some chose to get off the train rather than change. This is consistent with the experience of other organizations we know that are undergoing significant change. However, while we still regret the loss of knowledge and experience those people took with them, we felt it was more important to keep those with the new attitude that we needed. As Jack Welch points out, it isn't enough to perform well. You also need to have the right attitude and show the right values.

Since our founding, another major change occurred from a strategic focus on research and development to sales. As described in *The Discipline of Market Leaders: Choose Your Customers, Narrow Your Focus, Dominate Your Market* by Michael Treacy and Fred Wiersema, we decided that our corporate strategy would be customer intimacy. On a practical level this required us to shift our workforce from predominantly research and development to sales. For many years approximately half of our associates have been in sales, with 40 percent acting as sales representatives and 10 percent serving in direct sales support. We viewed fierce independence, the ability to work alone, and an entrepreneurial spirit as the prime characteristics we desired in our salespeople.

This mirrored their historical working environment as solitary sales representatives traveling to various customer sites, often without seeing another Buckman associate for months. Their primary contact with the company was via their computer and telephone.

However, the nature of our customers, and thus our sales environment, began to change. Increasingly, our customers became global. Rather than selling to one isolated mill in the backwoods of Maine, our sales representatives found themselves working with customers who were aware of our performance at other locations across the globe and expected the same level of performance at their mill. Additionally, customers began to focus on sole-source contracts across multiple locations. To make such sales, sales representatives needed to work as part of a team that often spanned national and linguistic boundaries. All of a sudden our sales representatives found themselves succeeding or failing as part of a team.

However, we had not hired people with the characteristics needed to work successfully in the new team-based environment. We had hired lone wolves. Accordingly, we worked with the guidance of our human resources department to redefine our requirements for our sales associates. We blended our historical entrepreneurial requirements with the new need to collaborate as we moved to team-based work. We also instituted a new award recognizing a team that made a significant contribution during each year. Finally, we developed work profiles that addressed the new competencies and actions that were needed. This change is still ongoing, as we also retained those hired under the old requirements. We do understand that this organizational change will take a number of years, although we already are feeling some effects.

These actions did not go far enough, though. We still needed a process for teaming itself. Working in conjunction with a cross-functional team, our HR department participated in the development of a teaming process. A critical enabler for teaming is the role of a facilitator. Facilitators concentrate on the group process of a team, rather than the content. However, when we started our teaming process we had only a handful of experienced facilitators within the company, and did not have any training for facilitators. Before we could train them, however, we had to find out who would be suitable for the role.

Human resources played a particularly critical role in the identification of potential team facilitators. We examined the current role of potential facilitators within the organization, although we didn't limit ourselves to the roles described in their work profile. We also looked at additional, sometimes unofficial roles associates played. For example, in one department an associate had developed training around teamwork and creativity for the department. Although not officially dubbed a facilitator, this individual clearly had both the skills and attitude necessary for facilitation. Human resources also coached us to look at an individual's growth potential, or what they could become with some coaching and assistance.

Another important step for our teaming process was the creation of a realignment of associate work profiles to recognize the importance of teamwork, and how each associate functions within a team environment.

As the requirements for our associates shifted, so did our managerial requirements. A new brief for our HR department became the creation of a management curriculum, the provision of coaching for managers, and the requirements to provide resources and support. The curriculum we created is mandatory. The development also continues, as we continue to work on assessing our needs and identifying new areas for development.

Over these years of change for our HR department, one subtle outcome has been the consistent coordination with other support functions to support organizational change efforts and communicate a shared message. No longer is HR carefully kept within traditional bounds; it is a vital part of our organization.

Looking to the future, we cannot predict exactly what paths HR at Buckman Laboratories will follow. We can, however, guarantee they will be standing shoulder-to-shoulder with everyone else to accomplish the goals of the global organization.

A Learning and Collaboration Infrastructure

Buckman Laboratories' HR department took a critical role in creating the climate and the tools to promote knowledge exchange. However, you may wonder how you might be given the same opportunity. In some cases, requests for training can be converted into the opportunity to build a knowledge infrastructure. Here's an example.

One of my clients approached me with a request to create web-based training on financial analysis. Their sales managers were going to be required to apply these skills in working with dealers, and a previous attempt at classroom training proved unsuccessful. It was expensive to bring the managers in from the field, and in an attempt to save time and money, too much material was crammed into a short course. Evaluation showed that most managers were unable to apply the complex material and formulas.

After some discussion, it seemed that conventional web-based training was not the right approach because:

◆ It would take too long to develop, and these managers needed to apply the skills immediately.
◆ The particular applications of financial analysis were undergoing constant revision.
◆ Many of the formulas really didn't need to be memorized; rather, applying job aids was a better approach than training.

What we developed was a prototype online collaboration and learning system called FAST for Financial Analysis System Tools (see Figure 5.5.) The website provided basic information on financial analysis, but in addition to this it included

◆ online job aids and downloadable spreadsheets (Figure 5.6).
◆ an online discussion board for managers to share questions and solutions
◆ an "expert" section through which users could contact a subject matter expert either via phone or e-mail
◆ examples of tools that were used by dealers in creating their business plans

Another similar situation arose when a client in the utility industry wanted to create some e-learning around new business processes. Instead of conventional training, I created the prototype interface, shown in Figure 5.7, that would let users:

◆ access short instructions for important business processes
◆ request that some new instruction or procedure be created if they could not find what they needed

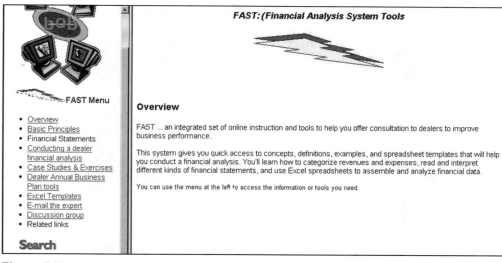

Figure 5.5
Main Menu from FAST, a Prototype Online Learning and Collaboration System

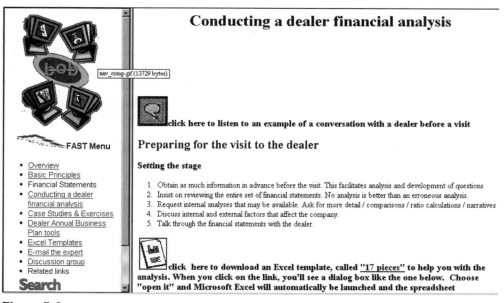

Figure 5.6
A Sample Page from the FAST System Providing Job Aids and Examples

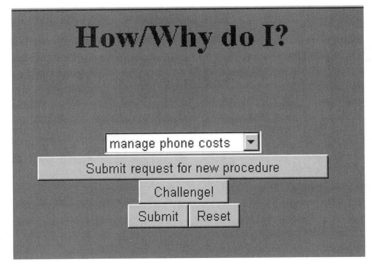

Figure 5.7
Online Tools Can Teach—and Challenge—Conventional Wisdom

♦ challenge the current procedures by asking questions or providing suggestions for a better procedure

However, online tools are certainly not the only method for capturing knowledge. Intel has made great strides in learning how to identify best practices and quickly spread them throughout their fabrication facilities. The following case in point explains their ABS system and its outstanding financial results.

CASE IN POINT

Intel captures expert knowledge
Frank J. Sanchez,
Intel Corporation, Rio Rancho, NM

Why is it that some people can perform a task with greater precision and accuracy than others? What knowledge do they possess that qualifies them as experts? How do they consistently out-perform peers who follow the same set of procedures? In the past experts were interviewed to get the answers to these questions, but this was not always effective because often experts "don't know what they know." A method was needed to capture the subconscious knowledge of the expert as well as skill proficiency. Accelerated Breakthrough Systems (ABS) is a methodology developed to do just that. The goal is to capture expert knowledge and document best-known methods (BKMs) through video-based observation, raising an entire work group's performance to the expert level.

Fab 9 (a wafer manufacturing site in Rio Rancho, New Mexico) was losing their "exemplary performers," those who exhibit skills unmatched by the rest of the organization. When these experts would leave their functional area, they would take the undocumented knowledge that allowed them to perform at higher levels than their peers. The problem Fab 9 faced was capturing the hidden knowledge and key learnings, as well as training other technicians to the same skill level before exemplary performers transitioned to other areas.

The ABS process was created by the training department and a consultant to remedy this problem. Here's how it works: During the project assessment phase, an informal group of one or two customers and an ABS specialist meet to decide whether ABS can help solve the customer's problem. This group discusses what exactly is occurring in the customer's work group, identifying a critical task that the customer's work group is not performing as well as expected. Once the critical task is defined, the project team is formed. Project team members include the project owner, the technical observer, the training observer, the exemplary performer(s), and the conventional performer(s).

During the ABS preparation phase, the team members meet to define the project parameters and create a timeline of the project. The team then reviews the critical task and reviews data measuring the current performance level of the customer's work group on the critical task. This data serves as a baseline against which improvements will be measured. Using the ABS project tracking sheet, all information for this phase is recorded. A typical Phase II entry is shown below.

Current documentation	Maintenance checklists
Performance indicator(s)	Performance indicator(s) Mean time between cleans less than 1,500 wafers
Performance goal and evaluation plan	Improve mean time between cleans to greater than 1,800 over a six-week evaluation period

In Phase III the ABS specialist separately videotapes the exemplary and conventional performers carrying out the critical task while the training and technical observers take notes. Following the videotaping, the entire team reviews the tapes and identifies technical or procedural differences between the exemplary and conventional performers. The differences are known as the key learnings. Our goal is to close the gap by sharing key learnings to create new BKMs with the work group.

Phase III, the most critical phase in the ABS process, is when subconscious knowledge is brought to the surface. While the performers are being videotaped, the key is to have no interruptions. The performers must perform the critical task as normal. They must not be interrupted with questions or suggestions. It is in this manner that the expert knowledge is captured. All questions and suggestions must be held until the review session with each performer and should be written on the ABS observation worksheet. An example of an observation worksheet is shown below.

Checklist/procedure	Recommended changes/comments	New text (BKM) comprised of key learnings
Attach plate to main body		Attach plate to main body
Insert O-rings into endplates	Lubricate O-rings	Insert lubricated O-rings into endplates
Attach shaft to bellows		Attach shaft to bellows
Lubricate shaft		Lubricate shaft
Screw shaft into bellows	Double-glove to prevent contaminants	Remove outside gloves and screw shaft to bellows

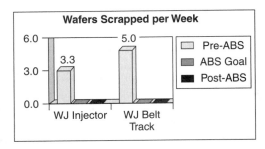

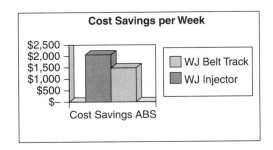

Figure 5.8
Results of ABS Intervention

Once the gap is identified and a new BKM is established, the project team meets to decide what type of training intervention will be used to close the gap on the critical task. Interventions can include spec changes, the creation or editing of training materials, job aids, training videos, and reference material, such as picture books.

The intervention selection stage is critical in that the intervention must match the need for both the target audience and the fluency of the task. If the task occurs only semi-annually, something more along the lines of a training video may be necessary. If the task is more frequent, perhaps a simple job aid may be all that's required.

One example of a project is an ABS performed on a tool called an Injector (see Figure 5.8). The Injector alignment had been the source of eighty-eight scrapped wafers, so an entirely new spec procedure was developed and implemented for training. Over the evaluation period, no wafers were scrapped due to the WJ Injector alignment. The graphs in Figure 5.8 indicate the number of wafers that were being scrapped before and after the ABS.

The combined savings of over $3,000 per week has resulted in over $109,000 during the evaluation period in 1999.

The ABS process is a proven methodology for capturing expert knowledge. The process is led by a certified ABS specialist and takes only minimal time and resources from customer groups. The key to identifying undocumented BKMs is through tapping into an expert performing a task to get to subconscious knowledge. ABS does this through videotape and analysis. Once the key learnings are captured, the best intervention for the target audience is developed and trained. Impact data results in justified training for the customer.

Feedback Systems

We usually associate the word "feedback" with something that a supervisor DOES to an employee that may cause anxiety, discomfort, and even resentment. But it doesn't have to be that way: feedback systems are much more varied and they also should have a positive impact on both performance and morale. These may be some of the most powerful and inexpensive infrastructure tools that organizations can adopt.

Several principles underlie good feedback systems:

1. Feedback SHOULD BE two-way.
2. It should be about the SYSTEM—not just the person.
3. It should increase—not decrease—the performer's sense of control and effectiveness.

There are several categories of feedback systems—here are some applications:

◆ personal
  ◆ to improve or maintain quality and/or quantity of individual performance
  ◆ to assess learning and its application to performance
◆ group
  ◆ to improve or maintain individual and team performance
  ◆ to provide a general understanding of one's role in the larger picture to guide performance and enhance commitment
  ◆ to maintain good communication that promotes a focus on performance and decreases rumors and anxiety
◆ system
  ◆ to track the causes of performance problems by isolating and tracking equipment and human functions
  ◆ to assess the performance of the human/machine system

As an example, the Ontario Lottery and Gaming Corporation uses scorecards to help supervisors and dealers track and improve their performance and also provides a means for supervisors to reward outstanding behaviors (see Figures 5.9 and 5.10).

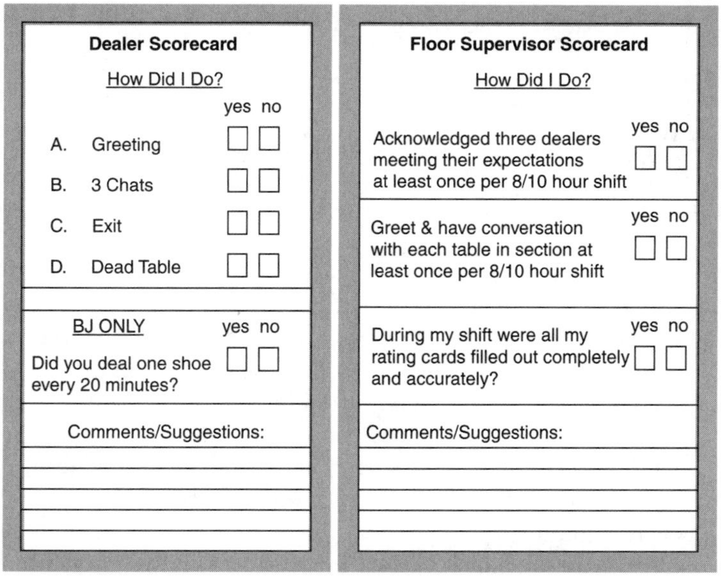

Dealer Scorecard

How Did I Do?

		yes	no
A.	Greeting	☐	☐
B.	3 Chats	☐	☐
C.	Exit	☐	☐
D.	Dead Table	☐	☐

BJ ONLY   yes no

Did you deal one shoe every 20 minutes?   ☐ ☐

Comments/Suggestions:

Floor Supervisor Scorecard

How Did I Do?

Acknowledged three dealers meeting their expectations at least once per 8/10 hour shift   yes no ☐ ☐

Greet & have conversation with each table in section at least once per 8/10 hour shift   yes no ☐ ☐

During my shift were all my rating cards filled out completely and accurately?   yes no ☐ ☐

Comments/Suggestions:

Figure 5.9
Feedback Scorecards from the Ontario Lottery and Gaming Corporation
Used with permission.

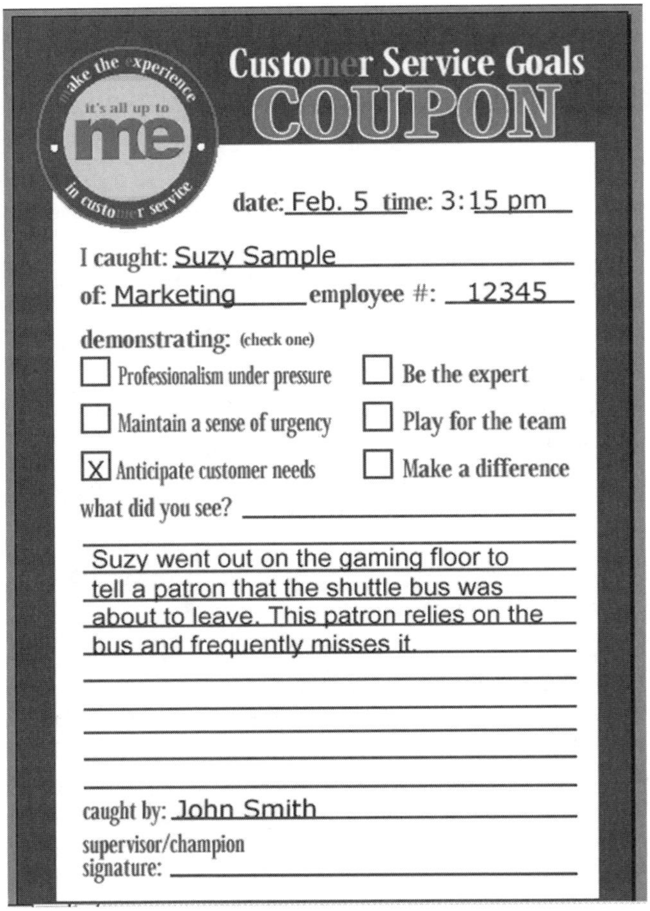

Customer Service Goals
COUPON

date: Feb. 5 time: 3:15 pm

I caught: Suzy Sample

of: Marketing employee #: 12345

demonstrating: (check one)

- [ ] Professionalism under pressure
- [ ] Be the expert
- [ ] Maintain a sense of urgency
- [ ] Play for the team
- [x] Anticipate customer needs
- [ ] Make a difference

what did you see?

Suzy went out on the gaming floor to tell a patron that the shuttle bus was about to leave. This patron relies on the bus and frequently misses it.

caught by: John Smith

supervisor/champion signature:

Figure 5.10
OLGC Encourages Positive Feedback When Employees Exhibit Desirable Behaviors
Used with permission.

Often it's effective to remove feedback from the personal level and provide accurate data about the efficiency of a system. In order to solve some complex production challenges, I helped one of my clients to develop feedback systems that tracked the status and productivity of a given machine in their factory. This helped in the analysis (to determine if it was an operator problem) to determine if it was a scheduling problem, or a problem with the machine itself. These graphs were frequently posted on a bulletin board in the work area and resulted in both effective interventions and an increased sense of control on the part of the factory technicians (see Figure 5.11).

Finally, closed-circuit television and computer monitors can be used to provide real-time feedback on performance status. Figure 5.12 shows a sample of the kinds of screens that can be displayed by a system from TargetVision, a company that provides an employee communication infrastructure.

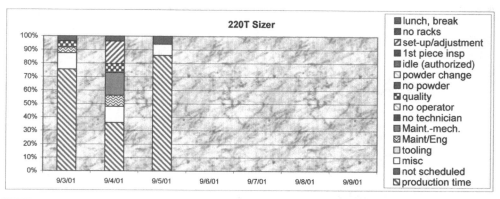

code		3-Sep	4-Sep	5-Sep	6-Sep	7-Sep	8-Sep	9-Sep	totals
	production time	18.1	8.6	20.6					47.3
	not scheduled								0
01, 21, 23	misc	2.9	2.9	2					7.8
02	tooling								0
03, 08, 09	Maint/Eng	1	2						3
04	Maint.-mech.		4						4
05	no technician								0
06	no operator								0
07	quality	1.1	1.6						2.7
10	no powder								0
11	powder change								0
12, 22	idle (authorized)								0
13	1st piece insp								0
14, 15, 16, 17, 20	set-up/adjustment		4						4
18	no racks								0
19	lunch, break	0.9	0.9	1.4					3.2
		24	24	24	0	0	0	0	72
	Machine Utilization	75.4%	35.8%	85.8%	0.0%	0.0%	0.0%	0.0%	

Cumulative Utilization: 65.7%

Figure 5.11
An Example of an Equipment Status Feedback System

Figure 5.12
A Closed-Circuit Corporate TV News System
(Courtesy TargetVision)

Probably the most effective performance management systems are those controlled by the people who perform the work rather than by supervisors. The next case in point from Timm Esque points out how and why these systems work.

Feedback and the performer information system

Timm J. Esque,
Esque Consulting, LLC., Tempe, AZ

With annual U.S. spending on information technology exceeding $400 billion per year, there is certainly no shortage of data in organizations. The primary designated users of all this data are managers and their analysts; however, some of it does eventually make its way back to the people doing the work. When performers get this data in a timely fashion and use this data to make work-related decisions, it is truly performance feedback.

Organizations could benefit from spending a little more of that outrageous sum on figuring out what data will best support each individual in contributing to the organization's goals.

Even when more organizations figure out how to effectively collect and channel performance data to their individual performers, another important source of feedback will likely be missing—self-monitored feedback.

Self-monitored feedback occurs whenever an individual takes responsibility for knowing how he or she is performing against specified goals at all times. Self-monitored feedback can rely on information technology but often does not. When individual performance goals are set properly, it is usually quite simple for the performer to track his own performance in a way that he can evaluate himself against the goals at any time. Properly stated goals focus on the quantity and quality of the output of work (versus the behavior or activities involved) and are referenced to short intervals of time. For example, in a factory, one individual's goal might be to assemble twenty components that meet two or three specific quality requirements (that the individual measures before they consider assembly complete) per hour.

Self-Monitored Feedback in a Call Center

The following real business case demonstrates how self-monitored feedback can be important even when much of the performance is being monitored through technology.

A work environment that increasingly impacts us as employees and as customers is the call center. Incidentally, the call center is a great information technology success story. Prior to call centers, it was relatively difficult and inefficient to connect customers with the information they demanded about products and services. Information technology has made it possible to get most of the information customers need out of the heads of a few experts and put it at the fingertips of good communicators who may or may not be experts in what they are communicating about. When managed well, call centers ensure that customers get reasonably consistent and accurate answers to their questions while freeing up the experts to produce more and better future products.

In this case, a large high-tech manufacturer used a call center to respond to all customer inquiries regarding their product lines. Potential buyers were channeled to one set of performers, people needing help with installation and maintenance to another set, and so forth.

Telecommunications technology has also played an important role in this call center. Not only did it allow for the fair and organized queuing up of customers, but it also recorded and "fed back" all transactions so that call center employees and managers could see how they were performing and learn from unsuccessful transactions (e.g., really ticking off a customer).

In addition to effectively addressing the caller's needs, the object of any call center is to fully utilize the employees' time while responding to customers in an acceptable amount of time. Two typical measures of success for a call center are wait time and abandon rate. In this case, wait time was measured as the average number of minutes that 80 percent of callers had to wait before their call was answered. Abandon rate was the percent of total callers that hung up before they were served.

These technology-generated data were being collected for the group and used as group feedback to improve performance to group goals. The wait time and abandon rate were talked about and posted in the work area at the end of each week. On a monthly basis, supervisors used recordings of actual transactions to coach employees on handling calls in an effective and courteous manner. For the purposes of this case, six months of wait time and abandon rate data have been summarized in Figures 5.13 and 5.14.

What immediately jumps out from the graphs is that performance improved significantly starting in July. This improvement was not due to a drop in the number of callers; call volume was actually 24 percent higher during the second three months and call center capacity (number

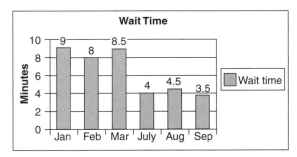

Figure 5.13
Wait Time Chart for a Call Center

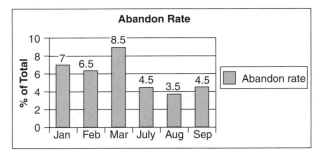

Figure 5.14
Call Abandon Rate Chart for a Call Center

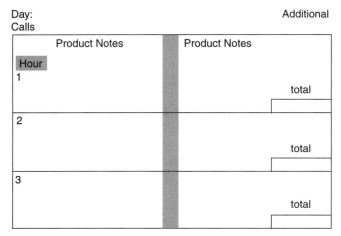

Figure 5.15
A Tool for Self-Monitoring of Performance

of person hours manning the phones) was increased only 14 percent. What changed in July was that, in addition to the automated performance feedback, all call center employees also started generating self-monitored feedback.

After attending a course on goal setting and feedback, the call center manager worked with a team of supervisors and employees to create a very simple self-tracking sheet (see Figure 5.15). The subteam agreed that it was reasonable for each employee to take six calls per hour on average and still be able to effectively and courteously handle each call. On simple uniform call tracking sheets, the employees began tracking their own calls per hour. To reinforce self-monitoring early on, the supervisors periodically checked in on each performer. If the self-tracking sheet showed the employee was "on track," the supervisor stamped the sheet to let the employee know she knew he was on track, without disturbing his current phone call.

The self-monitored data was anonymously aggregated for the team and posted on a daily basis so each individual could see how the call center was performing, and compare his own personal performance without the threat of being singled out. The quality of call handling continued to be reviewed and coached in monthly one-on-one sessions to ensure that there was no temptation to trade-off quality of calls for quantity of calls.

Legitimizing the Management Information System

Why did the addition of such a simple self-monitoring feedback system make such a big difference in performance? There are two primary reasons. First, the self-monitored tracking sheet greatly clarified the goal. The previous department goal, "Our department wants to minimize customer wait time and abandon rate," was translated into "I need to take six quality calls an hour." Second, although the performers were already getting feedback, there was too long a delay between the performance being tracked and the feedback on that performance. It was difficult to look at a week of abandon rate data and determine how to adjust individual performance. In contrast, with the self-monitored feedback, if someone had a slow morning he knew how much he would need to adjust in the afternoon to meet his goal. If he knew he couldn't adjust enough, he could let his supervisor know ahead of time that the goal was in jeopardy.

However, you may be thinking, what is so magical about the performer generating his own performance feedback? Couldn't we use the same sophisticated technology to automate individual performance data and make it available hourly instead of weekly? It is possible that you could, but it is not recommended that you do, at least until after self-monitored feedback has worked for a while. There is some reason to believe that self-monitored feedback increases worker motivation. Many performers who have had the opportunity to operate with self-monitored feedback would tell you that once they got over their initial resistance to change, the basic act of giving themselves credit for each accomplishment is very satisfying. For example, think about how you feel when you are checking completed items off your "to do" list. However, there is a more important reason that self-monitored feedback is so powerful.

A common name systems organizations create to collect, store, analyze, and report data is the management information system. Management information systems have evolved to tell management what is going on in their organizations. They are a primary source of the information managers use to make decisions about goal-setting, managing markets, developing products, and configuring resources to meet all these goals. They are also a primary source of the information managers use to decide who are the best and worst performers, who was present when a product was damaged, or who was there when a critical goal was missed.

Because management information systems are designed to tell management what is going on, and because non-managers inevitably feel that many management decisions are unfair (and/or biased), non-managers often do not trust the data in management information systems. Exacerbating this problem is that performers (non-managers) are the ones who input much of the data that goes into management information systems. If people believe that the data in a management information system may be used unfairly, and they have the opportunity, they will make the data look as favorable as possible. As counterintuitive as it may sound, self-monitored performance data is usually more accurate than the data in management information systems.

As technology becomes more and more sophisticated, this data integrity problem can be solved by leaving people out of the data collection process. However, the problem of performers not trusting the data in management information systems remains. Therefore, an important benefit of self-monitored feedback is that performers are more likely to use the data because it is their own data, and it is being generated solely to help them perform better and increase their personal (as well as the organization's) chances of success.

Going back to the case, the call center employees were originally not all that happy about a management information system listening in on every phone call. However, the self-monitored feedback system was clearly designed simply to help each individual be successful against the goals. Individual data was only used by the performer, and the aggregate data was fed back to the group and used *by them* to determine how they could perform even better. The self-monitored feedback was not a management information system, but rather a performer information system. Not only did the performers in this case benefit directly from self-monitored feedback, but they also began using the automated data more effectively when they realized it could also be a tool to help them succeed.

Given the current bias that performers have against management information systems, self-monitoring feedback systems are the first step toward engaging each and every performer in the effort to meet and exceed the organization's goals. Once performers experience the power of immediate and reliable feedback, they are much more likely to use other sources of feedback to their own and the organization's advantage. The key to getting a full return on our huge investment in information technology just might be getting every performer into self-monitored feedback systems as soon as possible.

Checkup 7: Re-wiring Your Training and Knowledge System

What is traditionally done and valued	What effective organizations need and value today	Notes to myself on this topic
Teach people how to do things	Give people advice on how to learn, find, sift through, and evaluate information on their own	
Thoroughly research and carefully develop courses	Supply fast, current information bites with little or no development time needed	
Provide polished speakers and stunning presentation support materials	Offer credible subject matter experts and on-the-job coaches	
Find and disseminate the "one best way" to do something	Provide divergent ways of thinking about problems	
Create materials and courses, and the appetite for more training	Reduce information overload and the need for externally provided training rather than individually motivated learning	
Do such a good job that people look to us as the source of knowledge and expertise	Provide a boost to individuals' confidence in themselves, their managers, and their colleagues	
Provide "edutainment"	Improve performance	

Self-Check

1. How do different learning theories inform the way that we design and participate in instruction, and judge what a "good" training system is like?
2. What are some of the hidden and dangerous "lessons" that the style and policies of training often inadvertently teach?
3. Where is training and performance placed in most organizations, and what are the trends in this field in terms of job responsibilities?
4. How have the concepts of the "learning organization" and knowledge management expanded and changed the roles of those who manage learning in organizations?
5. Define intellectual capital, intellectual property, and human capital and explain how we can build these assets.
6. What are explicit and tacit knowledge and how do we capture and nurture both of these?
7. What are some technology tools that can enhance the ability and ease of employees to learn and share knowledge, and moreover, to improve on current knowledge and processes?
8. What are some types and principles of feedback systems, and why is self-generated feedback even more powerful than management information systems?
9. What are some ways that we can technically and conceptually "re-wire" our learning systems to improve performance?

References

Esque, T. J. (1999). *No surprises project management*. Mill Valley, CA: ACT Publishing.

Gatto, J. (1992). The seven-lesson schoolteacher. *Dumbing Us Down*. Philadelphia: New Society Publishers.

Hawkins, S. (2002, December). The competence marketplace. *T+D, 56(12)*, 60–62.

Prusak, L. (1997). *Knowledge in organizations*. Boston: Butterworth-Heinemann.

Senge, P. (1994). *The fifth discipline*. New York: Doubleday.

CHAPTER 6 *Performance Analytics*

Overview

We need a new framework to manage communication and learning. Performance analytics is a set of processes that allow us to identify and assess performance gaps and find ways to close them using a variety of integrated approaches. The tools in this chapter will help you assess the effectiveness of your overall infrastructures and identify and solve specific performance gaps.

There is no shortage of communication and learning tools or vendors and articles that promote them. But as previous chapters have pointed out, unless they are aligned with an organization's brand and culture and unless they are specifically aimed at influencing critical behaviors, they are useless or even damaging.

I have frequently been called in to work with organizations whose executives are frustrated by what they perceive as an atmosphere of confusion and cynicism. Often, leaders, front-line employees, and supervisors engage in mutual finger-pointing when trying to uncover the cause. However, I've found that many—if not most—common patterns of ineffective and undesirable behaviors stem from inadequacies and disconnects in the learning and communication *system*, rather than individuals' skills, behaviors, intentions, or even their messages.

The performance infrastructure consists of the "rules and tools"—policies, procedures, norms, styles, and communication media—that support the ability of individuals to gain and share information. The infrastructure may make it difficult to provide the right information to the right people at the right time. Internal and external messages may be lacking in consistency and alignment. More importantly, the underlying themes embedded in the way that information is written and provided may be destructive to loyalty and performance.

We can attempt to engineer performance at several levels: the organizational infrastructure level, the group performance level, and the individual level (see Figure 6.1).

At the organization level, we need to assess and develop the performance infrastructure that includes:

- the tools that can be used for communication and learning, such as common databases, online courseware systems, user groups, internal meetings, Intranet applications, and so forth

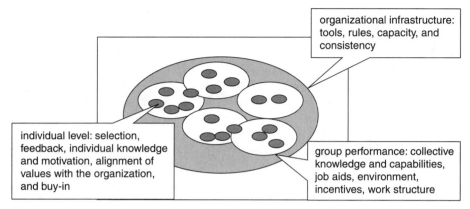

organizational infrastructure: tools, rules, capacity, and consistency

individual level: selection, feedback, individual knowledge and motivation, alignment of values with the organization, and buy-in

group performance: collective knowledge and capabilities, job aids, environment, incentives, work structure

Figure 6.1
The Levels of Performance Analysis and Intervention

- the rules that govern communication and learning, such as crisis communication plans, policies for who gets what kinds of training, norms for sharing organizational data at various levels, and so forth
- the capacity for the organization to grow, survive rough times, and change; this includes the level and type of staffing, the reputation and loyalty among employees and customers, and the willingness to try new approaches and ideas
- the consistency of messages and behaviors throughout internal and external communication

At the group performance level, we examine and try to influence the factors that impact teams, departments, or groups of people with similar responsibilities. These factors include:

- collective knowledge and capabilities, influenced by training, organizational design, and knowledge management practices
- job aids, which include memory aids, instructions, expert systems, and help systems
- the job environment, which includes the design of, and tools present in, the workplace
- incentives, which include compensation, bonuses, recognition and rewards, and group feedback and norms
- work structure, which includes the way that tasks are broken up and assigned to individuals, the way that collaboration and supervision are designed, and the amount and variety of work assigned to groups

At the individual performance level, there are also factors that should be considered, including:

- how individuals are selected for their jobs
- the feedback available to them on their performance and its role in the large organizational context

- the knowledge and motivation of the person as it impacts the work assigned
- how the individual's values are aligned with that of the organization and whether the individual performer "buys into" the organization's culture and mission

We'll begin with the "helicopter shot"—the application of various assessments to look at the overall organizational infrastructure that supports communication and learning.

Communication and Learning Infrastructure Audit

How can you tell whether an organization has a healthy communication and learning infrastructure? I look at a number of issues when I'm assessing an organization, as I find that I have to do a bit of probing. First, I talk with executives, first-line supervisors, front-line employees, customers, and training and communication professionals to see how well they feel the current tools and policies are supporting their goals. My team frequently observes employees at work or customers trying to buy or use the product. In a *Harvard Business Review* article about managing change, Richard Pascale, Mark Milliemann, and Linda Gioja (1997) identified four "vital signs" that they looked for in assessing organizational vigor:

- *Power.* (Do employees believe they really can have an impact on the organization and make things happen?)
- *Identity.* (Do employees identify more strongly with their professions or departments rather than the organization as a whole?)
- *Conflict.* (Do employees confront conflict constructively or avoid it and smooth over problems?)
- *Learning.* (Is the organization receptive to new ideas and experiments, or does it study everything to death before implementing it?)

These authors use the situation of Sears in the early 1990s to illustrate their points about organizational vitality. Few Sears employees had any sense of power, and most felt nothing but resignation. One regional manager remarked, "It was a company of salute and obey. Directives came from above, and we did our best to follow them." Feeling little support and enormous pressure to meet financial goals set for them by headquarters, management teams tended to concentrate on their own turf and form bonds with their own stores rather than the Sears umbrella. The company lost its capacity for constructive conflict; those who challenged ideas were accused of not being "team players." The company had lost its capacity to learn. When confronted with negative reports in the press, management called it "bad journalism" or said it was the victim of unfair treatment. "Sears is different" or "We tried that once and it didn't work" were frequent responses to new ideas (Pascale, Milliemann and Gioja 1997, pp. 130–131).

We see organizational behavior like this every day. Certainly, the reasons for this situation are complex. However, communication and learning systems can be a major factor in improving—or impeding—organizational vigor.

I've developed a communication and learning alignment instrument to help organizations see where their major stated goals and initiatives are consistent with their actual policies and practices. The first step in focusing positive energies on performance is in ensuring the highest degree of consistency among what the organization "says" and what the organization "does.".

Checkup 8: Communication and Learning Alignment

Check each initiative or approach that your organization currently is pursuing.

☐ Total quality management / Continuous improvement / ISO certification
☐ Employee empowerment
☐ Teamwork/self-managed teams
☐ Just-in-time manufacturing
☐ Diversity awareness/appreciation
☐ Environmental consciousness/protection
☐ Participatory decision-making
☐ Learning organization/continual learning
☐ Globalization
☐ Downsizing/rightsizing
☐ High performance workplace; performance-based compensation
☐ Relationship marketing

Number of checkmarks for this list: _____

Check the items that characterize your organization's *typical* communication and training practices.

☐ Employees are typically sent to training by managers rather than making the decision themselves.
☐ Training and employee communication programs are based on requests from managers who think they have a training or communication problem.
☐ People often throw out memos and newsletters, or delete e-mail and voice-mail messages, before even reading/listening to them.
☐ Policies and documentation are often not kept up-to-date.
☐ Communication/training/marketing staff are rewarded for the amount of materials or programs they produce rather than the return on investment.
☐ Training and documentation generally present one "best" way to approach a task.
☐ Company materials don't include or acknowledge input of employees or customers.
☐ Most learning activities consist of courses led by a professional instructor.
☐ Communication interventions like training and newsletters are evaluated (if at all) by "smile sheets" measuring how much the audience liked them.
☐ Websites and intranet pages are assessed by the number of "hits" on them.

☐ There's no established way to solicit and organize good ideas from customers and employees.

☐ The agenda of company news is decided by the communications staff.

☐ Most meetings with management consist of announcements and/or a formal presentation.

Number of checkmarks for this list: _____

How Did You Respond?

My experience with more than a thousand clients and workshop participants is that most people check off at least five items in both lists one and two. Did you?

If you checked off more than five initiatives in list one, you're in danger of falling victim to the *program du jour* syndrome where new management fads ride through the company, often distracting people from the core work of the organization. However, if you didn't recognize any of those themes in list one as factors that deserve some critical attention, you're probably working in a 1950s-style company that hasn't looked around itself lately.

How many descriptions of your communication and training system did you check off in list two? Each of these describes the typical practices in even the most progressive organizations today, but each one also represents a major threat to innovation and growth.

As you read over those statements, you probably realized that many of the practices in list two are actually at odds with the statements in list one. Can you identify some of these pairs?

We find that the practices of many training and communication departments actually contradict the content of what they may be teaching! For example, managers "send" employees to courses on empowerment, whether or not they want to participate. Or courses in diversity and teamwork are developed with the input of one subject-matter expert and attempt to teach the "one right way" to do something. Communication programs advocate total quality management, but they generally are assessed themselves by the number of pages or articles, or by how much the audience "liked" a publication or meeting. One of my clients said he knew their quality initiative was working because when he visited a manufacturing site, everybody was wearing their quality pins! Companies tout their sensitivity to environmental issues, yet waste tons of paper on memos and policies that nobody reads.

Unfortunately, many training and communication activities are sending the wrong messages to their participants about what's really important in the organization. Either the value statements (like empowerment, diversity, and participatory management) are not really supported or are unattainable, or the communication about these issues is at odds with the activities.

How Can We "Re-wire" Our Approaches?

Let's examine some of the common disconnects between typical organizational initiatives and typical practices.

Initiative(s)	Disconnects
Total quality management (TQM) / Continuous improvement / ISO certification	Communication interventions like training and newsletters are evaluated (if at all) by "smile sheets" measuring how much the audience liked them; websites are measured by "hits" without any idea of whether the information was used or not. (Is this any way to measure improvement or focus on quality?)
	Policies and procedures documentation is often not updated. (If we improve processes, why is this information often not accessible?)
	Communication/training staff are rewarded for the amount of materials or programs they produce. (Is this a good metric of quality?)
	We don't really know how much the company spends on communication and training each year (including the time of employees away from their "real" work). (Is this any way to manage resources?)
	There's no established way to solicit and organize good ideas from customers and employees. (How can we improve processes unless we capture these ideas?)
Employee empowerment	Employees are sent to courses or conferences by managers rather than making the decision themselves. (Empowered employees should make decisions about their own development.)
Teamwork/self-managed teams	Training and employee communication programs are based on requests from managers who think they have a training or communication problem.
Participatory decision-making	(Does the employee or team get to decide? Could there be other problems that are not training or communication-related, like the way that people or projects are managed?)

Initiative(s)	Disconnects
	Training and documentation generally present one "best" way to approach a task based on the input of one or two subject-matter experts. (Having a limited number of perspectives does not display the power of teamwork; learners should have some input into their own training.)
	There's no established way to solicit and organize good ideas from customers and employees. (Customers and employees should participate in important decisions.)
	Company materials do not include or acknowledge input of employees or customers. (Top-down communication is not compatible with self-managed teams.)
Just-in-time manufacturing	Policies and procedures documentation is often not updated. (If we can eliminate millions of dollars of inventory, we should be able to replace our old pages in manuals.)
Diversity awareness/appreciation Globalization	Training and documentation generally present one "best" way to approach a task based on the input of one or two subject-matter experts. (Most material should acknowledge and positively present differences in cultures, practices, and values.)
Learning organization/Continual learning	Most learning activities consist of courses led by a professional instructor. (The most important learning occurs in informal and peer-to-peer situations.)
	The agenda of company news is decided by the communications staff. (The audiences for information should set the agenda for what they want to know.) Most meetings with management consist of announcements and/or a formal presentation. (Two-way dialogue is needed to gather new information or challenge assumptions.)
	There's no established way to solicit and organize good ideas from customers and employees. (Organizations need mechanisms to continuously collect the best practices and innovative ideas from those closest to processes and products.)

Initiative(s)	Disconnects
Downsizing/rightsizing	We don't really know how much the company spends on communication and training each year (including the time of employees away from their "real" work). (How can we cut costs by laying off hourly workers yet spend untold resources disseminating information to those who are left?)
	Communication/training staff are rewarded for the amount of materials or programs they produce. (Do we reward waste?)
High performance workplace; performance-based compensation	People aren't rewarded for doing what they've been taught in training. (By ignoring or contradicting the investment in training, we just make people cynical and lower performance levels.)
Relationship marketing	Company materials do not include or acknowledge input of employees or customers. (Where can people see evidence of their own input in the partnership?)
	There's no established way to solicit and organize good ideas from customers and employees. (How can we forge relationships with people we don't really pay attention to?)

By completing this assessment, you may be able to begin pointing out inadequacies in the policies and practices that surround your own training and communication infrastructure. You can also modify this instrument to include important trends or initiatives in your organization, exclude those initiatives that are not being pursued, and also think of policies and practices that may conflict with important organizational goals.

Capacity for Change and Crisis

Executives can be lulled into complacence with their communication and learning infrastructures if the organization is not facing immediate change and stress. Typically, when a company begins, it is small and simple enough to get by with no formal communication channels, policies, or standards. However, as change and stress mount, if the proper systems are not ready, chaos and disintegration can happen suddenly. What happens when the unexpected accident occurs and there's no

**Communication Preparedness & the State
of the Organization**

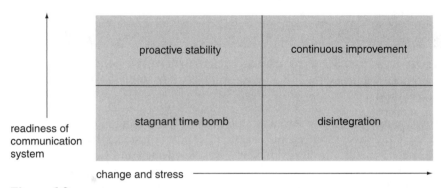

Figure 6.2
Communication Preparedness and the State of the Organization

crisis communication plan in effect? What happens when a community activist group suddenly decides to protest your new expansion? When layoffs need to take place, or when a key executive resigns, by what means is this discussed and processed with employees? When a product needs to be recalled, what happens? If the communication system is not prepared for significant changes, it's a time bomb—just waiting to go off (see Figure 6.2).

If the communication system is robust and ready, it can stay in a state of proactive stability during calm times, and jump into action to help with the enterprise's continuous evolution when the climate becomes more complex. If appropriate systems for learning, collaboration, feedback, and news are at the ready, the organization can actually profit from significant disruptions to its environment.

Checkup 9: Change and Crisis Capacity

☐ We have a crisis communication plan in place, including key media and spokesperson contacts, emergency plans, and backup communication systems.

☐ Our organization regularly conducts environmental scans to research trends and issues that might positively or negatively impact the organization.

☐ We have community and customer advisory boards or other mechanisms to regularly seek input and understanding with key constituencies.

☐ Our HR and training systems are aware of and ready to meet the future requirements of key positions and skill sets in the organization.

☐ There is a succession planning program in place that grooms individuals to step into leadership roles, if necessary, on an immediate basis.

☐ Employees are made aware of trends and competition in the industry on a regular basis through various types of meetings and news vehicles.

☐ Communication with executives is frequent and collaborative, so that employees develop a level of trust and understanding with leadership strategies and values.

☐ Ongoing assessments are done to determine the level of satisfaction among employees and customers and also to identify key opportunities and threats.

CASE IN POINT

Communication system key in crisis management

Mark Misercola, Tri-State Communications Director,
Deloitte & Touche, LLP, Norwalk, CT

Our internal television network normally serves as an electronic advertising billboard that promotes stories and helps reinforce key strategic messages on Deloitte & Touche's Tri-State intranet site. When our professionals are in our offices in New York, New Jersey, and Connecticut, they see a rolling slate of PowerPoint visuals with headlines that promote stories and other important messages, along with sports scores, weather, and breaking news from around the world.

Our headquarters in the World Financial Center is right next door to what was the World Trade Center. When the towers collapsed on 9-11-01, we were displaced from the building for several months and temporarily lost all of our primary electronic communications capabilities—e-mail, our intranet system, and voice mail. Fortunately, our television network (which operates remotely from our information network) remained in operation, and for a brief time it served as a primary communications conduit for reaching employees who worked at several sites throughout the region. We immediately began feeding critical information to viewers via the network . . . what to do, where to call for business recovery information, where to report their status and whereabouts, how to help clients, and where they could get counseling, among other issues. At a time of incredible uncertainty, the TV network served as a vital lifeline between senior management and our people. When other critical communications services were restored later that week, the TV network resumed its traditional role. However, we now see this capability in a whole different light, and it is a key component of our crisis communications plans.

Prior to 9-11, the TV network was probably the least utilized of our vehicles. We had upgraded the service by hiring TargetVision (a vendor of closed-circuit TV and computer-broadcast news systems), but it was not until we actually went through the experience of trying to implement a crisis communications plan with no e-mail, no intranet, and no extranet or voice mail that we actually saw the television network as a conduit that could fill a primary communications void.

The tangible benefits of the TV network (in our case) are twofold: On an everyday basis, it reinforces the messages on our intranet and other electronic channels and promotes them to users who might not otherwise look for them. It essentially helps us to ensure that our messaging gets through in one form or another to a very mobile population. The second big tangible benefit is it serves as an insurance policy in case we ever find ourselves in another situation where we don't have access to e-mail, voice mail, or our network.

The TV network is now a big part of our crisis communications plan. We specify that it will play a key role in disseminating critical information in a time of crisis. We spell out how it should be used in certain contingencies. We share contact names and numbers with other key leaders so that they can get messages on the network in the event that we're not available or able to work.

Conducting Communication Audits

Many organizations conduct communication audits to determine the level of satisfaction among employees and/or customers with their communication systems. Generally, these are done by a combination of surveys and focus group interviews. The focus of these studies is generally on employee opinions about the communication skills of their supervisors and the communication climate in general.

CASE IN POINT

Assessing communication in government

Christina Ragsdale, Public Information Officer,
Sacramento County Public Works Agency, Sacramento, CA

The Sacramento County Public Works Agency serves a community of over one million residents, approximately 250,000 households, and 2,500 employees. The county is large, only slightly smaller than the state of Rhode Island. The Agency provides a range of municipal services typically seen only in cities, and is unique among counties in the State of California. It provides transportation planning; design, operations, and maintenance services; water and wastewater services, including a large treatment plant; garbage and recycling services, including owning and operating its own landfill; building design; construction; construction management and inspection; infrastructure planning and financing; facility management; and more.

The Communication and Media Office for the Agency has conducted two internal communication audits; one in the summer of 1998 and one in the summer of 2000. The first audit utilized focus groups and executive interviews to identify preferred communication channels and relative effectiveness. The second utilized natural work groups and targeted interviews to identify needed communication tools and training.

The initial audit was done because the organization was experiencing major business problems that all agreed were a direct result of poor communication (skills, tools, and channels) throughout the organization. Major initiatives that came out of the first audit included a bi-annual series of employee meetings in the field with the Agency Administrator (CEO); a major revamping of the employee newsletter that included an employee editorial board; a weekly e-newsletter; and a new "communication skills" element in employee evaluations. Although there was already ample anecdotal evidence that these interventions were successful, a quantitative employee phone survey approximately one year after their introduction measured major improvements among employee perceptions about communication in the organization.

The second audit was done because there was a persistent concern about pockets of communication overload, areas where the new initiatives had not yet reached, and repeated employee requests for additional communication training. In response to this, new tactics including tip-sheets on the intranet, "Brown Bag" seminars, continued monitoring, and additional training opportunities have been offered on an ongoing basis.

Employee communication is as important to a public agency like this as it is to any other organization. Perhaps it is even more important to a government agency because they are open to greater scrutiny and are required to serve the broadest spectrum of customers. For the past few years, the organization has been competing against the private sector with significant success. Management attributes much of this success to improved communication in the organization, which has enabled rank and file employees a better understanding of the operations and realities of the business, as well as new opportunities for cooperation and collaboration.

The role of the Agency Communication and Media Office has continued to evolve since its inception in late 1997. Agency management relies on the office to bring solutions to the table, play an integrated role in active management of the business, and ensure employees and the organization's communication infrastructure are ready for future challenges.

Checkup 10: Communication System Map

This technique helps you get a literal picture of how primary audiences within an organization get their information. It also helps you to determine which message producers regularly collaborate with one another to coordinate those messages and media.

Draw a picture of the major communication sources and media in the organization. Draw arrows to show who their target audiences are, then draw dotted lines around those communication sources that frequently interact or collaborate on major message strategies and priorities. You may need to draw separate maps for different constituencies or areas of an organization. A simple example for a regional healthcare system is shown in Figure 6.3.

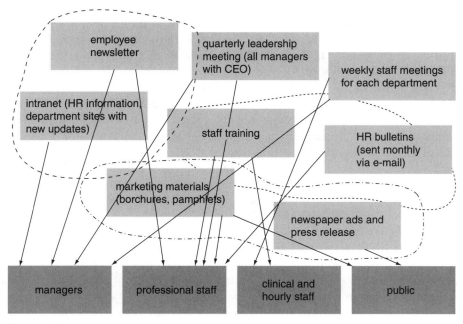

Figure 6.3
An Example of a Map of Messages and Media

1. Does the current system facilitate the coordination and prioritization of key messages?
2. Does the infrastructure support two-way communication and collaboration?
3. Does the company have and select the best information channels to provide targeted, quick, updated information to the right people?
4. Does the organization leverage various information channels to help support key messages from each area (i.e., does training reinforce key marketing concepts from the ad campaigns)?

Checkup 11: The "Person from Mars" Content Analysis

This is a process that identifies the underlying "personality" and messages that are sent by the writing style, layout, and visuals that an organization uses in its communication materials.

Get a representative assortment of communication materials from the company (newsletters, annual reports, recruiting brochures, training videos, benefits handouts, etc.). Pretend you're a "person from Mars" who has to figure out what the organization is like based on the materials you're examining. Describe the materials in terms of not only *what* they say, but *how* they say it. For example:

◆ Who is depicted in any photographs and illustrations, and what does this suggest to you about the organization in terms of who works there, what their settings are, and what the relationship among people depicted might be interpreted to be?

◆ How is the audience addressed, in terms of reading level (you can calculate this using various indices) and the manner in which they seem to you to be addressed (is the style collegial, authoritarian, friendly, etc.)?

◆ What does the layout of the material seem to "say" to you about the culture of the organization (i.e., formal, informal, old-fashioned, diverse, etc.)?

◆ What kinds of metaphors are used to describe the organization (e.g., mechanical: a lean and mean machine, biological: a family, a team)?

◆ Do the pictures or words only make sense to, or seem only to include, certain genders, races, types of people, and so forth?

◆ Does the assessment correspond with existing statements about the style of your organization? If not, what orientations need to be addressed and how?

Assessing and Managing Communication Overload

The managers of training and communication functions are often inadvertently rewarded for spending more money rather than for results. Think about it: Training managers get promoted when they have more instructors to supervise and communication managers get rewarded for dealing with increasingly large budgets for publications and lavish campaigns. Rarely are they accountable for the improvement of bottom-line performance, as are their peers in finance, production, or information systems.

Consider this case: A few years ago, while I was working on a training standards project with the Bank of Montreal, we explored the amount and coordination of instructional materials provided to the branches. We were introduced to a very insightful manager in the policies and procedures department who had undertaken a little study to see exactly how much information was being "downloaded" to the bank branches each month. He came up with what he called the "Change Management Calendar."

Basically, they determined how many "changes" were being communicated to the branch offices in a given month—how many memos about policy changes, new pages in operations and HR manuals, new training courses, and new marketing programs—and put an hourly estimate on each one to represent the typical time it would take to "process" each communiqué. What they found was that in some months, if branch employees really read each memo, viewed each video, and filed each manual update page, that they would have *no time to do their work!* They came up with a graph to indicate how many work hours were in a given month and plotted the communication load imposed each month. They found that, in practice, if the communication load rose above a certain level, the branches literally "yelled" in protest—so they labeled the value on the x-axis as the "yell line."

The graphic in Figure 6.4 is an example of how you can use this technique to tabulate the communication load in a department or location. First, collect all the materials that are sent to a particular constituency to read or view in a given period of time. Estimate how long it would take them to fully digest this information, if they had the time. Then add in the time that was taken in meetings, management updates, training classes, and so on. Calculate this in terms of hours for each type of communication and graph it. Figure 6.4 gives you an example of what this might look like.

We've exceeded the yell line in most organizations. People cope by *not attending to* all that expensive communication we're producing. In fact, if it gets too overwhelming, they quit. This is a powerful technique to show the impact of communications, training, and meetings on the available time for productive work.

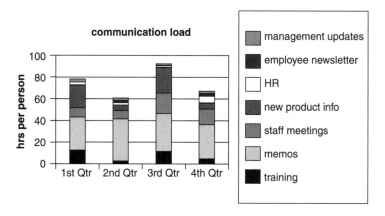

Figure 6.4
The "Yell Line" Showing the Communication Load on Staff

Assessing and Closing Group and Individual Performance Gaps

There is a saying about giving a child a hammer and finding out that everything suddenly looks like a nail. That's often the way we go about attacking performance problems in organizations. If you go to an ad agency, everything can be solved with a new campaign. Information technology and employee communication specialists push intranet sites or start planning a series of meetings. The training department offers to fix the problem with a course. Unfortunately, in many cases we are missing the mark instead of hitting "real" nails on the head.

Training and communication are typically trapped inside their respective silos. Both communication design and instructional design models start out with an analysis of the need and the audience. However, they assume that *one* type of well-designed intervention will solve the problem—like training, advertising, or information dissemination. Training people generally do not know anything about marketing or advertising, nor do communication folks typically study instructional design. Neither of them is generally involved with recruiting, incentive, or organizational development systems. This leads them to think that their own interventions are sufficient when, for most significant problems, a multi-faceted approach is necessary. However, they don't even know what other approaches to recommend, nor are they motivated to work with counterparts in other departments. For example, a training program may promote safe work practices, but if the work design, managerial communication, and performance appraisal systems do not reinforce these messages, they are likely to be ineffective. You can spend a million dollars on an ad campaign, but if employees don't understand and buy into the message and create the product and customer service environment as depicted in the ad, you've only created a dissatisfied and cynical customer.

Conventional practice in advertising, communication, and training assumes that the client has correctly identified the problem and the appropriate intervention—for example, that a performance gap is due to a lack of knowledge and that a two-day training course is needed. It's reactive rather than proactive. However, there is evidence that clients and sponsors often don't ask communication or training departments to deliver what they need; they ask them to deliver what they believe they can provide.

Here's the typical scenario: A manager notices a performance problem—such as a declining market share for a product or poor manufacturing quality. Based on past experience, budget, or convenience, the manager comes up with a possible solution, such as a new ad campaign, a training course, or an incentive program. Hopefully it will be something that can be accomplished quickly, because managers are generally rewarded for rapidly addressing problems and managing discrete projects to their completion.

The first department or vendor that's approached tries to land the job; they typically don't question the client's assessment of the problem or its causes because they are looking for potential work. They don't have any incentive to fragment the budget by suggesting that other kinds of solutions be considered. The client generally requests some slight variation of projects that have been before, something that doesn't have too many potential political ramifications. Stay within the budget, start a project that can be accomplished smoothly, and don't ruffle any feathers—that's the behavior that tends to be rewarded. However, we've seen ample evidence of why this is disastrous: It's estimated that a third to a half of training programs are a wasted effort, and the same can safely be said about internal and external promotional campaigns.

The way that CEOs manage professionals in the various "islands" of communication does not encourage them to learn about each other or to cooperate. Vice-presidents of marketing, HR, employee communication, and training manage messages only within their own domain, and have little interaction with other "communicators." In an environment of uncertainty and downsizing, these individual departments are competing with each other for budgets, headcount, and credibility with management. Furthermore, many of these functions have been outsourced, and vendors certainly have no stake in sharing scarce resources or possible glory with competitors.

The Performance Engineering Model

An alternative model for managing communication and learning is **human performance engineering** (see Figure 6.5). This approach selects and evaluates solutions based on changing specific performance outcomes. Measuring success by outcomes, rather than on creativity or just "taking action," is an important step.

A very general description of the human performance engineering process includes the following:

◆ identify performance goals in operational and measurable terms
◆ identify current performance
◆ assess the causes and cost of the performance gap
◆ recommend solutions to close the gap and determine their potential return-on-investment

A High-Level Walkthrough of the Performance Engineering Approach

Most performance improvement projects start with a "presenting statement" from the client or requestor. Often, this is a rather fuzzy goal or problem like "Our retail sales staff need to be more customer-oriented" or "We need to improve sales." Frequently, it even starts out with a specific request for an intervention: "I would like a two-day seminar on time management for our department managers." All too often, however, the solution has not been determined using a systematic approach. So here's how to turn that presenting statement into some hard data that you can use to start the analysis and determine the potential return on a solution.

Human Performance Engineering Process

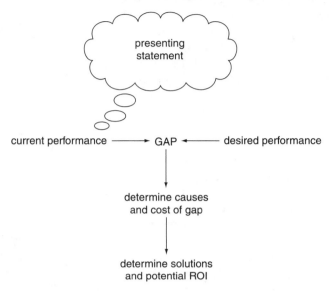

Figure 6.5
The General Performance Improvement Model

First, the desired performance goal is developed, such as "Our goal is to have five proposals accepted each month, generating at least $26,000 worth of business," or "Nonconforming parts from the production line will be reduced to no more than 1 percent." It's important that these goals are observable and measurable. Unacceptable goal statements might be "We want to improve the image of our company," or "Our employees need to become empowered," or "The efficiency of the purchasing department needs to be improved."

Next, the current performance is specified. Again, this statement needs to be measurable and observable, based on real evidence. For example, you might say "Currently, we average one proposal accepted each month and we are generating an average of $6,000 per month," or "Currently 3 percent of VX production line output are not in conformance with our engineering specs." It's important here to be as specific as possible about the current performance—for example, are we not generating enough proposals, or are we generating an adequate number of proposals that are not accepted at a sufficient rate?

Once you know the desired and current performance, it's easy to articulate the gap. But again, it's critical to measure the gap and assess its cost. Sometimes closing the gap is not worth the cost. For example, it may cost more to generate winning proposals than the revenue from them would justify. Likewise, it may only cost $30,000 per year to throw away 3 percent of the output of the production line, which would mean that any solutions to close that gap would need to be pretty inexpensive. Sometimes you may find that there's really no way to measure the cost of the gap. For example, we were once asked to produce a video program for bank tellers about how to dress more professionally. This request emanated from a vice-president who walked through the lobby of one of the rural branches and was horrified by the casual dress of many of the tellers. He knew what the desired performance was, and he could articulate the current performance. The only problem was that nobody had any idea whether that gap cost the bank any money. In fact, he may have felt uncomfortable about the dress of the tellers, but their customers may have found their appearance to be quite appropriate, if they even stopped to notice. So even though the bank could have spent $30,000 on a video, and probably twice that in terms of the time for all their tellers to sit down and watch it, how would they know if it was worth the investment?

Next, the causes for the gap are examined. Why are we not generating more successful proposals? Do account managers have a skill deficiency in proposal writing? Do they need to learn more about their potential clients and the competition? Are the proposals fine in terms of content, but presented to the clients too late? Do we have the right product at the right price? Are performers adequately rewarded for generating successful proposals, or are there hidden disincentives (for example, do we give commissions or bonuses to account reps when they bring in a new client, or do we merely give them more proposals to write)?

In the case of nonconforming products, is it a problem with the work setting—the production line tools or the cleanliness of the environment? Do workers have the adequate training to maintain the equipment and can they spot defects? Are there incentives to produce quality products, or is the incentive to work quickly and produce quantity? Are there differences among workers, or are the defects pretty well spread out over workers and equipment? Is there a good feedback system to let employees know how they're doing and why nonconforming products are a problem to the company and ultimately to their jobs?

Once the costs and causes for the gap are identified, you can begin to look at solutions. Again, a multi-faceted approach is generally needed. Let's take the proposal acceptance rate problem first. You should attempt to interview clients who accepted proposals and those who turned down proposals. What were their criteria? To gain more winning proposals, perhaps your company needs more name recognition with potential clients; or perhaps the product, price, and proposal construction were adequate, but the buyer had never heard of your company and was afraid to take a risk. You then need to consider advertising or public relations solutions. Maybe the proposals themselves are badly constructed—they may be difficult to understand or do not address the true needs of the customers. The proposal writers then need training and/or better templates as well as access to information that would help them understand their clients' business needs. If your proposals are mostly being accepted, but there are too few of them, you might want to consider what it would take to generate a greater number. What's the solution? Is it incentives for generating more proposals, better templates or knowledge banks that would speed the process, or a different division of labor so that some employees focus on customer sales calls while others stay in the office and write proposals? Perhaps you need to consider whether you have the right people for the job and examine your recruiting and selection system.

For the product conformance case, perhaps the line workers could produce better quality if they wanted to; in that case, it's not a training problem, but an incentive problem. Are they rewarded for doing quality work, or do they even know its importance? Perhaps just a feedback system or a relatively inexpensive incentive system would take care of the problem.

Once potential solutions are brainstormed, it's critical to assess the total cost of implementing them. While a training program or series of meetings might appear to cost $20,000, if you add in the time of employees away from their work, it could escalate tenfold. Is the solution more expensive than the problem?

You can see how this bottom-line analytical approach differs from the conventional practice of communication and training. It's based on hard data, is systematic, and focuses on performance.

To offer these kinds of performance-based, integrated communication interventions, a team or a multidisciplinary approach is necessary. It requires competencies in message design, training, persuasion, incentive systems, business process re-engineering, media/information technology, marketing, employee selection, and performance assessment. This sounds like more than any one person could master. The solution is to use a performance analyst who knows a little about a lot of interventions because the analysis needs to be done by someone who's informed and not biased in terms of what solutions are selected. Sometimes you can bring together a team of people who represent the skill set, and certainly a team approach is almost always required when it gets to the point of execution. This team or person works with the client and a representative constituency of the target audience to analyze the situation and to prototype and evaluate interventions. The team may exist within one department, or may be an interdepartmental work group.

Proposed solutions are based on how they affect the sustainability and competitiveness of the organization. All communication systems and messages are aligned around meeting market needs and the bottom line. This is why a data-based analysis of the goals and gaps is critical. In order for everyone in the organization to develop the big picture of how and why they may need to change their behaviors, share information, or learn new skills, they must first understand the "business of the business," and all messages must relate to improving the viability of the organization. A successful organization breeds satisfied employees.

The range of solutions is broad. They should center on communication-related functions rather than elements like product, pricing, or equipment. The key here is that the entire spectrum of interventions needs to be considered, and they need to be tightly integrated. Anything that's proposed has to be done within the context of the organization's style and culture, and with knowledge of other concurrent initiatives and messages. This is rarely done, increasingly because so much of training, advertising, and communication is outsourced and/or managed in silos.

Performance Engineering in Detail: The ComADD Model

There are many process and project management models that have been developed over the years by practitioners and researchers in performance improvement, organizational development, training, communications, and industrial/organizational psychology. I've developed my own to reflect the processes that I use when I work with my clients and teach the process to my students: The ComADD model, or Communication Analysis, Design, and Development.

The ComADD model consists of a series of questions, or filters, to help you move from a fuzzy problem statement to the selection of one or more communication, HR, and learning interventions.

The process involves a number of stages that you might visualize as a filter. At the top of each filter, we start with some "raw material" and gradually refine it by asking questions that eliminate some of the extraneous or irrelevant factors or solutions.

The entire process starts with a presenting statement, as previously described. In many cases, a client, potential project sponsor, or executive approaches you with a problem. However, you should not merely rely on this type of reactive approach. In addition to being responsive to requests, you might take some proactive steps such as:

- Do a survey of managers and employees to see what performance problems or barriers to performance they encounter. For example, you might ask:
  - What problems have you experienced on the job lately?
  - What are our biggest sources of wasted time and expenses?
  - What would make it easier to do your job really well?
  - What information or skills do you need to develop your career and effectiveness?
  - What behaviors really please or really annoy customers and affect sales or loyalty?
- Observe employees at work to determine frequent mistakes, best practices, and barriers to effective performance such as poorly designed work areas or difficulty in accessing needed information
- Examine records (productivity, safety, turnover, re-work) to determine patterns or trends
- Research best practices and benchmarks in similar businesses or tasks

The first filter consists of refining the presenting statement into a performance gap with an associated cost (see Figure 6.6). The steps are:

1. Operationalize the goal. Refine the presenting statement into some goal that can be observed and measured.
2. Operationalize the gap. Describe, in detail, the desired performance. Then contract the desired performance goal with the current performance, which then becomes the gap. Again, this needs to be measurable and quantifiable.

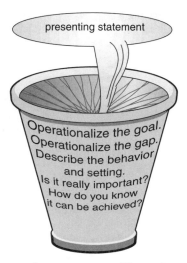

Figure 6.6
The ComADD Model Filter One

3. Describe the behavior and setting. What specific behaviors are occurring and what specific behaviors are desired? Here, you need to specify both the individual behaviors and other characteristics about it, such as how frequently it should occur, with what accuracy, and so forth. At the same time, describe the behavior setting. Where do the performers work? What is the nature of the space and the tools that they work with? Are there distractions? What is the design of the workspace like?

4. Ensure that the problem and desired behaviors are really important. Although a client or sponsor may have many "pet peeves," try to narrow down problems to those that are most critical to address in terms of potential return-on-investment.

5. Determine that the goal really can be achieved. Are there performers in your organization or in other organizations who are achieving the desired performance level? Is it possible to achieve that level of performance with the workers and the environment you have or could reasonably hope to achieve?

Out of this, you should have one or a few specific performance goals that you believe are both important and can be achieved . . . and you should know the exact, or at least estimated, cost of the current performance gap.

The second filter helps to identify the cause(s) of the gap and identify potential solutions (see Figure 6.7).

1. Do the performers actually know what performance is desired? Are they told what the priorities are and do they know what their current performance level

Figure 6.7
ComADD Filter Two

is? Perhaps they need a better feedback system. Do they understand the business and its goals and values? If not, investigate employee communication systems, better methods of orientation, training in basic business concepts, and articulation of mission and vision. Sometimes they are just focusing on the wrong activities or they're not aware of how their current performance differs from what is expected.

2. If the target group *really had to,* could they exhibit the desired level of performance? If they could not, is it a lack of skill or are there other barriers? If they could exhibit the desired performance, they do not need training; look for other impediments such as task interference or a lack of motivation.

   a. Does a new skill need to be learned or concepts/facts memorized? Investigate various methods of training and development if memorization is necessary.

   b. If memorization is not necessary, consider job aids, performance support systems, online help, databanks, and so forth.

3. Did the target group *ever* meet the performance goal in the past? If so, why has the performance slipped? If they never have achieved the goal, are you sure it's possible? Are they being distracted by other tasks or the environment? Are they getting lazy or out of practice? Are the best performers recruited and selected for the job? If not, investigate public relations, recruiting, and testing interventions.

4. What are the barriers or disincentives to performing well? Look for opportunities to change the culture to one that values high performance and doesn't inadvertently reward poor performance.

a. What are the incentives for performing well? Do they "work" for your target group? Investigate what kinds of rewards and feedback are meaningful to your target group (i.e., publicity, monetary incentives, job perks, etc.).
b. Are there disincentives? Do good performers get "punished" by being put on difficult or undesirable tasks? Are they ostracized by their peers?
c. What are the important sources of feedback, social support, and coaching? Can you redesign the performance appraisal system, make families and communities more supportive of employees, and teach managers to be better coaches?

5. Could the job, work process, or environment be redesigned? Could the job be made less complex? Could jobs be divided up differently? Are all the steps really valuable? Is the environment conducive to the type of work performed and to the personal styles of the workers?

The following table summarizes some of the typical causes for performance gaps and some of the types of interventions that might be used.

Causes	Interventions
No consequences	Feedback and communication
Lack of incentives	Coaching
Wrong people	Incentives
Lack of skills	Improved environment
Poor environment	Better recruiting and selection
Punishment of excellence	Training/education
Lack of timely information	Job aids and tools
Unrealistic expectations	New policies and procedures
Bad management of resources	Culture change/reorganization

From filter two, you should have a list of probable causes for the performance gap, along with potential interventions that could close the gap. ComADD filter three now helps you decide among potential solutions (see Figure 6.8).

1. Are there any solutions that already exist, either in your organization or in off-the-shelf programs or products, that could be bought from vendors?
2. What are the potential costs of the various solutions—both in terms of out-of-pocket costs and also the time of the project managers and participants?
   a. Which have the best ROI?
   b. Which might also provide the infrastructure for other interventions? (For example, if you choose to license a tool to help you create online help files, can that tool be used again for other similar projects?)
3. Do you have the resources to pull off the intervention? For example, if you choose web-based training as a solution, do your participants all have access to an appropriately configured computer? If you choose a mentoring program, can you gain the time of experienced coaches?
4. Will the proposed solution cause any unanticipated negative effects?
   a. Does it fit the organizational culture?

Figure 6.8
ComADD Filter Three

b. How does the potential intervention interact with other existing communication and performance systems?
c. Are there political ramifications? (For example, if you create a new bonus program for one group of employees, will other groups become jealous?)

From this process, one or more usable solutions should emerge that, when integrated correctly with the organization's brand and goals, will increase performance.

Getting the Results You Want

The ComADD model is a general problem-solving method to help you systematically address performance gaps. Because of the rigor involved, it's generally used where the problem is at the group level (a work team, department, or a number of people with the same task or role).

A simplified version of this should really be in every front-line supervisor's toolkit as a way to look at coaching and helping individual contributors.

Thomas Gilbert (1978), a pioneer in the human performance engineering movement, wrote a seminal book called *Human Competence: Engineering Worthy Performance*. In that book, he developed the Behavior Engineering Model (BEM), which outlines six factors that underlie performance and divides them up between environmental or infrastructure factors and individual factors. Table 6.1 presents Gilbert's factors, along with some examples of how each might be influenced.

Table 6.1

Gilbert's Factors with Examples of How They Might Be Influenced

---

Environmental factors

Information (clear instructions, goals, feedback, mechanisms for performers to track their own progress)	**Resources** (equipment, materials, access to appropriate information and job aids, enough time to do the job, good processes)	**Incentives** (appropriate compensation and other rewards, removal of disincentives, clear consequences for good and for poor performance)

Individual factors

Knowledge (skills and concepts previously attained through education and experience, opportunities to develop knowledge through training, coaching, developmental job opportunities, etc.)	**Capacity** (physical, intellectual, and emotional capacity that the individual brings in general and specifically given particular life events, engineered through proper selection and then sustained through employee wellness and employee assistance programs to deal with emotional and psychological difficulties)	**Motivation** (engineered through proper incentives, the right job opportunities to match interests and goals, matching individual values to corporate values, and the proper work climate to foster social needs)

One of the biggest challenges in getting the performance engineering approach accepted in organizations is explaining it to executives and managers. By presenting a simple graphic like the one previously shown, you may be able to use it when you are asked to produce some sort of training or communication intervention. Furthermore, many organizations are now offering training to supervisors based on these performance engineering ideas.

This is the first step in creating a process that is itself an important value-adding infrastructure element in your organization. By having a systematic approach to learning and communication, you can avoid wasteful interventions and ensure that your projects directly impact important behaviors and accomplishments.

Self-Check

1. What are the three levels at which we need to engineer performance, and what factors do we need to design at each level?
2. What are some typical "disconnects" between organizational initiatives (such as continuous improvement and teamwork) and actual practices and policies in communications and learning—and how does this affect organizational performance?
3. What systems and practices need to be included in the learning and communication infrastructure to cope with change and possible crises?

4. "Information overload" is a common complaint in organizations. Describe at least two tools and management practices that you could use to assess and better control the current load and flow of information within a particular department or function.

5. Describe two evaluation methods that you could use to assess the quality and consistency of messages within an organization, and discuss possible interventions that could improve these areas.

6. When performance is less than desired, managers often blame employees for being lazy or they believe that it's because they lack knowledge. Discuss the performance engineering approach for analyzing performance problems, listing at least eight possible causes for poor performance.

7. The vice-president of finance for MyState University asks you to develop a course on cost control for department chairpersons. She states that these chairs are faculty members who generally have no background whatsoever in finance, and that they are ordering supplies and equipment that are much more expensive than necessary. Often, they go over budget at the end of the academic year. She would like you to develop a two-day course in purchasing and the basics of accounting so that they can do a better job in managing their budgets. Use the ComADD model to develop at least six questions or areas of investigation that you would pursue before you developed any type of training (or other solution) to this performance problem.

References

Gilbert, T. (1978). *Human competence: Engineering worthy performance.* New York: McGraw-Hill.

Pascale, R., Milliemann, M., & Gioja, L. (1997, November–December). Changing the way we change. *Harvard Business Review 75(6),* 127–139.

CHAPTER 7 Translating Data to Dollars: Calculating and Communicating the Value of Learning and Communication

Overview

It is critical for professionals in communication and training fields to demonstrate the value of their work and the systems they manage. This chapter will present models for calculating return-on-investment (ROI) as well as an approach to assessing the valuation of ongoing infrastructure assets.

Where Is 1 Million?

One of my colleagues, Jim Hill, a past President of the International Society for Performance Improvement and the Director of Sales Acceleration for Sun Microsystems, uses a powerful exercise to demonstrate the level of financial impact that professionals in learning and performance need to achieve in order to establish credibility in large organizations.

In conference presentations, he presents the graphic in Figure 7.1 and asks participants to quickly "find 1 million" . . . that is, to place a dot on the line—with 1 at the left and 1 billion at the right—to show where 1 million would fall.

Most people put their dot somewhere about one-quarter of the way up the line. However, the correct placement is much, much closer to the 1. As you can see from the graph in Figure 7.2, 1 billion is 1 thousand million. Therefore, 1 million is only one-thousandth of the way from 1 to 1 billion. You may ask, so what?

1   1 billion

most people put their
dots somewhere in here

Figure 7.1
Where's 1 Million?

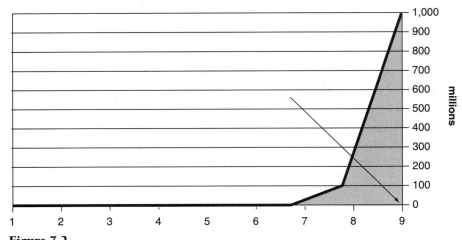

Figure 7.2
One Million on a Scale of 1 to 1 Billion

The point here is that many of us would be very proud if we could say we saved our company $100,000, or if a project we did for our client increased productivity by a half a million. However, in many of the organizations in which we work, executives' heads are operating in the millions and billions of dollars. A few hundred thousand dollars is lunch money.

We face two giant hurdles in showing return-on-investment in training and communication projects:

1. Knowing what we need to measure to show ROI, and tying our project directly to any result.
2. Determining, even if we can figure out some measure, the numbers that are really impressive.

Because of these hurdles, projects are often not assessed at all. When they are, however, professionals often approach them as one-off interventions. The returns, even on a highly successful meeting, software purchase, or training course, are generally not all that impressive. In addition, it begs the question of whether the next intervention will be as successful. Sadly, in this era of change and competition, you are often only as good as your last project.

Therefore, in the following sections of this chapter we will examine the need for evaluation, as well as the various levels at which projects in an infrastructure can be assessed and managed.

When communication and training are not assessed, a vicious cycle of ineffectiveness is initiated (see Figure 7.3). Many communicators and trainers don't really know how to evaluate their interventions; they may not have been trained in statistical methods or other quality control techniques. They may also be afraid to evaluate their projects, lest they show negative reactions or no real results. Often clients and requestors don't allow assessment to take place; they won't pay for

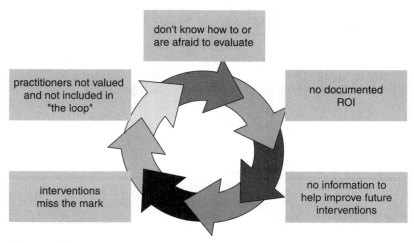

Figure 7.3
The Vicious Cycle of No Evaluation
Copyright 2002 Gayeski Analytics.

the time it takes, and they also may not really want to get answers other than knowing that a project was completed on time and on budget.

If assessment is not done, no return-on-investment can be calculated. Designers and producers don't have the feedback they need to improve the current project or future ones. Therefore, they get more and more "out of the loop" and removed from real performance data and business needs.

Management sees them as low-level wordsmiths and meeting planners rather than strategists, and communicators lose whatever chance they may have had to get a seat at the table. Of course, this makes them more defensive and more afraid to evaluate their work, so the cycle continues.

Levels of Project Evaluation

Typically, communicators and trainers don't evaluate programs. When they do, the most common methods are:

- ◆ questionnaires that solicit an audience's satisfaction, such as their opinion of a course, a meeting, or a newsletter;
- ◆ readership studies, where communicators interview a sample of the audience to see which memos or newsletters were read, or which articles within those media were read or ignored;
- ◆ media exposure, where communicators calculate the column-inches in magazines or newspapers that their press releases generate (called earned media value), or tabulations of "hits" on Internet or intranet pages;

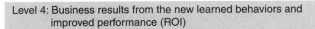

Figure 7.4
Kirkpatrick and Phillips Levels of Evaluation

- ◆ tests of knowledge administered after courses or online training;
- ◆ focus groups and individual interviews, to determine what the audience likes or wants to have changed, or how they've used information or training provided to them.

One of the best-known classifications of evaluation, developed by Donald Kirkpatrick, was first presented in 1959 in a series of *Training and Development Journal* articles, and were published in book form in 1999. His levels (see Figure 7.4) are:

- ◆ **reactions** (measures of satisfaction and impressions of learning gathered from participants)
- ◆ **learning** (measured by written or performance tests)
- ◆ **transfer** (documentation of whether learning actually is applied on the job)

Jack Phillips, in several articles and books, extends Kirkpatrick's models to "level four" or results—sometimes called ROI (see Figure 7.4).

- ◆ **results** (do the new behaviors being applied on the job actually result in financial benefits)

It is difficult to determine ROI because, in most cases, business performance is determined by a whole range of variables. For example, if sales increase after a sales training course or an ad campaign, was it because of those interventions, or because the price was lowered or the economy got stronger?

To get around the difficulties in demonstrating ROI, we can use benchmarks of the financial success of companies that have various approaches to communication and learning. As we saw in Chapter 1, studies done by firms like Watson-Wyatt have found that there is a positive correlation between good human capital practices and company profits. Other intangible assets that can affect organizational vitality and shareholder value include

- ◆ a positive reputation with stakeholders and customers
- ◆ employee loyalty

- ◆ strong branding and identity
- ◆ innovation and knowledge

A recent study by the accounting firm, Ernst & Young, found that these intangible assets represent anywhere from 30 to 50 percent of a company' s market value. Surveys of 275 buy-side investors and analysis of 300 sell-side reports showed that the more analysts use non-financial measures, the more accurate their earnings forecasts. Ernst & Young concluded: "How skillfully companies manage key non-financial areas of importance and then communicate related successes to outside constituencies—shareholders, investors—will have a powerful effect on how they are valued." *Fortune* magazine reaffirmed the importance of reputation as it published its seventeenth annual ranking of "America's Most Admired Companies." Chosen in a poll of 10,000 corporate officers, directors, and industry analysts, the top ten most admired companies had a total return to shareholders of 70.5 percent, compared to a 27.1 percent average return for the S&P 500. The ten least admired had a return of −26.8 percent (Bergen, 2002).

Other innovative ways exist to measure communication and training effectiveness. The Body Shop assesses employee communication by trying out new approaches on experimental groups and comparing employee behavior to control groups that have not received the programs. Sears and Roebuck correlates employee attitudes and behaviors to customer satisfaction, as measured by surveys and mystery shopper analyses. Through modeling techniques, Sears has determined that there is a positive relationship between the way they provide information and feedback to employees that results in employee behaviors that have a direct impact on the bottom line (Gray, 1999).

At Dow Chemical, marketing communication is measured by achievement against strategy for each communication activity and by achievement of productivity goals. For example, their goal for 1995–2000 was to demonstrate $45 million of productivity from better access to information and the application of new communication technologies. FedEx measures results by performing an analysis for every marketing promotion, and then comparing results with the business plan. At Fidelity Insurance, they measure costs per inquiry, per lead, and per conversion and break it down by their different promotional campaigns (McGoon, 1998–1999).

New communication and technology strategies can often be measured in terms of cost savings. At SoftChoice, a Toronto-based software reseller, an online employee newsletter reduced their volume of e-mails, which were putting a drain on their system's bandwidth. They estimated that each e-mail cost the company $150.00 in terms of hardware and support. GTE Corporation saw a 200 percent return-on-investment when it replaced paper-based documents with an online library and saw an 800 percent ROI when it created an online staffing system for hourly employees. They were able to reduce headcount in human resources while providing the same or better service (The hardest question, 1999).

Going Beyond ROI—Infrastructure Analytics

Although it's important to measure the impact of individual projects, it's not sufficient. That's because:

◆ As we've seen, it's difficult to correlate some change in business results to a given program or intervention.

◆ Even when you can do this correlation, the impact in dollars is often not very large.

◆ Finally, many of the activities and investments of training and communication groups are ongoing infrastructure assets rather than individual programs that have beginnings and ends.

Professionals in human resources and communications want to show value, and financial analysts would love to be able to get a better handle on these "intangible assets" that form an increasingly large portion of the valuation of so many organizations. The U.S. Securities and Exchange Commission (SEC) report *Understanding Intangible Sources of Value* said "The Sub-Group concluded that new disclosures are necessary. These changes reflect the shift from a tangible, asset-based economy to one that emphasizes technology and services. Much of today's corporate value is associated with intangible factors. The recommendations call for immediate disclosures of managements' perspectives on drivers of aggregate corporate value, including intangibles."

I've developed another category system for assessing human performance improvement interventions, the Gayeski (E)valuation Model. The name indicates that it includes types of assessments that evaluate projects as well as get at ongoing systems that add to an organization's valuation.

Rather than calling the various types of assessments "levels," I prefer to think of them as "layers." The surface layer is "smiles," which is a shorthand for measures of audience and client satisfaction with a particular project. Examples of smiles are the typical student evaluation forms used after training classes, and surveys of clients to determine what they thought of both the process and the output of a particular project.

The next layer is quick fixes. This kind of assessment looks at immediate results from some kind of intervention. For example, if you do a webcast for technicians showing a new method of troubleshooting one of your devices, you might measure whether their average repair times were reduced, or whether they were using fewer replacement parts in their work. There are many organizational situations where a relatively short intervention is designed to make an immediate impact, even though the results of this might not continue very long, either because attention and motivation may fade after time or because the work situation changes, making the content no longer relevant. Nevertheless, this type of intervention and evaluation are important.

A different kind of situation and set of assessment methodologies are used for longer-term goals. For example, an organization might institute a coaching system

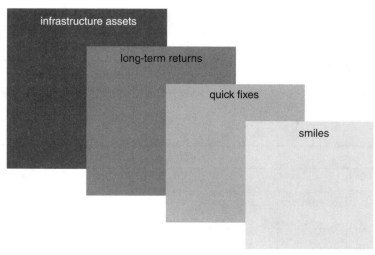

Figure 7.5
The Gayeski Analytics (E)valuation Hierarchy

for women and minorities aimed at reducing turnover among this population and increasing their numbers among management ranks. In order to be effective, this type of program would have to be done over a period of years—maybe even indefinitely. Furthermore, to show any kind of impact, you would certainly have to wait years.

Just as "smiles" are the surface layer, "infrastructure assets" are the core. An analogy to the bricks-and-mortar tangible property of a company can be made: The wallpaper and carpet are the surface layer. They are important, and probably catch immediate attention, but are not expected to last very long. Underneath them are walls and floors that are much more permanent. Supporting all of this, however, is an invisible infrastructure such as electrical wiring, plumbing, and foundation. It is upon this infrastructure that you can add other amenities such as lighting, appliances, and even other rooms (see Figure 7.5).

Doing the Numbers: Methods of Calculating Value

There are a number of calculations that can be performed to put a dollar value on training or communication interventions. Perhaps the simplest is the benefit/cost ratio.

Benefit/Cost Ratio

results (benefits) / out-of-pocket costs

Example: Leading focus groups and creating posters on best practices cost $20,000 and resulted in efficiencies yielding $60,000.

60 / 20 = 3:1 benefit/cost ratio

A slightly more sophisticated form of the benefit/cost ratio is an ROI (return-on-investment) calculation. Instead of dividing the benefits by out-of-pocket costs, the ROI calculation considers fully loaded program costs. "Fully loaded" means accounting for expenses such as the time of participants that's taken in meetings or training courses. This time could be represented as a portion of their salaries, or include the opportunity costs of having them out of commission during the program (such as lost sales).

ROI Calculation

$$\text{ROI\%} = \frac{\text{net program benefits}}{\text{fully loaded program costs}} \times 100$$

net program benefits = program benefits − program costs

For example, let's say a new intranet knowledge base for sales reps costs $50,000 to produce. When it was introduced to the company, it took six days of an in-house trainer's time to prepare and conduct three-hour workshops for 100 employees. We calculate the trainer's expense at $500/day or $3,000. We calculate the salary of employees at $30/hr, and therefore the cost of their attending the workshops is $9,000. In addition, we estimate lost sales during the time that the reps were being trained at $2,000. After the knowledge base was in place for a year, the reps increased the volume of their sales by $200,000.

$$\text{ROI\%} = \frac{\$200,000 - \$50,000}{\$50,000 + \$3,000 + \$9,000 + \$2,000} \times 100$$

ROI% = $150,000/$64,000 × 100 = 234 percent

You probably have no difficulty in following those formulas. Unfortunately, it is not this easy in most real-life situations. The typical problem we have in showing ROI is isolating the effects of any particular intervention. Several authors (Fusch, 2001; Phillips, Stone, & Phillips, 2001) have come up with some methods to help us estimate the percentage of value that each element of a coordinated intervention may provide. In addition, it includes a confidence level for this estimation. For example, you might ask:

> *"How many more sales do you feel you can close per month using the techniques you have learned in training? How confident are you of this on a scale from 0 to 100?"*

Let's take another example: a performance improvement intervention that's aimed at increasing recycling and therefore reducing the cost of processing waste in a manufacturing cell. The intervention has several components: training on methods to reduce scrap and how to recycle, an incentive and motivation program that the communication department is coordinating, giving prizes to employees who come up with innovative methods for reducing waste, and finally, the institution of some new procedures that reduce the consumption of paper.

Intervention	Isolation factor	Confidence	Adjusted value
Training	50% = $50,000	× 70%	35% or $35,000
Motivation and incentive plan	20% = $20,000	× 90%	18% or $18,000
New procedures	30% = $30,000	× 50%	15% or $15,000

After-Tax Calculations

When we calculate the cost of various systems, it's important to remember to factor in the impact of taxes. While a new intervention will certainly cost money, it will also reduce net income and, therefore, reduce taxes. As shown in the table below, a new system (let's say, an online course management system) may cost $200,000. That might seem like a $200,000 impact to the organization, but since it reduces taxes, it really only "costs" $120,000. (This assumes that there is no increase in revenue or decrease in operating expenses with the new system, which would probably be the case for its first year.)

	No new system	With new system purchase
Revenue (income)	$1,500,000	$1,500,000
Operating expenses	−765,000	−765,000
Purchase of new system	0	−200,000
Income before tax	$735,000	$535,000
Tax (40%)	−294,000	−214,000
Net income	$441,000	$321,000
	$120,000 difference	

Similarly, when you look at the benefits of some new project or system, you must calculate the impact of taxes. If a newly designed website brought in $30,000 more in sales, the impact of your intervention is softened by the taxable amount of that profit.

Profit before new system	$70,000
Added profit after new system	+30,000
New before-tax profit	$100,000
× 36% tax	−36,000
After-tax profit	$64,000

Depreciation is another tax factor that should be considered. While many projects or systems are "expensed" in a year, many of them can be considered ongoing assets that should really be written off over a period of time. Let's say you invested $200,000 in a new intranet. That investment, consisting of hardware and software, might be written off in five years, taking $40,000 off your profit each year.

First-year balance sheet assuming $200,000 written off over five years

	No new system	With new system
Revenue	$1,400,000	$1,400,000
Operating expenses	−450,000	−450,000
Depreciation	0	−40,000
Income before tax	$ 950,000	$ 910,000
Tax (40%)	−380,000	−364,000
Net income	570,000	546,000
		$24,000 difference

Multi-Year Systems

Let's say that you develop an online job aid that you feel has a useful life of three years. Each year you plan to add some features to it that should increase employee productivity and make it even more valuable, and as employees become more proficient with it, their performance will become even higher. However, there will be some ongoing costs to updating and maintaining the system, as well as training new employees on its use. You would need to calculate a cash flow that looks something like this:

	Year 1	Year 2	Year 3	Total
Benefits (savings)	$ 10,000	$20,000	$30,000	$60,000
Costs to develop/maintain the job aid	$ 20,000	$ 5,000	$ 5,000	$30,000
Net cash flow	$(10,000)	$15,000	$25,000	$30,000

More Complex Financial Considerations

As you can gather, there's more to calculating ROI than might at first meet the eye. The purpose of this book is not to make you an accountant—if anything, I want to encourage you to collaborate with your colleagues in finance. As we get into some of the more complex financial concepts in this chapter, I have intentionally oversimplified the calculations. You should use these as starting points to ask questions of your own financial professionals, since they will have the latest figures to work with, and they know how your organization handles specific kinds of financial accounting.

Present Value

Money in your pocket today is worth more than money coming in tomorrow. You should remember this simple rule, sometimes called the "time value" of money, when you're trying to assess multi-year interventions.

Discounted cash flow is the value at a point in time of a stream of receipts to be received in the future. For example, if you deposited $1,000 today into your savings account and were able to get a 10 percent interest rate, you would have $1,611 at the end of five years. This effect is called compounding, and you're undoubtedly familiar with it from your own personal banking experience.

Present value is expected future income discounted back to today.

Another way to look at this is that $3,000 in your pocket today is worth more than getting $1,000 each year for the next three years, because you would be missing out on getting interest on the whole amount.

The formula for an expected future payment or present value is:

$$\text{present value} = (\text{future value})/1.0 + \text{interest rate}^n$$

The exponent n is the number of years over which the project will last. Table 7.1 shows you the value of $1 paid back over one through five years, given three different interest rates.

Net Present Value

Net present value (NPV) is a discounted cash flow technique where all cash inflows and outflows are discounted to the present time, using a discount rate. Generally, only projects with positive NPVs are acceptable.

For example, a new training program will require an initial investment of $480,000 and is expected to result in a decreased labor cost (savings after tax) of $130,000 per year for five years. The company will use a discount rate of 8 percent. *As shown in Table 7.2, you do not simply multiply $130,000 × 5 and assume that you are saving $655,000. Rather, the present value of the savings is $519,090, and the net present value (the present value of the savings minus the present cost of the new program) is $39,090.*

Table 7.1
Present Value Table Showing the Value of $1 Over Various Payback Periods

	Interest Rate		
# of years	8%	10%	15%
1	.926	.909	.870
2	.857	.826	.756
3	.794	.751	.658
4	.735	.683	.572
5	.681	.621	.497

Table 7.2

Present Value Example: $130,000 of Savings Over Five Years at 8 Percent

# of years			
1	$130,000 ×	.926	$120,380
2	$130,000 ×	.857	$111,410
3	$130,000 ×	.794	$103,220
4	$130,000 ×	.735	$95,550
5	$130,000 ×	.681	$88,530
Present value of savings			$519,090
Present value (cost) of new program			−$480,000
Net present value			$39,090

Combining NPV and ROI

Let's say you are comparing two software systems for group collaboration and decision-making. In this case, you need to consider both NVP and ROI.

Example

Software system A costs $80,000 and has an NVP of $4,480.
Software system B costs $37,000 and has an NVP of $3,774.

It appears that system A is the better investment. But look at ROI.

Software system A ROI $4,480 / $80,000 = 5.6%
Software system B ROI $3,774 / $37,000. = **10.2%**

Working with Vendors

Professionals in training, HR, and communications often need to work with vendors of potential systems to project the value of some new program, hardware, or software. Table 7.3 presents the results of a spreadsheet used by TargetVision, a Rochester, New York-based company that provides electronic company news and feedback data systems. This spreadsheet is used to help their prospective customers calculate the potential benefits and savings resulting from installing an employee information system in a call center; this system would provide company news as well as the status of calls being processed.

Note that the spreadsheet makes use of research showing that improved communication can reduce absenteeism and turnover as well as reduce time lost to poor communications (such as employees spending time on rumors or searching for information that they need). It makes some modest assumptions in the system's ability to close some productivity gaps, since no system will ever result in perfect performance or a complete turnaround in absenteeism and turnover. Even so, you can see that a system can result in over $100,000 in savings if your workforce is large enough.

Table 7.3

Inbound Call Center ROI with TargetVision

Call Center Variables*		Notes
Number of agents in call center	100	1
Annual salary cost	$32,000	2
Cost to recruit, hire, and train new agent	$10,000	3
Number of days worked per year	240	4

	Before TargetVision	After TargetVision		Potential Cost Reduction
Performance Issues*				
Agent turnover rates per year	26%	23%	5	
Absenteeism rates per year	8%	6%	6	
Average agents absent per day	8	6	7	
Annual cost of absenteeism per agent	$2,560	$2,048	8	
Annual cost of absenteeism per call center	$256,000	$204,800	9	$51,200
Annual cost of recruitment for call center	$260,000	$234,000	10	$26,000
Productivity Issues*				
Lost time due to poor communications	14.0%	12.5%	11	
Workforce lost time due to poor communications	$448,000	$400,000	12	$48,000
Other Costs*				
Additional customer variables			13	$0
Total annual cost reductions				$125,200

Other factors that can accelerate ROI projections are:

*consideration of overhead costs (benefits, utilities, rent, etc.) that are associated with each agent

*improved customer satisfaction as a result of improved morale

Assumptions and Calculations Applied in ROI

1. This is a customer-defined field. For the purpose of this exercise, 100 was used for the number of agents based on the following information.

   "There are approximately 7,000,000 agents now working in 70,000 call centers in the US, with an annual growth rate of up to 20% in agent positions."
   Source: Davox, citing F.A.C./Equities, 1998.

2. & 3. These are customer-defined fields. For the purpose of this exercise, $32,000 was used for the salary cost and $10,000 was used based on a mid-point of the following recruiting and training costs.

   "Average agent compensation is now at $32,000 per year. . . . The average cost for recruiting and training a call center representative is between $5,000 and $18,000."
   Source: Dr. Jon Anton, Benchmarking Study, 1998.

4. This is a customer-defined field. For the purpose of this exercise it assumes:

$$5 \text{ working days} \times 48 \text{ weeks}^*$$

* This includes deductions of ten working days for holidays and ten working days for vacation and miscellaneous absences, but excludes sickness.

5. These are customer-defined fields. For the purposes of this exercise, 26 percent was used for the "Before TargetVision" variable as quoted in the following statement.

"Inbound centers have an average annual turnover of 26% for full-time reps, and 33% for part-timers. Nearly half of all centers said that part-timers handle 5% or less of their total calls."
Source: 1999 Call Center Benchmark Report, Purdue University Center for Customer Driven Quality.

The "After TargetVision" field is a customer-defined field. Based on TVI's thirteen years of experience and the typical expectation of our customers, we have used a 10 percent reduction of employee turnover.

6. The "After TargetVision" field is also a customer-defined field. Based on TVI's thirteen years in the business and the typical expectation of our customers, we have used a 20 percent reduction in absenteeism as a direct result of improved employee communications that unifies your workforce and speaks to the needs of your agents.

"Of the 106 U.S. companies surveyed, the range for annual absenteeism was 1.2% to 72%, with the mean at 8%."
Source: Response Design Corporation, Leap Frog!™ Call Center Metric Study 1998–1999.

7. This field uses the following calculation:

average absentee rate per day × number of call center agents

8. This field uses the following calculation:

annual absenteeism rate × annual salary cost

9. This field uses the following calculation:

annual cost of absenteeism per agent × number of call center agents

10. This field uses the following calculation:

annual number of agents needed to replace turnover
× cost to recruit, hire, and train agent

11. This field represents the lost time/productivity due to poor internal communications, as per the following statement.

"Executives say 14% of each 40 hour workweek is wasted because of poor communication between staff and managers, based on a Septem-

*ber survey by OfficeTeam. That amounts to a staggering seven work-
weeks of squandered productivity a year."*
Source: Money, September 30, 1998.

The "After TargetVision" field is a customer-defined field. Based on TVI's thirteen years of experience and the typical expectation of our customers, we have used a 10 percent improvement in productivity.

12. This field uses the following calculation:

14% lost time × total annual salaries

13. This is a customer-defined field. Items that may be inserted here are costs associated with the publication of newsletters, paper, and so forth.

Translating This to Stockholder Value: Turning $100,000 into $1 Million!

Imagine that your company was about to announce an IPO or was about to be sold. You will get a hefty portion of stock or 1 percent of the selling price. You need to come up with a pitch about the value of your training and performance systems that you will present to the financial analysts hired to come up with a valuation of the company. How would you do this?

The key to really impressive results is, when possible, to show how a particular communication or learning system can expect to yield relatively permanent increases in revenue or decreases in costs. You can then multiply this benefit by the current applicable price-to-earning ratio in the stock market. Table 7.4 shows how a program that is expected to yield $100,000 of permanent savings per year results in a more than $1.5 million increase in shareholder value!

Table 7.4
Worksheet for *Simplified* Method of Determining Increase in Shareholder Value Based on Permanent Expense Reduction

Pre-tax profit or savings (a)		$100,000
Tax rate	36.0%	
After-tax income	$64,000	
Applicable PE ratio	24.1	
(S&P 500 average 12/2002)		
Indicated increase in shareholder value		$1,542,400

(a) Assumes permanent savings after all applicable adjustments for overhead and other fixed expenses.

CASE IN POINT

Pitching an e-learning system in a company turnaround

Steve Jensen, Managing Partner,
Deep Dive WorkSolutions, San Diego, CA

Before becoming a partner in my current consulting firm, I had been vice-president for learning and performance for years in an organization that has gone through tremendous turmoil and change—mergers, acquisitions, spin-offs, and many changes of ownership. This large retail automotive company had ten different CEOs and/or presidents over the course of about four years. This revolving door of top management presented many challenges in selling performance improvement interventions, but has given me lots of experience in selling the concepts to top management.

Prior to when the company filed for Chapter 11 bankruptcy protection, I had pushed through and implemented an ASP e-meeting/e-learning platform on a small scale, while we were developing standards and protocols to use on a larger scale later on. The company was still operating using two separate operating systems (one mainframe, and the other a costly client server system). Bringing two different parts of the company onto the mainframe was estimated to save millions in operating expenses per month by IT folks. Thus, we used this as a central turnaround strategy that the president and CEO pitched to the bankruptcy court and Creditor's Committee.

I started my pitch process with live e-learning demos to the CEO and chief turnaround officer, so they could get an idea of what the platform could do to train and communicate to the employee base during a very difficult time. NOTHING beats getting them to touch, see, and feel the thing! This was key, since the IT people wanted nothing to do with implementing e-learning when they had their hands full with converting to a single operating system. They thought we could just train people with manuals or traditional classrooms. However, when we had the CEO hooked, they had to go along.

The ROI included four different options to implement the system conversion project, which the CEO challenged IT to complete in less than a year. One brand/company had rolled out the client/server system just two years previously, and I had detailed expense information on that training, such as how they set up very expensive temporary training centers in hotels and airport locations throughout the continent, pulled people out of their jobs for ineffective crash course training, tore down the temporary centers, and moved on to the next town. The training was often done weeks and even months before they would "go live" on the new system. We extrapolated those numbers for the parameters of this very similar project, made projections of the number of training hours by job group needed, determined how many trainers would be needed, and so forth.

The cost of this brick-and-mortar approach was astronomical, with no residual value compared to the investment in an e-learning infrastructure that could be leveraged for other performance improvement interventions. The other two options were printing books and sending them out (which was not really an option though I costed it out) and a hybrid distance learning approach using computer-generated slides on the intranet and conference calls. This latter hybrid approach would have resulted in a huge expense in conference calls and a much less interactive and engaging experience as compared to the e-learning platform that we recommended, which used voice carried over the Internet technology.

With the momentum gained from the top two decision-makers' support, we enlisted a financial analyst to crunch projections and costs and figure out what could be capitalized. We also estimated monthly cash flows (which is very important when you're in Chapter 11!). We worked closely with IT management and IT financial analysts to round out the ROI—investments in PCs, routers, LAN upgrades, and tons of other stuff. The CEO presented the intervention to the bankruptcy judge as an integrated part of the entire system development plan, so it was relatively seamless. As far as I know, it's still on track.

My biggest lessons learned come down to this short list:

1. Senior leaders have a standard perception of our profession that must be broken. We don't just respond to requests to solve problems by pumping out training programs. You have to prove yourself by being as knowledgeable of the business as finance, operations, sales, or any other key function in the company. When we take out our stethoscopes and take a look at a productivity or expense control problem, we don't just look at skill and knowledge gaps, but also all the other components that lead to deficiencies: equipment and environmental factors, policies and procedures, standards and metrics, incentive systems, and so forth.

2. Do your homework, be able to discuss your assessment findings, and pitch your solutions in the language of the boardroom or shareholders' meetings. Do an ROI analysis that leaves no stone unturned. I was recently faced with a turnaround situation where the company had three years of costly mistakes and negative profit margins in a poor economic environment. Not surprisingly, the turnaround strategy involved radical changes in systems and business processes that would require new skills and capacities from the workforce. A distance learning intervention, while costly in start-up expenses, made the most sense. We did an extensive ROI that included five years of cost analyses, monthly cash flows, and comparisons to other delivery methods (see Table 7.5). The CEO approved it because it made good business sense.

3. Pick your supporters, both individuals and functions, carefully, and then do everything you can to show how their support with senior management will benefit them as well as you.

4. Carefully measure the results of the interventions you implement. It makes the sell job that much easier the next time if you can show the contribution your last performance improvement intervention made.

Table 7.5

ROI with Cost Analyses, Monthly Cash Flows, and Delivery Options

Delivery options (to train 10,000 on new operating system)	Costs (low-med-high)	Time to market (shorter-longer)	Quality of learning (low-med-high)	Return-on-Investment (low-med-high)	Associated risks (low-med-high)
Option A e-learning Infrastructure Blended "distance" delivery structure using virtual classroom environment and LMS Total Costs: $8.3 million	**Medium** • IT costs are PC hardware/software & circuit upgrades • P&L (performance & learning) costs are content development, EPSS for mainframe, and virtual ASP hosting/maintenance	**Longer** • IT estimates 45 days to complete upgrade of network and PCs once approval is received • P&L will take phased approach to begin delivery during network upgrade process	**High** • virtual class provides benefits of face/face class w/o travel, much fewer trainers, better retention, and follow-up • allows optimal structure to make changes to content, as system development changes impact user interface and navigation training materials	**High** • e-learning infrastructure can be leveraged ongoing for other turnaround strategies (quality training, operations merger training, improved communication)... • start-up costs in training and travel cost savings will be recouped in 14 months	**Low** • risks to the business are minimal, other than time and resources to implement
Option B Temporary CBT Classroom "Traditional" facilitated delivery Total Costs: $14.9 million	**High** • IT/facility costs are hardware/software, data lines, construction of temporary training centers • P&L costs are content, materials, instructors, and T&E expense	**Longer** • estimated 45–60 days to coordinate training space, system set-up/tear down, and hiring and training of trainers	**Medium** • facilitated instruction allows training of business practices, workarounds, and functionality • lower ability to react to program/business process changes during system quality assurance & testing	**Low** • substantial costs with shift coverage during training, temporary classroom, temporary trainers needing ramp-up training, and T&E expense, with no residual value to the company	**High** • greater potential for business disruption from lag between class training and going live without a follow-up support component, and training not able to quickly mirror changes during quality assurance & testing

Option	Cost	Time			Risk
Option C • "Low Tech" distance structure • Intranet Power-Points • 3rd party hosted Conference Calls • Blended "distance" delivery Total Costs: $9.9 million	**Medium** • IT costs are PC hardware/software & circuit upgrades • P&L costs are content development, increased print costs, and conference call expense	**Longer** • number of trainees requires additional PCs for intranet access, training capacity, and associated circuit upgrades • same 45-day estimate as e-learning option	**Low** • reduced facilitator controls and thus learner retention without collaborative component offered with e-learning option • less accountability for training completion without tracking mechanism	**Low** • substantial costs for conference calls, with no residual value • similar network upgrade investment without residual value of e-learning platform to leverage for other training and communication needs	**High** • greater potential for business disruption from lack of proper learning and understanding of business process changes and workarounds
Option D • Low Cost Solution self-directed with written manuals Total Costs: $ 2.4 million	**Low** • printing and shipping • content development	**Shorter** • time to print and ship to locations, plus additional shipments and/or printing for manual updates as program and business process changes are made	**Low** • no facilitated instruction and lack of accountability for learning creates poor retention of concepts and behavior changes	**Low** • low training investment relying on learner control potentially more than offset in resulting business disruption costs due to lack of proper knowledge of operating system	**Extremely High** • a low touch approach to a major change in business processes with many workarounds could cause major disruption to the business

Are You Leveraging Your Communication and Learning Assets?

In addition to improving the productivity of your organization by producing interventions and developing systems, you should think about how you might extend the value of what you produce and manage. There are a variety of ways that you might accrue additional value to your projects.

♦ *Re-purpose.* Projects or parts thereof can be developed so that they are easy to re-use for other in-house purposes.
♦ *License or sell.* You might think of actually creating a revenue stream from your projects. For example, if you develop a training course on managing difficult customers, you may be able to license or sell it to other companies. Stock video footage or graphics may also be useful to other companies who produce business programs or multimedia.
♦ *Donate.* Once you are through with some hardware, software, or some other sort of media, you might consider gaining a tax advantage by donating it. A computer that's too old for you might be perfect for a school. A series of videotapes on your company history might be quite welcome by your local museum.

Summary: How to Determine the Value of an Infrastructure Project

Here's a quick formula to keep in mind when calculating the value of a new system, based on an article by Christopher Gardner and Ray Trotta (2002) that is designed for chief information officers who want to show the value of a new information technology investment.

$$\frac{\text{benefits} - \text{total cost of ownership} - \text{tax}}{\text{years} \times \text{annual discount rate}} = \text{value}$$

Benefits include potential increases in revenue or decreases in cost. You need to consider a revenue stream across a number of years that you envision the system's viability to continue.

Total cost of ownership includes the cost of purchasing and/or developing the system as well as the costs of operating it. This includes necessary upgrades, training of users, and maintenance on the system.

Taxes represent the tax that you must pay on the difference between the benefits and the total cost of ownership. You can minimize tax on profits by amortization and depreciation of the system.

Time and risk factors must be considered as well. Risk is accounted for in the **annual discount rate**; this figure accounts for both a present value calculation (each dollar expected in the future is worth less than one dollar in your pocket at the present) as well as the risk associated with the investment. This is a figure that will come from your finance professionals. Risky projects may be assigned a 50 percent discount rate while lower-risk projects might be assigned a 10 percent discount rate. All of this needs to be considered across the number of years that the expected system will be in place.

To find the total value to the bottom line, add up all the annual cash flows expected to come from the new system, while adjusting them by time and risk. For a publicly held company, you can take this total value number and divide it by the number of outstanding shares to get the increased value in the stock price per share. So, let's say a new intranet system has a total expected value of $2 million, and the company has 1 million shareholders. The current price of the stock is $10. That yields a 2 percent increase in the stock price, bringing it to $12.00 per share.

Checkup 12: Are You Making the Most of Your Assets?

Check off the activities and policies that you currently engage in to increase the value of your communication and learning assets.

- ☐ Do we document our media and training assets? Do we have a list of programs, video shots, graphics, and learning objects that are categorized so that they can be accessed?
- ☐ Do we save media and training assets in standard format so that they can easily be re-used or re-sold? For example, does our multimedia training meet industry standards for format and tagging?
- ☐ When we create assets, do we make decisions about content and format with possible future re-purposing, licensing, or sales in mind?
- ☐ Do we encourage and actively review mechanisms for copyrighting and patenting of works that we produce?
- ☐ Do we document performance gaps and financial costs/opportunities before creating projects so that we can create convincing evidence of the value of our interventions?
- ☐ Do we regularly measure changes in behavior after our projects?
- ☐ When we decide on what projects to undertake, do we strategically tie programs into reducing important costs, such as turnover, waste, and accidents?
- ☐ Have we created systems for soliciting, storing, and leveraging new ideas from employees and customers?
- ☐ Do we actively seek to add knowledge to our products in order to increase the value/price of what we offer to our customers?
- ☐ Do we have crisis plans in place to minimize risks?
- ☐ Do we vigorously protect licenses, brands, copyrights, and logos?
- ☐ Do we create systems that are scalable to allow rapid growth of our company?

Self-Check

1. Research shows that training and communication programs are frequently not evaluated at all, or if they are, they are done at a superficial level. Discuss the various "levels" of evaluation possible, as well as the long-term outcomes of *not* evaluating programs and projects.
2. Why is it difficult to evaluate programs at "level four" or ROI?
3. What is the difference between attempting to show ROI of an individual project and doing an infrastructure analysis?
4. Explain and contrast benefit/cost ratio and ROI, giving a hypothetical example for a training or communication project.
5. Outline an approach for showing the relative impact of a set of related interventions (such as a project to improve the quality of products by instituting a training program, a set of job aids, and re-designing the production line).
6. Discuss the impact of taxes on new projects that involve the purchase or licensing of capital assets.
7. How do you apply the concepts of "present value" and "discount rate" to show the financial impact of a multi-year project or a long-term asset?
8. How do you project the increased shareholder value of a new system that is expected to show a relatively permanent cost savings or increased revenue?
9. Give an example of how you can use research studies and financial formulas to estimate the projected ROI of a new infrastructure asset, such as an electronic information system or a learning management system.
10. What are some approaches for turning "intangible" assets such as an internal training program into a more "tangible" asset that may actually generate revenue or result in a tax break?

References

Bergen, J. (2002). MBA careers in public relations firms. Retrieved March 22, 2003, *www.prfirms.org/career/career_info/mbacareer.asp*.

Fusch, G. (2001). What happens when the ROI model does not fit? *Performance Improvement Quarterly,* 14(4), 60–76.

Gardner, C., & Trotta, R. (2002, November 21). How to determine the value of a project. Ref# VM001. *CIO Insight.com*. Retrieved March 22, 2003.

Gray, R. (1999, December/January). Measuring behavior change: the real destination. *Total Communication Measurement, 1(1)* 6–9.

The hardest question: Does your company's intranet save time or money? (February, 1999). *Ragan's intranet report*. Chicago: Lawrence Ragan Communications.

Kirkpatrick, D. (1999). *Evaluating training programs: The four levels.* San Francisco: Berrett-Koehler.

McGoon, C. (1998–1999, December/January). Cutting edge companies use integrated marketing communication. *Communication World 16(1),* 15–19.

Phillips, J. Stone, R. & Phillips P. (2001). *The human resources scorecard*. Boston: Butterworth Heinemann.

CHAPTER 8 *Getting There:* How to Start Managing and Communicating for Value

Overview

In order to manage communication and learning systems as business assets, several steps are necessary. The first is to create the right infrastructures to support an integrated and strategic approach. That infrastructure consists of "tools" (such as databases, media channels, and information technology resources) and "rules" (such as policies, templates, and procedures for the preparation and dissemination of communication and training). To move from traditional approaches to these functions, executive support is needed; this chapter presents several case studies and consulting models to help you get started.

Creating the Strategic Structure

As you have read in the previous chapters, the key to creating and demonstrating value is to move from a "project" approach to an "enterprise infrastructure" approach to communication and learning. These structures consist of "rules and tools" that make the everyday design, creation, dissemination, and evaluation of messages more efficient and effective. You might think of this as the hard side (technologies, data) and the soft side (templates, policies, and know-how) (see Figure 8.1).

One example of the kind of infrastructure that's needed for integrated, performance-based communication and learning is provided by Stuart Goldstein, a director of corporate communications at the Depository Trust and Clearing Corporation (Goldstein, 1999). He points out that professionals in departments such as media relations, philanthropy, government relations, and the like traditionally have their own separate administrative databases. Even when they want to cooperate, the design of the data and technology may limit their ability to share information and coordinate work. As depicted in Figure 8.2, an integrated database would allow communication professionals to leverage opportunities such as:

- ◆ tracking reporters who have written about your company or an issue important to it
- ◆ finding grants and government officials who can provide assistance around issues important to the company

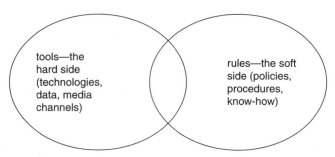

Figure 8.1
The Infrastructure Consists of Rules, Superimposed on Tools

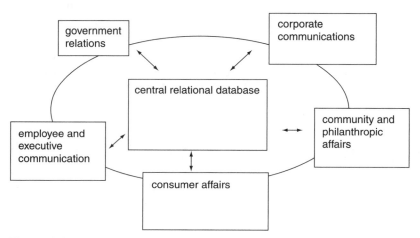

Figure 8.2
An Integrated Database Structure

- ◆ providing PR people with information on your company's philanthropic activities so that this can be fed to the press and elected officials
- ◆ maintaining an integrated database of news clippings, photo files, press contacts, executive statements, and so forth

Goldstein predicts that the corporate communication infrastructure of the next decade will be a set of interrelated technologies and information sources (see Figure 8.3). The centralized relational database is the tip of the pyramid, supported by a diagnostic database that measures the effectiveness of messages, a set of online distribution channels, and underneath it all, an online resource library.

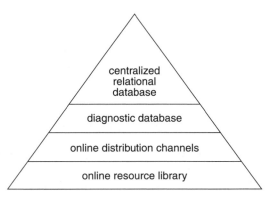

Figure 8.3
Electronic Infrastructure for Integrated Communications

As powerful as online research tools and integrated databases are, they can be sinkholes for money and time unless the right processes to design, distribute, and evaluate messages are in place. An example of creating the right rules is the development of standard information-sharing templates that speed both the creation and the reading of documents.

CASE IN POINT

Effective information sharing

Sheryl Lubbock, President,
Trimatrix Management Consulting Inc., Toronto, Ontario

Companies that have not built effective information-sharing systems often have to spend excess time (and money) searching for information, updating it, reinventing it, duplicating efforts, and/or creating content separately for every communication.

For example, a newly formed line of business within a large corporation needed to quickly pull together a multitude of information from various sources regarding their business strategy. They wanted to immediately communicate it to their clients, a number of executives and others in the company, and over 1,100 employees. The audiences were in numerous locations across the country and had varying degrees of access to technology. Ongoing communication through various channels, media, and within a mix of operating cultures was a critical part of laying the groundwork for behaviors and performance.

Stage 1

The first step was to assess the situation. Talented team members were working on the many critical business start-up programs. Present resources did not have time to spend in meetings or creating and reviewing documents. So, we gathered the mountain of fabulous information already available— brainstorming notes, presentations, program information, employee booklets, spreadsheets, and more (when printed, this amounted to about one foot of paper). We reviewed all existing material and interviewed the leadership team, and others. We researched industry best practices; reviewed business operations, organization and roles, culture, technology, and processes; and asked follow-up questions to help us effectively connect the relevant knowledge to the business needs.

Stage 2

Next, we drew the outline for the information set required for this line of business at this time. We systematically evaluated information gaps, overload, and linkages across the organization and among the various programs underway. After identifying cross-impacts, relationships, and synergies, we began to draw the information-sharing matrix. This was used to organize, cross-reference, and package the business information into discrete components. In this case, we included: vision/mission/mandate, strategic directives/business plan, and programs (people, process, and I/T).

We then input the necessary information, creating a uniquely designed and streamlined set of information components. In this case, it took the form of a business strategy document, which provided a clear, comprehensive, and integrated picture of the new business and its strategic priorities and programs, with links to supporting information. This information set provided the foundation for moving forward—from leadership to clients-facing—consistent information and communication across the organization (see Figure 8.4).

Information was organized into modular components to facilitate building, rebuilding, updating, and distributing communications, depending on the audience, situation, location, and output media.

Stage 3

Groups in various parts of the country were at different stages of transition. There were a number of different cultures. At the senior and junior levels of the organization, the depth and breadth of information required was quite different. The access to technology was not the same in all locations, and the hours of work varied depending on one's role.

We invented ways to immediately share information with various audiences at the same time through assorted communications drawn from the one core information set—the Strategy Document. The core information package provided all the relevant information and the tools to help people readily use and/or relay critical information, according to the situation in which it was to be communicated.

Only required components of information were output in various communication forms. Information and messages were easily added, subtracted, and/or adjusted to deliver information based on specific audience needs and situations, in various regions of the country, and across the business operation—effectively communicating required information to everyone at the same time (see Figures 8.5 and 8.6).

Three immediate and different outputs enabled sharing of information with a wide variety of audiences, including:

Executives   The Strategy Document was distributed in booklet format.

Managers   Illustrations in the Strategy Document were output as presentation slides, appropriate content was used for speaker's notes, and refined for situation, culture, and style.

Each component on each page is created with its own document type definition. Is it strategic, business, operational, process, etc. information? Is it title, content, support tool, or illustration?

Illustrations, forms, commitments, synergy maps, global business information, etc. are linked as supplementary data pieces, in such as appendix files.

Each page is created as if it were a separate document, linking to its respective category.

Table of contents delineates categories of information for index-type retrieval and/or linkage to business operation, e.g., Is it a governing policy? A program? A specific process? Where would you link to the business, for example on the internet/intranet?

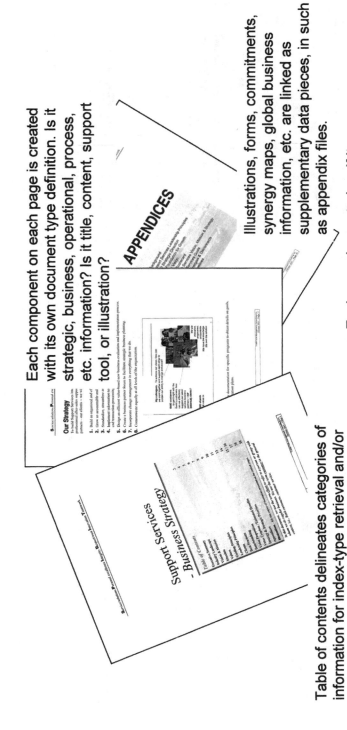

Figure 8.4
The Business Strategy Document

177

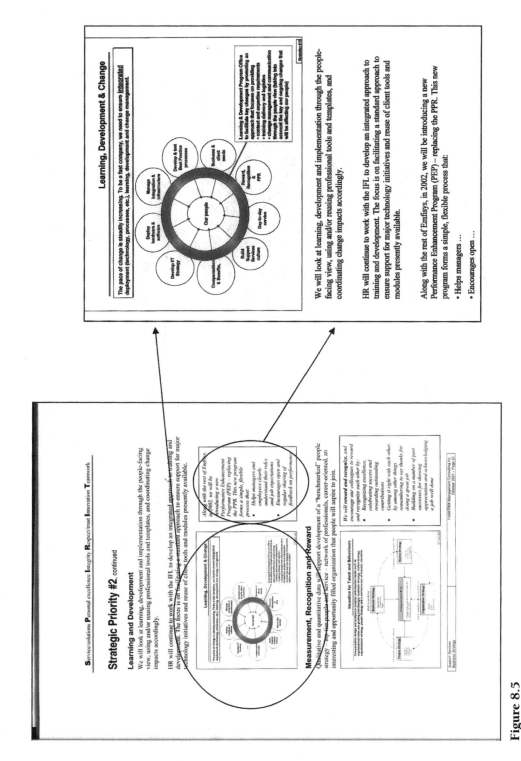

Figure 8.5
Relevant Information Components Reused and Refined, According to Use

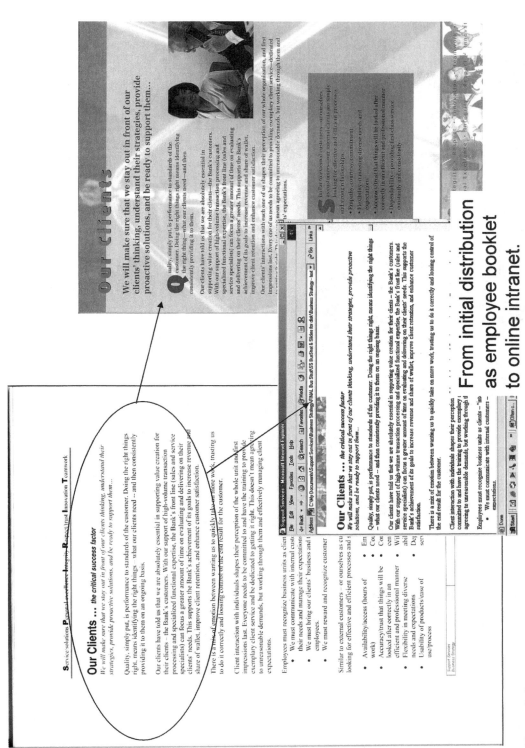

Figure 8.6
Relevant Information Components Inserted and Refined, According to Audience

179

Print-based booklet[1] provided all employees with timely and equal access to strategic, behavioural and human resource information, such as company values, leadership commitment, performance measurement. It included a calendar to support continuous communication regarding critical organizational milestones.

The illustrations formed the slides for a manager presentation. Modular content from the Strategy Document was readily inserted as speakers notes.

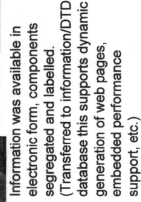

Information was available in electronic form, components segregated and labelled. (Transferred to information/DTD database this supports dynamic generation of web pages, embedded performance support, etc.)

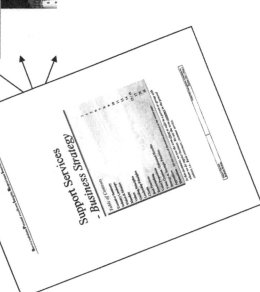

Figure 8.7
An Integrated Communication Approach

Employees   Relevant content was literally inserted into an employee handbook and calendar. [Shortly after, pertinent content from the core information set was reused to output web pages via the company intranet.]

As a last step, we defined how to easily update the information, a critical ingredient for growing the business and evolving its operation, through dynamic performance-driven communication. Each part of the information-sharing matrix—in this case, embedded presentation slides, modular and tagged information components—could stand on its own (see Figure 8.7).

As the business evolves, information can be easily updated, deleted, and/or added, component by component, just like "plug and play" components on a PC. Business owners do not have to reinvent and/or rework the entire set of information when they need to communicate. And, they can be sure they have a complete set of relevant business information from strategy to process and from support tools to behaviors and performance.

In Summary

Information can be an extremely valuable asset when it is:

◆ collected within a framework that specifically defines the information required for a given situation, group, or business
◆ organized into modular components, which are linked to the business operation
◆ assembled in such a way that each information component can be:
  ◆ readily adjusted
  ◆ integrated with other components
  ◆ disseminated dynamically to various audiences through multiple delivery mechanisms

How Do You Pitch a New System?

As a manager in communication or learning, you will often be faced with doing a feasibility study and "pitch" for some new system. Here are some ways to approach this task.

◆ *Sell it as an infrastructure asset.* As I've stressed throughout this book, it's important to sell something not as a short-term project but as an infrastructure asset and actually try to make it as "tangible" as possible.
◆ *Use one or more case studies.* When executives want to know what value something can bring to the organization, it's often hard to predict. Use one or more case studies from your own organization, or from other sources. Read your professional magazines and network among your colleagues in the field.
◆ *Show long-term value.* Use the models presented in the previous chapter to show the return-on-investment over a period of years, using the present value methodologies.

◆ *Consider tax implications.* Can the system be amortized over a number of years?

◆ *Show how it can be leveraged by others (i.e., training, safety, production).* Often, some new system can be used by other departments besides your own. For example, if you are in a communication department and decide to create portals for the delivery of company news, this same system can also be used to deliver training updates. Or, if you're pitching a new synchronous web-based training delivery system, you can show how this can be used by the sales staff to make virtual product presentations or hold sales meetings.

Making the Case for Change

I'm often engaged by organizations to be a "change agent": perhaps somebody in a leadership role understands that new approaches are needed, but they themselves may not have the credibility—or they may not really know how to approach their executives or colleagues without making them defensive. Because I'm an outsider, I often start discussions purposely *without* knowing a lot about the specifics of the organization. Rather, I present what I've found as general trends or challenges in business life today. I then ask the clients if any of these problems resonate with their own situation.

Magically, most clients feel both relieved and interested in exploring new options. One way that I proceed is to show them a list of common organizational challenges that I have encountered, and ask them to check off the ones that are most important to them.

Checkup 13: Organizational Challenge Inventory
Here are some observations that people frequently make about their organizations. Check off the factors that you think are honest characterizations of *your* organization's situation and might be most important to your organization's success.

☐ Customers and employees seem to be becoming more cynical toward the company's formal communication (advertising, newsletters, speeches, etc.).

☐ Employee communication, advertising/PR, training, information systems, and marketing are all separate departments and don't work together.

☐ People often complain of information overload and perform important tasks less well or less frequently because of it.

☐ Often our employees work hard, but spend their energy on the wrong tasks.

☐ We lag behind our competition in innovation or efficiency.

☐ We have a tougher time recruiting and retaining good employees than our competition in our region or industry, and it doesn't seem to be an issue of compensation or working conditions.

☐ We don't do a very good job in documenting the experiences and advice of employees and customers.

☐ There is no regular mechanism for communicating company news and its values and culture to contractors, vendors, and business partners.

☐ Employees are often unaware of new products or company events until they hit the mass media.

☐ Most employees couldn't identify the strategic objectives of the company, what factors make it most profitable, and who its major competition is.

Here's how to follow-up on the reactions you might get from using the challenge inventory.

◆ From your observations and conversations with various constituencies, see which of the items most people identified as being typical in the organization. Note the ones that were particularly sensitive and pay special attention to those. You might want to highlight or color-code these "hot" items on your survey.

◆ Next, follow-up on these hot items, and explore some root causes and possible alternatives.

◆ For each hot item, a number of follow-up questions and actions are implied. I use a five-step system diagnostic model to probe the situation (see Figure 8.8). I call it the HICCUP model to be funny and to help remember the steps.

Let's see what this HICCUP model might sound like in use by showing a snapshot of a conversation between a performance analyst and a client.

ANALYST: So you feel that we don't do a good job in (**hot item**) documenting the experiences and advice of customers and your fellow sales reps. Can you give me some examples?

SALES MANAGER: Sure. A lot of our customers have talked to us about extending the range of data input on the framis calculator, and one of them even wrote his own software patch to do it. But somehow, these ideas just get lost and never seem to make it back to engineering.

ANALYST: So what's the **consequence** of not capturing this kind of information from our sales reps and customers?

SALES MANAGER: Well, in the example I just gave you, I bet we could sell that calculator routine to a whole new set of customers who are doing animal studies if we had that extended data range. But that's just one example. We could get smarter about our competition and I'm sure we could develop better pricing models if we really got input from the sales reps who have to face objections every day. And our customers probably have more ideas for extending our product line than our own R&D folks.

ANALYST: So what **causes** this situation? Why don't we seem to document and share these ideas?

SALES MANAGER: I guess there are a couple of reasons. First, the sales folks are always out in the field; R&D and engineering are all back at headquarters, and these groups simply don't know each other or even think of communicating. Second, sales reps are under the gun to close deals and make calls. Writing

Five-Step (HICCUP) System Diagnostic Model

Hot Item (e.g., we don't do a very good job in documenting the experiences and advice of employees and customers)

Consequences: What do you think are some of the results of this? How does this affect the performance of the organization?

Causes: Why do you think this situation exists? Are some people actually benefiting from the current state? Do the benefits to those people outweigh the opportunities for change? Are people aware of the current situation and its consequences? Are people aware of alternative ways to manage the situation?

Uncover Opportunity: If this situation were different, how would it improve our position as individuals and as an organization? What would it look like if we could magically correct this? What resources would it make available for other opportunities?

Possibilities: What would it take to change the situation? Who could do it? If you could wave a magic wand, how would you change the way that we communicate, share information, provide instruction, or develop promotions that might make a difference? Do you know of any new tool or policy that we might institute?

Figure 8.8
Five-Step (HICCUP) System Diagnostic Model

down good ideas and trying to figure out where to send them just takes too much time, and frankly, doesn't add to their commissions.

ANALYST: I can see how it would be difficult and not very rewarding to capture all this kind of data. Do you think people are aware of the situation, and is it worth it to change?

SALES MANAGER: Sure, we could all benefit from better pricing structures and new products. I guess there's just no easy mechanism to do this, so it doesn't get done.

ANALYST: If we did a better job of documenting ideas from sales reps and customers, how could it improve our position? Do you see some **opportunities** that are worth **uncovering?**

SALES MANAGER: Yes, I do. I think that this is especially true in the area of expanding our traditional market. You know, the agricultural management sector of the economy is shrinking, and our share of the market is being eroded by some newcomers. We need to get smarter about where the research funds are going, and how we might develop some products that would be attractive to some of these new biotech start-ups. If we had some hot new products, everybody would be a lot happier—it's fun to sell new stuff, and of course the sales force is driven by bonuses and commissions.

ANALYST: So it seems like we'd all benefit if we could make better use of some of the information that's right under our noses, especially regarding new products and markets. But we have a barrier to overcome regarding the mechanism to do that, without taking up too much of the sales reps' time. Can you tell me about any **possibilities** that come to mind that would improve this situation? What would a more ideal state look like?

SALES MANAGER: Well, I am still concerned that the sales reps get face time with customers. I don't want them co-opted to be quasi-staff members in marketing or engineering. But I think we have some tools that we could make use of. For example, they all just got laptop computers and they send in e-mail sales reports to me every week. We could add a reporting line to include any new ideas for products or customers that they uncovered that week. My brother works for a company that has their sales force call in ideas to a voice-mail box and the best idea of the week wins a gift certificate. You know what would *really* be cool would be to have some sort of little application programmed into our little digital assistants . . . just some place to scribble ideas or sketch out new product designs. Then those ideas could be uploaded to the headquarters' server, and the folks from R&D and marketing could collaborate with us. . . .

Well, you get the idea. This kind of analysis can reveal a gold mine of valuable input about ways to improve your communication and learning infrastructure.

What the CEO Wants You to Know

The important thing to remember is to think like the CEO. According to Ram Charan, author of *What the CEO wants you to know* (2001), the things that are important to the vigor of a company are the following:

♦ cash generation
♦ return on assets (margin and velocity)
♦ growth
♦ customers

◆ P/E ratio (a P/E ratio of 7 means that for every dollar of earnings per share, the stock is worth seven times more). This represents expectations for growth and value.

Questions to Ask the CEO

◆ What were sales last year?
◆ Is the company growing?
◆ What is your profit margin and how does it compare with the competition?
◆ What is your return on assets (or equity?)
◆ Is cash generation increasing or decreasing?
◆ What are your primary goals and strategies for the next few years?

Communication and learning professionals are playing a much larger role than in previous decades. Instead of merely communicating the strategy created by executives and training employees in tactical skills to implement the strategy, we are now important creators and managers of the systems that drive innovation and growth. Enlightened executives understand this, as we will see from the following case in point.

CASE IN POINT

Engineering the flow of communication within Pitney Bowes

Marie Henshaw, Director, Global Strategic Employee Communications,
Pitney Bowes, Stamford, CT

How does the employee communications system need to change to support and drive growth?

This was one of many questions raised when Pitney Bowes adopted a new growth planning process in 2002. Following several strategic changes to focus on our company's core capabilities, senior leadership announced a change to our growth planning process. Instead of developing an individual plan for each part of our business, we would develop one integrated growth plan to leverage our company's combined capabilities and potential.

Over twenty cross-enterprise, global task forces were created to participate in this endeavor. Some were responsible for exploring growth opportunities and plans. Others examined how various "organizational enablers" would have to change to support and drive growth.

I was a member of the Organizational Enabler Task Force, which was led by Pitney Bowes Chairman and CEO, Michael J. Critelli. This task force was responsible for developing recommendations to align culture, organizational design, facilities, and employee communications with growth plans.

At the onset, the Organizational Enabler Task Force divided into four smaller groups. I led the employee communications team, which consisted of the vice-president of public relations, a manager and a director from our total rewards department, the safety director, and a finance manager.

After setting overall goals, timelines, and responsibilities with the larger Organizational Enabler Task Force, the communications team began meeting weekly to develop recommendations for aligning employee communications with growth plans.

Getting Started

Up front, we defined two key objectives:

1. develop a strategy to educate employees about our integrated growth plan and motivate them to take action to drive progress
2. recommend how to better align employee communications with growth goals

Since it would be several months before the growth plan was far enough along to develop a communications strategy, we focused on the alignment objective first.

It's important to understand that up until that time employee communications were handled the same way as our growth planning process. Each business and function developed its own plans for communicating with employees. The corporate employee communications department was solely responsible for corporate messages and infrastructure. No governance or infrastructure existed to manage all of the information sent to employees. And, as the communications task force confirmed in the months to come, this minimized communications effectiveness throughout the organization.

Our team began by defining the "as is" state of communications, in terms of governance, infrastructure, goals, and measuring success. Based on the preliminary growth plan—which was shared with us through a Lotus Notes database, Organizational Enabler Task Force meetings, and a two-day update meeting—we also defined how communications needed to operate in the future. Looking at the current and future states, we identified gaps that needed to be addressed.

Starting with this baseline information, we agreed to conduct a more thorough analysis, via executive interviews, an employee survey, and employee focus groups. Upon learning that the culture team was planning similar actions, we agreed to combine our efforts.

Refining Our Approach

The culture team had already spoken with a number of external consulting firms to learn about more concrete ways to define the current and future culture, as well as identify gaps. One firm's model and survey tools looked like a good starting point. So, we agreed to leverage them for the assessment stage of employee communications as well.

To clearly define the *current state* of culture and communications, the two teams conducted an all employee survey and employee focus groups worldwide. To identify priorities for the *future* states of culture and communications, we surveyed the company's top 300 managers, conducted executive interviews with the twelve members of the management committee, and held focus groups with emerging leaders.

While the survey enabled us to gather general perceptions, the face-to-face forums gave us an opportunity to obtain detailed examples that illustrated how culture and communications affect employees' ability to get their jobs done.

Initial Findings

Several members of the culture and communications teams facilitated the interviews and focus groups. During that one-month period, I learned more about how our company works and how communications are used than during my five previous years with the company.

I knew that "information overload" existed throughout the company. What I didn't know was how employees dealt with it. They often took matters into their own hands, prioritizing the information they received into three major buckets:

1. information I need to do and keep my job
2. information that affects me personally—such as benefits and compensation
3. everything else

Unfortunately, many of the messages about the company's direction fell into the "everything else" bucket and were often discarded and not read. The same would hold true for the upcoming growth plan communication, if we didn't do something fast.

Findings also reinforced the importance of aligning all aspects of a company to support and drive growth. Focus group discussions revealed disconnects between messages about the company's direction and the company's rewards system, decision-making process, and more. Perhaps most important, discussions highlighted opportunities for employee communications to drive business results.

In a nutshell, a simple solution like giving advance notice of marketing materials, along with a contact name for questions, would save our call center, sales, and service employees a lot of time and enable them to be more responsive to customers.

However, the executive interviews brought the conversation in another direction. While many acknowledged the existence of information overload and the importance of communicating effectively, it was difficult to define how communications should change to support future growth and success.

Our Recommendation: Information Management

Armed with all of this information, the communications team identified a number of tactics to address a variety of gaps. Yet, we lacked an overall framework to explain the future direction for communications. That's when we came across Diane Gayeski's work in relation to information management.

Diane took a complex issue and brought it down to a few simple ideas: The world has changed and businesses have changed, yet we're communicating the same way we did years ago and, as a result of the emergence of new technologies, we're communicating more frequently and via more channels than ever before.

A solution can be found in taking a step back and looking at it from an "information management" point of view. How do you get the right information to the right people via the right medium to drive business results?

Diane summarized the question we had to answer at Pitney Bowes. We engaged Diane to help us develop an information management strategy to align communications with future growth plans.

Diane spent time going through our research findings and initial recommendations. She agreed to introduce the "information management" philosophy to key senior leaders and to facilitate a discussion with communicators across the organization about how we could work together to use "information management" to improve effectiveness.

The philosophy and discussion were accepted with open arms.

Then came our final deliverable: sharing our recommendations with our Chairman and CEO, Michael J. Critelli.

Obtaining Senior Management Support

We sent Mike an advance packet of materials, which included:

- a summary of the "information management" philosophy and approach
- "day in the life" profiles of key employee segments—like sales, service, call center, and managers—revealing what a typical workday is like and how communication fits in
- a summary of recommendations, which included "case studies" that illustrated how the way we communicate would change if we adopted different recommendations
- raw data of what employees said during focus groups

At a meeting, we quickly reviewed the previously mentioned items. Mike focused much of the conversation on how to address the issues raised by different employee segments, as reflected in the "day in the life" profiles.

"The day in the life scenarios clearly illustrated genuine challenges employees face trying to balance all aspects of work, much less taking time to review company communications. Like all people, they have finite time and bandwidth to receive and process all of the messages coming at them," explained Mike. "Because I believe that capturing the minds and hearts of employees is critical to obtaining their support and commitment—especially during these uncertain times—we had to take action to ensure employees received and understood communications about our company's plans, why the company needed to change, what was changing and what they could do to support the change."

Of the many recommendations proposed, Mike identified three to get started on:

1. develop a communications calendar that everyone can reference to identify opportunities for integration, to avoid conflicts, and to help prioritize messages
2. create an assessment process that would help anyone with a communication need identify how to get the right message to the right audience via the right vehicle
3. develop one integrated communications strategy for rolling out our growth strategy and related initiatives

This last one was vital. You see, at the same time that the growth strategy was being created, the company had separate task forces working on a one-company vision, operating principles to define the behaviors to support growth, and a rejuvenated brand strategy. The communications team recommended that instead of taking the same approach as in the past—where the owners of each initiative would develop their own strategy for communicating their initiative—we develop one integrated strategy.

Mike immediately sent a memo to senior leadership, along with copies of our "day in the life" profiles, indicating that he supported this recommendation and asked for their cooperation.

That was in October of 2002. We had exactly three months to develop a strategy, obtain approvals from each initiative owner, and begin execution.

Our Integrated Communication Strategy

Shortly thereafter, we contracted with a vendor to facilitate a communications strategy session, with representatives from each of the initiatives and employee communicators throughout the organization, as well as leadership development and change management professionals. By bringing in an outside party to facilitate the session, we showed that no one's initiative or charge would be given preferential treatment; we would have to break out of our silos to develop one integrated strategy together.

By November, we were presenting the "information management" philosophy, along with the integrated rollout strategy, to senior management for review and approval.

Next, we were onto execution. An umbrella theme was created to link all of the separate initiatives and was incorporated into all communications.

On January 2, our Chairman and CEO kicked off the campaign. Here's what followed:

- ◆ a weekly voice mail from a senior leader, introducing a new initiative and how it works with the other initiatives to create a stronger company for the future
- ◆ corresponding weekly e-mail newsletters and intranet content to provide more details about the initiatives
- ◆ a senior leadership toolkit, containing a communication strategy template, change management tools, and sixteen different presentations for rolling out the message to different employee audiences
- ◆ a three-hour communication planning session at the company's annual Senior Leadership Conference, where leaders were required to outline audiences, how they would deliver messages, and what were the most appropriate points of focus for each audience
- ◆ a "name that program" contest, where employees were invited to submit ideas for the name of a new reward program being created to recognize employees who embody behaviors that bring our vision to life
- ◆ a manager toolkit, equipping managers to hold a staff meeting on the day of our new brand launch and discuss the campaign and employee questions or concerns
- ◆ a moratorium on all internal newsletters initiated by the chairman and CEO, who facilitated a discussion with his top thirty managers about establishing governance to manage the flow of information
- ◆ a subsequent discussion with the company's top thirty managers about how the face-to-face cascade was working, what wasn't working, and what else was necessary to ensure communications success
- ◆ many other initiative owners—like those responsible for our PAC and employee referral programs—have come to us to link their activities, messages, and communications to the larger campaign, rather than develop independent campaigns
- ◆ a collaboration with non-U.S. communicators to modify and roll out materials to employees worldwide

In addition, the umbrella theme and brand guidelines were incorporated into our existing communications infrastructure and forums.

- ◆ The Chairman Online intranet site was transformed to Leadership Online, featuring different executives introducing their initiatives and responding to employee questions.

- The umbrella theme and related key messages were used for the management presentation at our annual jobholders' meeting (where senior management and employees met to discuss the state-of-our-business and conduct a Q&A session).
- PB People Powering Business—a content area in our intranet—was being changed to reflect our new theme and featured employees who embody the new direction of our company.
- The intranet was updated to reflect the new brand guidelines, and a special content area was set up to house new brand nomenclature and guidelines.
- Employees were invited to write-in their thoughts/reactions to each initiative, and their responses—good, bad, or indifferent—were posted on the intranet.

Feedback to Date

We're planning to do a survey within the next few months to measure our progress and effectiveness. Employee feedback and questions submitted via the intranet show an initial level of interest and engagement. Perhaps the most indicative sign of how we're doing to date is the tone of the jobholders' meetings and employee questions. Despite benefit cuts, downsizing, and constant change to drive progress, employees' questions primarily focused on the state-of-our-business and future plans, rather than the items that were personally affecting them. This is a big departure from the tone of meetings in years past.

What's Next?

Senior leadership has created several task forces to oversee execution of our growth plans and enablers. One team—which will be led by our senior vice-president of human resources, group president, executive vice-president of marketing, and our chief financial officer—has been assigned responsibility for overseeing execution of the many recommendations the communications team developed in 2002.

At the time that I'm writing this, it has been almost one year since the growth planning initiative started. The company has already made tremendous progress aligning communications with growth plans, with its recent integrated communications rollout. In addition, the stage has been set to drive further progress in the upcoming year.

Valuation Concepts for Not-for-Profits

Throughout the book I've given many examples of management and measurement methods and case studies, most of them involving publicly held corporations. It would be a major mistake to infer that the approaches and tools related to the "infrastructure asset" approach are not applicable to not-for-profit organizations and government agencies. In fact, communication and training professionals in organizations that draw their support from taxpayer funding or from donors probably are even more pressed to "show value" than their for-profit colleagues.

One example comes from the North Suburban Library System (NSLS), a client with whom I conducted a communication audit to refine their image and mechanisms of communication with their membership. NSLS is a consortium of over 650 academic, public, school, and special libraries in north suburban Chicago funded by the State of Illinois. NSLS provides shared services such as continuing education, book circulation among libraries, policy analysis and development, group purchasing and insurance packages, and networking groups for library professionals in their area.

In 1999, a comprehensive analysis of NSLS's member services was completed by an outside consultant. This study highlighted several areas concerning communication that might need improvement. At the same time, many communication tools and techniques had been added and modified by NSLS, and of course, the information technologies available to member libraries had also expanded. With this in mind, NSLS engaged me to conduct an assessment of its communication system with its member libraries to ascertain the perceived effectiveness and preferences of librarians with regard to the media and methods NSLS used to communicate with them. The study used two methods:

◆ An expert review of printed, interpersonal, and electronic methods that NSLS used to communicate with its members (i.e., the Blue Sheets, the NSLS website, meetings, fliers, etc.). Materials were reviewed for their format, readability, style, or "personality," and consistency.
◆ A phone and mail survey of a selected sample of about 100 member librarians.

The members surveyed reported a high degree of satisfaction with the content and format of most NSLS services and communication vehicles. However, as the information landscape of member libraries changed, they desired an increased use of electronic communication, with information aggregated and individually targeted as much as possible. Our analysis concluded that their website needed to be redesigned and better leveraged. Finally, personal contact among NSLS staff and member library staff was very much appreciated; organizations needed to retain and even enhance this aspect of their service.

We found that the "brand" and "personality" of NSLS was perceived to be professional, credible, friendly, and responsive but that those traits needed to be sharpened and made consistent throughout communication—whether in person or mediated, and whether broadcast or targeted to one person. As the staff at the member libraries changed, the newer people did not have a strong sense of NSLS's offerings—and sometimes people became confused about NSLS's role. Most importantly, because the design of their communication system was not as efficient as it could have been, many librarians didn't even use or know about many of the resources that NSLS could offer them.

The most urgent recommendations from this first communication audit were to redesign NSLS's website, bundle a lot of their print and electronic bulletins into one e-newsletter, and conduct an image analysis and redesign. These were undertaken in phase two.

Our team facilitated an "image / personality / brand" identification through online brainstorming plus an on-site half-day meeting with a team of NSLS staff and representative members. When we asked focus group members what words came to mind when describing NSLS, they responded with terms like: *"Teacher, leader, innovator, bureaucratic, invisible to the public, deliverer of goods, responsive, flexible, proactive, receptive, evolving, vital, caring, helpful, down to earth, imaginative, interested, collaborative, advocate, nurturing, gracious, sharing, motivating, welcoming, informative, professional, active, concerned, supportive, facilitators, partners, leading edge, cooperative, goal-oriented, growing, outreach, busy, accessible low cost, pragmatic, listening, risk taking, dedicated, serious, traditional, fragmented."*

This exercise revealed a couple of important facts:

◆ Members were generally very positive toward NSLS.

◆ However, there appeared to be an important dichotomy between members who expected NSLS to exhibit forward-thinking, proactive, professional leadership and those who expected NSLS to function more like a quick-responding, reactive staff service organization.

While these two images were not necessarily incompatible, these perceptions could lead to a level of dissatisfaction and confusion for both NSLS staff and its members. For example, should NSLS maintain an image of being the proactive leader and expert, or should it represent itself as more reactive and oriented to acting quickly on member requests? In other more blunt terms, are NSLS staff members expert consultants or an outside "pair of hands" ready to respond to members' demands?

We used an electronic group decision support system (GDSS) to collect ideas from a focus group and then a wider constituency of staff, member librarians, and board members. This brainstorming focused on what services and image would make NSLS most useful to members in the future. A graphic representation of the results of this exercise, generated by the computer, is shown in Figure 8.9. The various "islands" are clusters of individual statements that were generated in the brainstorming stages. The height of the "stack" for each cluster represents the level of importance rated by the participants.

We then conducted a usability study of the NSLS website (see Figure 8.10). Since the original survey found that many members found it difficult to find information on the website, we designed a specific exercise to uncover what made it difficult and what search strategies typical member librarians liked to use. The website had also been criticized for its overall look, including the logo. Some staff and members felt that the tree image in the logo did not make a connection with NSLS and that it looked outdated.

Our team used the input from the web usability study to develop a prototype logo, home page, and electronic newsletter (see Figure 8.11). In order to drive traffic to the website and consolidate a number of print and electronic bulletins, they created an e-newsletter that is now e-mailed weekly to members. By clicking on links in the newsletter, the user is brought directly to the relevant web page (see Figure 8.12).

After an eighteen-month process of analyzing and redesigning its communication system and "voice," both NSLS staff and members appreciated the improvement in information efficiency and consistency. Mary Witt, Assistant Director of NSLS, said, "As a leadership organization, our success depends on

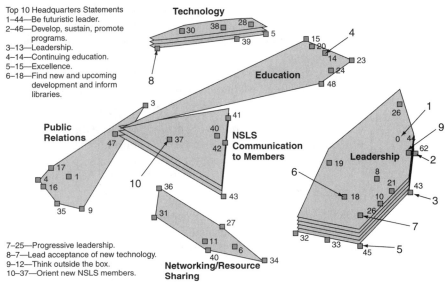

Figure 8.9
Output of Brainstorming About NSLS Role and Brand

effective communication with our members. Our new Web site and e-newsletter have helped us to achieve this goal. Our new logo is a much better reflection of this leadership image as well."

Reporting to Stockholders and Financial Analysts

The Holy Grail of human resources management and communications is the ability to actually place the value of intangible assets on "the books." Although standard accounting procedures (such as GAAP in the United States) have really not determined procedures for accounting for and reporting these assets in detail, many organizations have made strides to communicate these "softer" but critical assets to their stockholders and other financial analysts.

One approach to measuring and reporting on initiatives and assets in communication, HR, and learning is called the balanced scorecard, developed in the early 1990s by Robert Kaplan and David Norton (1996). Recognizing some of the limitations of current reporting formats, the balanced scorecard approach is both a management system and a measurement system that enables organizations to clarify their vision and strategy and translate them into action (see Figure 8.13).

Figure 8.10
NSLS Old Website Design
Used with permission of North Suburban Library System.

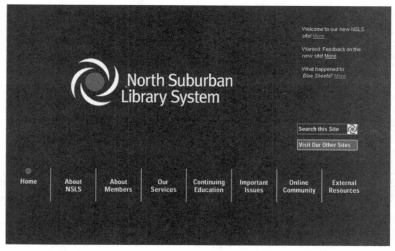

Figure 8.11
NSLS New Home Page
Used with permission of North Suburban Library System.

What Do You Think?

Tell us what you think of our new Web site and nsls.info, our new weekly e-newsletter. "Kick the tires," "check the engine" and take it for a "test drive," then let us know what you like and what we can improve.
More

Desperately Seeking SUSi

SUSi, our member information database, has been melded into the new Web site. We're working to create a way for members to easily access their information directly from the home page. Until then, all the information previously found in SUSi can now be found in the "About Members" and "Online Community" categories. In "About Members," create queries by clicking on "Create and View Statistical Reports" and update your information by clicking on "Membership Directory." In "Online Community," click on "My NSLS" for RBP info, to edit your profile and to check today's Library News.
More

Challenging the Internet Filtering Law

The American Library Association and American Civil Liberties Union are challenging the constitutionality of the Children's Internet Protection Act (CIPA). CIPA, which becomes effective on April 20, requires public libraries to use and install Internet filtering software in order to qualify for federal funding. CIPA is the third attempt by Congress to restrict Internet access. You can find specific information and guidance on CIPA and how it affects libraries at ALA's CIPA site.

Visit ALA's CIPA Site

What's Your Knowledge About Knowledge Management?

Interact with colleagues from a variety of library settings to explore common

Newsletter Links:

Positions Open
Meetings/Training/CE
Discounts
Legislative
Announcements
Free
For Sale
Closings/Movings
Submit Newsletter Items

Subscribe

NSLS Links:

About NSLS
About Members
External Resources
Important Issues
Our Services
Online Community

Credits:

Christina Johnson, Editor

Printable Version

Figure 8.12
NSLS E-Newsletter
Used with permission of North Suburban Library System.

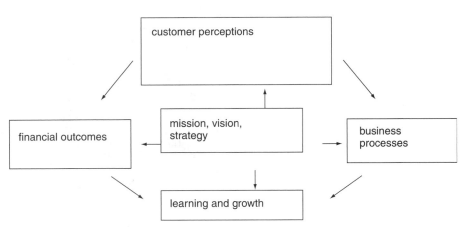

Figure 8.13
The Perspectives Measured By the Balanced Scorecard Approach

Kaplan and Norton describe the innovation of the balanced scorecard as follows: *"The balanced scorecard retains traditional financial measures. But financial measures tell the story of past events, an adequate story for industrial age companies for which investments in long-term capabilities and customer relationships were not critical for success. These financial measures are inadequate, however, for guiding and evaluating the journey that information age companies must make to create future value through investment in customers, suppliers, employees, processes, technology, and innovation."*

The balanced scorecard approach uses a format to present data from

♦ the learning and growth perspective
♦ the business process perspective
♦ the customer perspective
♦ the financial perspective

Skandia, a global financial company based in Stockholm, uses its own model of the balanced scorecard, called the Skandia Navigator. This tool facilitates comprehensive planning, management, follow-up, and communication of the company's long-term profitability. Financial as well as non-financial key ratios are weighed together, and traditional budget reporting has been done away with. In the late 1990s the company completed a major transformation from a traditional insurance company to a global savings company.

Coloplast, a Danish consumer healthcare product company, also includes statements about value creation from knowledge management, shareholder, and customer relationships in its annual reports. If you can influence the contents of your company's annual report, you can make a significant impact in getting the company as well as its stakeholders to understand the value of infrastructure assets (see Figure 8.14).

A One-Year Plan

Now it's time for you to get to work. If you're ready to make your own job more exciting and strategic, if you're ready to share your interest with executives and colleagues, if you're ready to make some changes to impact organizational performance, you need a road map.

By now you know that I'm not going to recommend a cookie-cutter approach to "re-wiring" your infrastructure. However, I have coached many organizations through these deliberations and changes, and here's a plan that's realistic. I've found that several factors are essential:

♦ Get initial enthusiasm and support from at least one key executive.
♦ Make it a team effort with communication, learning, media, information systems, public relations, marketing, and as many other related professionals as possible.
♦ Get at least three outside "experts" to help endorse your analysis and recommendations; it doesn't have to be a long and expensive consulting engagement,

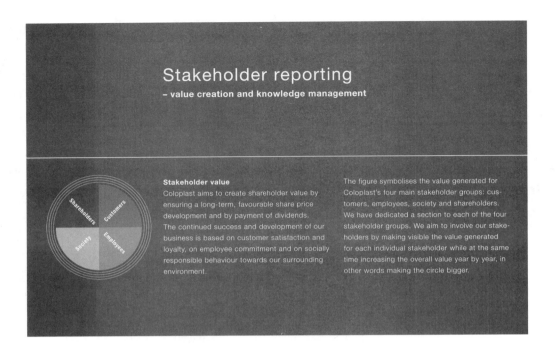

Stakeholder reporting
– value creation and knowledge management

Stakeholder value

Coloplast aims to create shareholder value by ensuring a long-term, favourable share price development and by payment of dividends. The continued success and development of our business is based on customer satisfaction and loyalty, on employee commitment and on socially responsible behaviour towards our surrounding environment.

The figure symbolises the value generated for Coloplast's four main stakeholder groups: customers, employees, society and shareholders. We have dedicated a section to each of the four stakeholder groups. We aim to involve our stakeholders by making visible the value generated for each individual stakeholder while at the same time increasing the overall value year by year, in other words making the circle bigger.

Structure of intellectual capital accounts

This report uses text, figures and illustrations to show the value generated by Coloplast. The indicators reported on were chosen because they relate to our Mission, Values and business objectives. Coloplast's Mission is printed on the inside right-hand cover flap.

By entering into a dialogue with our stakeholders we can share expectations and attitudes in a mutual process and generate shareholder value.

From this process, we shall get valuable feedback telling us if we are meeting the expectations of our stakeholders. This continuous dialogue promotes our prompt understanding of new signals from stakeholders.

The indicators are grouped by value drivers and value propositions using the EFQM Excellence model, with which Coloplast has been working since 1995. The model is based on our ability to define the correlation between value drivers and results. It rests on the belief that only when the chosen strategies and activities achieve good financial results plus increased satisfaction and a positive effect on society, is the company optimally managed, with balanced results for all stakeholders. Stakeholder reporting also has an internal, managerial purpose as measuring of the chosen indicators will be integrated into Coloplast's planning process.

EFQM Excellence model

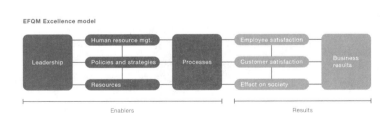

Figure 8.14
Coloplast Annual Report

Employees

Employee value

Employee loyalty and motivation are vital to corporate growth. We wish to attract and retain the best employees, people who take responsibility, are quality conscious and deliver value to our customers. Our management believes in mutual respect and trust, and values the personal and professional development of the individual employee. Communication of relevant information has a high priority in the organisation.

One of the objectives stated in Coloplast's HR policy is that the majority of managers should be recruited internally. We believe that a challenging job is the best training you can get. We encourage job rotation to enable the individual employee to add qualifications in various job functions and professional competences. Finally, we believe that decisions are best made where they are to be implemented. This management approach generates value and creates employee satisfaction and commitment.

Value chain for employees

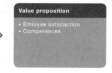

Mission	Value drivers	Value proposition
• Attract and retain best employees • Show empathy for user needs	• Working conditions • Personal and professional development • Knowledge management	• Emloyee satisfaction • Competences

Employee satisfaction measurement

Denmark

Point

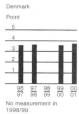

No measurement in 1998/99

Working conditions

The job becomes a learning process when the individual employee is offered development opportunities and challenges. The majority of production workers in Denmark work in self-managing teams, representing 65% in 2000/01, up from 60% the year before. This move towards self-management is a process which aims to increase job satisfaction and make production more efficient.

Health and safety-at-work is handled decentrally in groups supported by trained safety managers. Work at reducing the various risks continues in close cooperation with the public authorities. During its visit in May 2001, the Danish Working Environment Service assessed Coloplast as a level 1 manufacturer, the best rating.

In Coloplast, we regularly measure job satisfaction. Employee satisfaction measurements have been made since 1994, including working conditions, health and safety at work and other factors.

Since Coloplast became listed on the Copenhagen Stock Exchange in 1983, employees have been offered employee shares at a favourable price six times. These shares create motivation and increase commitment in daily work.

Employee development

At yearly development talks, the quality of working results is discussed by a manager and each of his team members. They also discuss job norms and plans for the coming year. Depending on the job and plans for the future, a training programme is prepared.

Our HR department organised 65 courses and seminars in Denmark in 2000/01. In the international context, Coloplast Academy has developed a programme consisting of 27 courses within four competence areas with constant training needs. Included in this programme are eight courses dedicated to managerial training. In 2000/01, 11 such courses were held within the Academy framework. In Denmark, 72% of vacant managerial positions were filled by internal candi-

Figure 8.14 *continued*

A staff party with a theme is a challenge. There was a multitude of creative costumes at the Aladdin party in 2000.

When the US breast care division developed its latest website in 2001, their IT people went to Denmark for sparring and training by Corporate IT and the Danish e-business specialists.

dates, the figure for subsidiaries being 53%. Our objective of filling the majority of managerial positions by internal candidates was met. The average amount of time spent by Coloplast employees on training and development in 2000/01 was 4.4 days, slightly below the level of last year. The cost of training came to DKK 6,855 per employee. Job rotations remained at last year's level.

Coloplast is present at recurring job fairs for students in Denmark. Last year we had a stand at the VIP fair addressing engineers, organised by Denmark's Technical University. We were also present at the SICEF fair addressing students of economics and finance. The total number of visitors to the two fairs was 13,000.

Knowledge management

Knowledge management is an important competition parameter, and we aim to give Coloplast employees the best level of information, allowing them to do their job optimally. All employees are responsible for developing, documenting and communicating their knowledge about issues and relations which may affect Coloplast's competitiveness. Nearly all employees have IT access and Coloplast's intranet, InSite, which was introduced in year 2000, is increasingly used for knowledge sharing. At the time of writing, some 20,000 visits per week are reported for InSite.

Employee satisfaction

During the year, employee satisfaction was measured in 13 companies including more than 2,800 people. The response rate was 86% and the surveys showed that general satisfaction has increased to an all-time high of 3.75 compared to 3.60 last year. This increase is due to a dedicated effort to make improvements in those areas where results were low in previous surveys. The figure reflects a rating on a scale from 1 to 5, 5 being the maximum.

Staff turnover dropped from 9.9 to 9.0% for salaried employees and from 16.7 to 15.5% for production workers. Absence was low both for salaried employees and production workers, reported as 2.1% and 6.3%, respectively, during 2000/01.

In 2000/01 the number of accidents in our Danish factories, where most manufacturing activities are located, decreased from 51 to 46. This caused a drop in the rate of accidents recorded from 18 to 15 accidents per million working hours. Accidents causing more than one day's absence are included in the figure.

Stability

%

Staff turnover, salaried

Staff turnover, hourly-paid

Accident rate

No. per mln working hours

Employee satisfaction, Denmark 2000/01

On a scale from 1 to 5	Salaried	Hourly-paid
Persoal development	3.82	3.29
Development talk	3.97	3.65
Job commitment	4.50	4.43
Pay and working conditions	3.25	3.02

Figure 8.14 *continued*

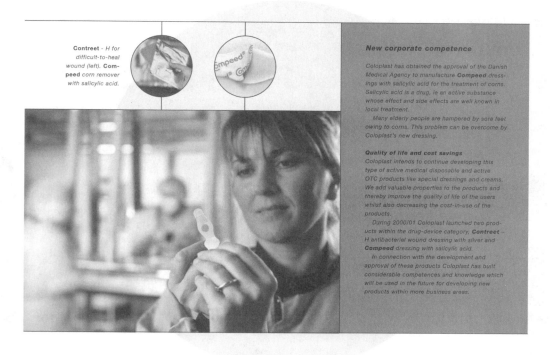

Contreet - *H for difficult-to-heal wound (left).* **Compeed** *corn remover with salicylic acid.*

New corporate competence

Coloplast has obtained the approval of the Danish Medical Agency to manufacture **Compeed** dressings with salicylic acid for the treatment of corns. Salicylic acid is a drug, ie an active substance whose effect and side effects are well known in local treatment.

Many elderly people are hampered by sore feet owing to corns. This problem can be overcome by Coloplast's new dressing.

Quality of life and cost savings

Coloplast intends to continue developing this type of active medical disposable and active OTC products like special dressings and creams. We add valuable properties to the products and thereby improve the quality of life of the users whilst also decreasing the cost-in-use of the products.

During 2000/01 Coloplast launched two products within the drug-device category, **Contreet** – H antibacterial wound dressing with silver and **Compeed** dressing with salicylic acid.

In connection with the development and approval of these products Coloplast has built considerable competences and knowledge which will be used in the future for developing new products within more business areas.

The employee satisfaction measurement showed that safety and working environment score high on satisfaction, 4.14 for salaried employees, 3.64 for production workers.

Employee satisfaction affects Coloplast's ability to attract new employees. The number of unsolicited applications was more than 3,000 in Denmark, the same level as the year before. This is considered very satisfactory considering the high employment rate.

Competences

Coloplast's competences are based on specific knowledge about own products, manufacturing processes and business processes. It is therefore difficult for our competitors to copy our products. A number of new competences are being developed to met our strategic objectives. Special systems have been developed for managing knowledge and developing competences in the most important areas, such as understanding customer needs, technology, innovation, marketing and providing services.

This figure shows how our Mission, Values and business objectives are integrated in employee development.

COLOPLAST 2000/2001 (40) EMPLOYEES

Figure 8.14   *continued*

Society

Generating value for society

We recognise our shared responsibility for a sustainable development. We practise this responsibility through social commitment and environmentally responsible behaviour. We find it important to get feedback on ways to prevent and reduce the environmental impact of our activities and ways to enhance our social responsibility.

We cooperate with research and educational institutions in all professional fields where we can either provide or get access to special competences, and we aim to influence developments within trade, research, training and education as well as legal and regulatory affairs.

Value chain for society

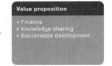

Mission
- Social responsibility
- Environmental consciousness

> **Value drivers**
- Social commitment
- Environmental management
- Partnership

> **Value proposition**
- Finance
- Knowledge sharing
- Sustainable development

Social commitment

We wish to contribute to supporting a flexible labour market, both at home and abroad. At the local level, we help integrate ethnic minorities and are involved in programmes aiming to provide opportunities for the unemployed. During the last five years, Coloplast's Danish locations have found trial job openings for 50 such persons. The programme involves temporary employment for periods of three months.

In 2000/01 Coloplast offered trial jobs to 18 persons, five of whom have subsequently obtained permanent jobs on standard terms.

Coloplast has an open dialogue policy with local communities through local newspapers, and representatives of Coloplast's management are often interviewed in the radio or on television.

Environmental management

Coloplast's five manufacturing sites in Denmark and our Amoena subsidiary in Germany have obtained certification according to the international environmental management standard DS/EN ISO 14001. Since 1998 the Danish sites have complied with the EU Eco Management and Audit System for environmental management, auditing and reporting, EMAS. Our envi-

ronmental management system is the main tool for maintaining and improving quality in our environmental work. Our environmental efforts have led to a reduction of the effects caused by our products and production processes.

In the past year we have put special focus on integrating environmental considerations into product development. This approach offers the greatest potential for changing the overall environmental impact of a product. The environmental department has built up considerable competences in this field. The development departments of the product divisions now have their own environmental department contact. As early as possible in the development process, the contact person gives advice on the choice of materials and processes, often based on a assessment life cycle.

Each year a thorough review is made of the environmental status of each factory. Based on legislative and environmental criteria we determine which aspects are significant and deserve special focus. These then become the basis for the environmental improvement goals set for each factory.

The most important environmental objective for 2000/01 was met, as polymer process waste was reduced by 7%. However, the consumption

Figure 8.14   *continued*

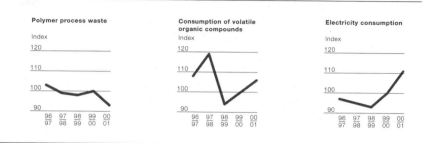

1999/2000 is index 100

Contact person for environmental affairs
Jørgen Fischer Ravn,
Corporate Environmental Manager.
Tel + 45 49 11 13 08
E-mail: dkjfr@coloplast.com
Environmental statement
for 2000/01 at
www.coloplast.com
Select: Company Information, then Environmental Statement

of volatile organic compounds rose by 6% while the consumption of electricity rose by 11%. This development is not satisfactory. In future, environmental objectives will therefore be set for each factory in more detail.

Being an environmentally conscious company involves more than simply being on good terms with the surrounding community. Our efforts must also be based on the commitment of employees and their demands for improvement. The most recent employee satisfaction measurement confirmed that our environmental consciousness is of increasing importance for our employees and that we are meeting their demands in this field. A total of 130 people make up the environmental organisation.

Partnerships

We aim to have influence on all decision-making processes which affect our business. We have entered into partnerships and are cooperating with a number of companies, institutions and private individuals. The contractual relationships range from the supply of raw material to machine purchases, contractor agreements, distribution agreements, research and development agreements. The transactions for many of these supply agreements are based on common IT systems.

Economic value

Coloplast has developed along a continuous growth curve. Since its establishment, there has been no single year without growth in turnover and operating profit. In 2000/01 Coloplast created 233 new jobs in Denmark and 199 new jobs abroad. At year-end the number of employees

was 4,203 converted into full-time equivalents. Most of the economic value generated through Coloplast's operating profit in Denmark benefits society through company tax, capital gains tax and personal income tax. In 2000/01 the total tax liability was DKK 708 mln, or 41%. Employees received 26% of the value. The remainder went to shareholders or was added to reserves to safeguard future operations.

Knowledge sharing

Awareness of the potential for utilising new knowledge is decisive to Coloplast's ability to complete research and development projects and technological strides within short periods of time. We are involved in a number of national and international activities, bilaterally or through consortia. Current major partnerships include a centre programme under the auspices of the Ministry for Commerce and Industry, an EU framework programme and two Research Council programmes under the Danish Ministry for Research. In Denmark we participate in the technical and professional work of our trade association, the Danish Medical Device Industry, whose chairmanship is held by Coloplast executive Mogens Pedersen. These activities support the exchange of knowledge and building of competences.

Sustainability

At investor meetings, inquiries are regularly made about Coloplast's rating in the social, ethical and environmental fields. Coloplast is included in the Dow Jones Sustainability Indexes and the FTSE4Good, the world's two leading sustainability indexes for shares.

Figure 8.14 *continued*

but you will need to point to research and unbiased expertise when you get challenged. "Experts" can be peers in other companies, briefings, or outside audits by respected authors, researchers, consultants, and so on.

♦ Find enlightened colleagues for your executives to network with—perhaps the CEO of another regional company has taken an interest in new communication approaches, or you can take your boss to a conference when another executive makes a presentation about her company's innovations. I've found that CEOs are much more candid with and willing to learn from their counterparts—especially if you can arrange it so they do not feel threatened.

♦ Set up a one-year timeline for yourself. Fill out the following action item list, and post it somewhere you can't overlook.

Checkup 14: Your One-Year Roadmap

Action Item	Who Will Do It?	When?
Write a one-page paper on one or two key performance gaps caused by having an outdated learning and communication system and outlining possible ways to close those gaps.		
Get input from and support of at least three internal colleagues—at least two of whom are in different departments.		
Get endorsement of your ideas and coaching from at least three outside "experts"—they can be peers in other companies, briefings or outside audits by respected authors, researchers and consultants, and so forth.		
Get at least one key executive to "buy into" acknowledging the shortcomings in the present communication and learning system and to exploring more contemporary approaches.		
Form an interdepartmental study group or strategic planning task force.		
Find colleagues in other organizations who are at an equal level with your key executives and who are also exploring new ideas regarding learning and communication.		
Develop descriptors of an "ideal" communication or learning infrastructure.		

Action Item	Who Will Do It?	When?
Select a prototype project—design and develop it using "re-wired" philosophies and technologies.		
Show the prototype to internal clients and executives and get their buy-in		
Hold a conference, open house, celebration, or "learning day" to share your experiences.		
Ask for executive approval for resources necessary to re-design your system.		

I wish you success and welcome your comments and questions; contact me at diane @ dgayeski.com.

Self-Check

1. In order to effect change and heighten performance, both the "rules" and "tools" of learning and communication systems need to be engineered. Give examples of rules and tools.
2. One obstacle in integrating a common approach to information and performance improvement is the lack of coordination among various company databases. Describe the ideal system for integrating corporate communication databases and how these data would be shared across functions.
3. In order to "sell" the value of a proposed infrastructure asset, it's necessary to influence executives. Explain the steps of the HICCUP model, giving a typical example of a training or communication proposal.
4. What are some very general questions to ask company executives about what drives the finances and goals of their company?
5. Typically communications and training specialists are brought in by executives to "communicate" or "announce" change. Explain an alternative "information management" approach to effecting organizational change and re-framing the role of communications and training personnel.
6. Explain how the concepts of valuation apply to engineering the learning and communication system of not-for-profit organizations.
7. What is the "balanced scorecard," as well as other similar measures for actually reporting non-financial measures?
8. Outline a one-year strategic plan for re-engineering one important infrastructure asset in an organization, discussing the reasons behind your approach.

References

Charan, R. (2001). *What the CEO wants you to know.* New York: Crown Business.

Gayeski, D. (2001, September). Beyond level 4: Tying HPT to valuation of intangible assets. *Performance Improvement Journal, 40(8).* 7–9.

Goldstein, S. (1999). Information preparedness. *Strategic Communication Management 3(1).* 6–10.

Kaplan, R. S., & Norton, D. P. (1996). *The balanced scorecard: Translating strategy into action.* Cambridge, MA: Harvard Business School Press.

INDEX

A

Accelerated Breakthrough Systems (ABS), 112–114
ACE Group of Companies, 62–63
Acquisitions, 87
Advertising, 46
After-tax calculations, 159–160
Air Canada, 51
Altruism, 85, 86
Annual discount rate, 170
ARCS model, 9
Arthur Andersen, 64
Assembly line approach, 12
Assets
  infrastructure, 1
  intangible, 1–3
  intellectual, 6–7
  leveraging, in communication, 170
  making most of, 171
  tangible, 2
Audits
  communication, 48, 65
  learning infrastructure, 127–129

B

Balanced scorecard, 194, 197
Behavior Engineering Model (BEM), 148
Behaviorist approach to learning, 95, 97
Benefit/cost ratio, 157–158
Benefits, 170
Best-known methods, 112, 114
Body Shop, 155
Brand extension, 87
Branding, internal, 78
Brands
  corporate, 88–89
  defined, 73
  mega, 87
  value of strong, 74
Brick-and-mortar approach, cost of, 166
Buckman, Stanley J., 106
Buckman Labs, 35, 106
  organizational knowledge management at, 106–110

C

Call centers, self-monitored feedback in, 118–120
Capital
  human, 3–4, 7, 105
  intellectual, 105
  social, 7
Cascade model, 47
Cash flow, discounted, 161
Caterpillar, 78–84
Centralized relational database, 174
Century 21, 103
Change
  capacity for, 132–134
  making case for, 182–185
Chaos theory, 13
Charismatic leaders, 86
Chief executive officer (CEO), getting information from, 185–186
Chunking, 96
Civic virtue, 85
Closed-circuit television, 61, 116
Cognitive approaches to learning, 96
Cohen, Don, 7
Collaboration, 6–7
  internal, 59–61

Collaborative decision-making, 13
Coloplast, 197
ComAdd model, 144–148
Communication, 51
   alignment of, 128–129
   assessing, in government, 135–137
   assessing and managing overload,
      137–138
   crisis, 64–65
   customer relationship, 55–56
   customer/supplier, 61
   defined, 51–52
   defining success of, 53–54
   dis-integration of, 36–38
   downward, 66
   elements of strong infrastructure,
      59–63
   employee, 48, 135–136
   engineering flow of, with Pitney
      Bowes, 186–191
   external, 45–47
   financial, 46
   fit of, in organization, 43–45
   integration of, 49–51
   HR assessment and, 65–71
   internal, 47–48, 84
   islands of, 36–38, 49
   as key in crisis management, 134–135
   lateral, 66
   leadership and supervisory, 61–62
   learning infrastructure audit and,
      127–129
   leveraging assets in, 170
   obstacles to effective corporate, 20
   organizational, 43–45, 57–59
   supervisory, 48–49
   supportive, 62
   technology in, 49
   transportation model of, 51–53
   upward, 62, 66
Communication audits, 48, 65
Communication system map, 136–137
Communication theory, 51
Company intranet, 47
Company turnaround, e-learning system
   in, 166–169
Complexity theory, 13
Compliance, 100
Computer monitors, 116

Confidence, 8–9
Conflict, 127
Connectedness, 55
Conscientiousness, 85
Constructivism, 96–97
Continual learning, 131
Continuous improvement, 130
Cookie-cutter approach, 197
Co-orientation, 62
Copyrights, 105
Corporate brand, 88–89
Corporate communication, obstacles to
   effective, 20
Corporate culture, 84–85
Corporate reputation, 49
Corporate universities, 97
Courtesy, 85
Cracker Barrel Old Country Store, 74–77
Credibility, 7–8
   building, 3–5
Creo, 103
Crisis, capacity for, 132–134
Crisis communication, 64–65
Crisis management, 46–47
   communication system key in,
      134–135
Critelli, Michael J., 186
Culture, 9
   corporate, 84–85
   engineering, 87
Customer relationship communication,
   framework for, 55–56
Customer relationship management
   (CRM), 14, 38–40
Customer/supplier communication, 61
Cynicism, 101

D

Data
   customer, 65
   profitability, 65
   self-monitored, 120
   technology-generated, 119
Decision-making
   collaborative, 13
   participatory, 130–131
   rule-based, 97
Delahaye Group, 8
Dependence, 100

Depository Trust and Clearing Corporation, 173
Depreciation, 159
Discounted cash flow, 161
Dishonesty, 101
Distrust, 100
Diversity, 129
    awareness/appreciation of, 131
Dove, 87
Dow Chemical, 155
Downsizing, 6, 132
Downward communication, 66

E

E-learning system in company turnaround, 166–169
Emerson Electric, 58
Employee communication, 135–136
    objectives of, 48
Employee forums with the CEO, 13
Employee newsletter, 47
Employees
    assessing knowledge of, 4
    effectiveness of, 49
    empowerment of, 17–18, 130
Empowerment, 129
    of employees, 17–18, 130
Engineering culture, 87
Enterprise infrastructure approach, 173
Enterprise training systems, linking, to value, 102–103
Ernst & Young, 155
Expert knowledge at Intel, 112–114
Expert system, 99
Explicit knowledge, 106
External communication, 45–47
Extranets, 61
Extreme Logic, 34

F

Fayol, Henri, 12
FedEx, 155
Feedback
    negative, 62
    performer information systems and, 118–122
    self-monitored, 118–122
Feedback systems, 114–118
    categories of, 115

Fidelity Insurance, 155
Financial Analysis System Tools (FAST), 110–111
Financial analysts, reporting to, 194–197
Financial communications, 46
Fractal organization, 14
Functional silos, 14

G

Gatto, John, 100
Globalization, 131
Government, assessing communication in, 135–137
Government relations, 46
Group decision support system (GDSS), 193
Group performance level, performance infrastructure at, 126
GTE Corporation, 155
Guthrie Healthcare System, 102

H

Hawthorne Studies, 13
Hewlett-Packard (HP), 26–27, 89
HICCUP model, 183–184
Hicks, Tim, 7
High performance workplace; performance-based compensation in, 132
High performance work teams, 13
Hugo Boss store, 56
Human capital, 3–4, 7, 105
Human Capital Index (HCI), 29–33
Humanistic school of management, 13
Human performance engineering, 140
Human performance management, 17–18, 104
    in creating value, 26–27
Human resources, subspecialties of, 25

I

Identity, 127
IMPSYS©, 90–93
Individual performance level, performance infrastructure at, 126–127
Information management, 188–189
Information sharing, effective, 175–181
Infrastructure, assessing the current, 20–22
Infrastructure analytics, 156–157

Infrastructure assets, 1
Infrastructure project, determining value
    of, 170–171
Initiatives, 194
Instructor, characteristics of a good, 98
Intangible assets, 1–3
Intangibles
    need for measuring, 4–5
    professions that create and manage, 3
Integrated communication strategy,
    190–191
Integrated infrastructure for perform-
    ance, 9–11
Intel, expert knowledge at, 112–114
Intellectual assets, 6–7
Intellectual capital, 105
Intellectual property, 105
Interactive websites, 61
Interbrew, 87
Internal branding, 78
Internal collaboration, 59–61
Internal communication, 47–48
    future of, 84
Intranet broadcasts, 61
Investor relations, 46
ISO certification, 130

J

Just-in-time manufacturing, 131

K

Kelleher, Herb, 9
Keller, John, 9
K'netix©, 107–108
Knowledge
    assessing employee, 4
    expert, 112–114
    explicit, 106
    as intangible, 4
    management of, 105–106
    markets for, 106
    promoting exchange of, 110
    tacit, 106

L

Labatt Breweries, 49
Lateral communication, 66
Leadership
    charismatic, 86

effectiveness of, 49
    implications of managerial, on organi-
        zational citizenship behavior, 85–87
    supervisory communication and,
        61–62
Lean staffing, 27
Learner, characteristics of a good, 98
Learning, 127
    alignment of, 128–129
    behaviorist approach to, 95, 97
    cognitive approaches to, 96
    continual, 131
    defined, 95
    leveraging assets, 170
    organizational, 2, 95–101
    team, 104
Learning experience
    characteristics of a good, 98
    reflecting on last, 99–101
Learning organization, 104, 131
Learning systems in practice, 101–102
Learning theory, behavioral and cognitive
    approaches to, 95–96
Levi Strauss, 49
Licensing, 105
Low self-esteem, 100–101
Loyalty as intangible, 4

M

Management
    crisis, 46–47, 134–135
    customer relationship, 14, 38–40
    humanistic school of, 13
    human performance, 17–18,
        26–27, 104
    implications of leadership in, on orga-
        nizational citizenship behavior,
        85–87
    information, 188–189
    of knowledge, 105–106
    open book, 59
    participatory, 129
    scientific, 12–13
    teamwork, 6
    total quality, 129, 130
    by walking around, 5
Management information system, legit-
    imizing, 120–122
Manpower Inc., 6

Marketing, 46
   relationship, 132
Markets for knowledge, 106
Market value, 2
Mayo, Elton, 13
McDonald's, 19, 73
Meaning, 51
   shared, 54
Media exposure in project
    evaluation, 153
Media relations, 46
Megabrands, 87
Mental models, creating and
   challenging, 104
Mergers, 87
Messages, 51
Mindshare, 36
Motivation, ARCS model for, 9
Multi-year systems, 160

N

Negative feedback, 62
Net present value, 161–162
News, 61
Nordea, 87, 88–90
North Suburban Library System (NSLS),
   192–194
Not-for-profit organizations
   communications in, 46
   valuation concepts for, 191–194

O

Objectivists, 96
Ontario Lottery and Gaming Corpora-
   tion, 115
Open book management, 59
Organizational challenge inventory,
   182–183
Organizational change, 5
Organizational citizenship behavior
   (OCB), 85
   implications of managerial leadership
    on, 85–87
Organizational communication, 43–45
   ideal system for, 57–59
Organizational internal connectedness,
   38–40
Organizational knowledge management
   at Buckman Labs, 106–110

Organizational learning
   communication and, 2
   conceptualizing and assessing,
    95–101
Organizational training, 97
Organizational trust, 8
Organization level, performance infra-
   structure at, 125–126
Organizations, factors driving future of,
   16–17
Outsourcing value, 40–41

P

Packard, David, 89
Paine, Katie, 8
Participatory decision-making, 130–131
Participatory management, 129
Patents, 105
Performance
   integrated infrastructure for, 9–11
   traditional practices and, 35–38
Performance analytics, 125–149
Performance consulting, focus on, 104
Performance engineering
   ComAdd model of, 144–148
   high-level walkthrough of, 140–143
Performance engineering model,
   140–143
Performance gaps, assessing and closing
   group and individual, 139–140
Performance infrastructure, 125–127
Performer information systems, feedback
   and, 118–122
Personal mastery, nurturing, 104
Philanthropy, 45
Pitney Bowes, engineering the flow of
   communication within, 186–191
Portals, 61
Power, 127
Present value, 161–162
Pricing agreements, 105
Profitability data, 65
Program du jour syndrome, 129
Project approach, 173
Project evaluation, levels of, 153–156
Property, intellectual, 105
Prusak, Laurence, 7, 106
Public relations, 45–47
   measurement of programs in, 46

Q

Qualcomm, 49, 51
Quality circles, 13
Questionnaires in project evaluation, 153

R

Readership studies in project
    evaluation, 153
Reciprocity, 106
Relationship communication system, 55
Relationship marketing, 132
Reputation as intangible, 4
Rightsizing, 132
Risk-aversiveness, 101
ROI calculation, 158–159
Rule-based decision-making
    processes, 97

S

Sacramento County Public Works
    Agency, 135
Scientific management, 12–13
Sears, 59, 127, 155
Self-directed work teams, 13
Self-managed teams, 130
Self-monitored data, 120
Self-monitored feedback, 118–122
    in call centers, 118–120
Senge, Peter, 104
Service quality, 86
Shared meaning, 54
Shared vision, building, 104
Silja Line, 39–40
Skandia, 103, 197
Social capital, 7
SoftChoice, 155
Southwest Airlines, 9, 35, 62
Special events and sponsorship, 62–63
Sportsmanship, 85
Springfield Remanufacturing Corpora-
    tion, 58–59
Stewart, Thomas, 7
Stockholders, reporting to, 194–197
Stockholder value, 165
Strategic event sponsorship, 63–64
Strategic structure, creating, 173–174
Supervisory communication, 48–49
Supportive communication, 62

Suspicion, 101
Sveiby, Kaarl Erik, 2
Synergy, 6
Systems, focusing on, 27–28, 104

T

Tacit knowledge, 106
Tangible assets, 2
Taxes, 170
Taylor, Frederick, 12
Team-building workshops, 13
Team learning, fostering, 104
Teamwork, 130
    management of, 6
Technology-generated data, 119
Time and motion studies, 12
Time value of money, 161
Total cost of ownership, 170
Total quality management, 129, 130
Traditional practices, performance
    and, 35–38
Training
    conceptualizing, 95
    linking enterprise to value, 102–103
    organizational, 97
    reducing costs of, 103
    web-based, 110
Transportation model of communication,
    51–53
Tylenol, 64

U

Uniformity, 101
Unilever, 87
Upward communication, 62, 66
Upward distortion, lack of, 62
User groups, 61

V

Valuation concepts for non-for-profits,
    191–194
Value
    determining for infrastructure project,
        170–171
    human performance management in
        creating, 26–27
    linking enterprise training systems to,
        102–103

methods of calculating, 157–160
  outsourcing, 40–41
  stockholder, 165
Value statements, 129
Vendors, working with, 162–165
Video news updates, 61

W

Web-based training, 110
Wegman's Food Stores, 62

Welch, Jack, 108
Wheatley, Margaret, 14
Work teams
  high performance, 13
  self-directed, 13
WorldCom, 64

X

Xerox, 87